D0082135

The Pyramid Builders of Ancient Egypt

By the same author
The Ancient Egyptians: religious beliefs and practices

THE PYRAMID BUILDERS OF ANCIENT EGYPT

A Modern Investigation of Pharaoh's Workforce

A.R. DAVID

LONDON AND NEW YORK

First published 1986
by Routledge & Kegan Paul plc

First published in paperback 1996
by Routledge
11 New Fetter Lane, London EC4P 4EE

Simultaneously published in the USA and Canada
by Routledge
29 West 35th Street, New York, NY 10001

© 1986, 1996 A.R. David

Typeset by Intype London Ltd
Printed and bound in Great Britain by
T.J. Press (Padstow) Ltd, Padstow, Cornwall

All rights reserved. No part of this book may be reprinted or
reproduced or utilized in any form or by any electronic,
mechanical, or other means, now known or hereafter
invented, including photocopying and recording, or in any
information storage or retrieval system, without permission in
writing from the publishers.

British Library Cataloguing in Publication Data
A catalogue record for this book is available from the British Library

Library of Congress Cataloguing in Publication Data
David, A. Rosalie (Ann Rosalie)
The pyramid builders of ancient Egypt.
Bibliography: p.
Includes index.
1. Kahun (Ancient city)   2. Egypt—Social life
and customs—To 332 B.C.   3. Egypt—antiquities.
4. Pyramid of Sesostris II (Egypt)   5. Fayyūm (Egypt)—
Antiquities.   I. Title.
DT73.K28D38   1986   932   85–10775

ISBN 0–415–15292–5

Contents

Illustrations

Plates (between pages 174 and 175)

Figures

Acknowledgments

Preparation for this book has been in hand for several years, and has drawn upon the help, skills and advice of many people. I would like to express my gratitude to those who made the initial studies possible: the Director of the Manchester Museum, for enabling me to publish the Kahun material in the collection; the Petrie Museum at University College London, for granting permission both to study their Kahun artefacts and to examine the diaries and excavation reports of Sir William Flinders Petrie, from which several extracts are quoted in this book. I would like to thank my colleagues, Mrs Joan Allgrove McDowell, Dr G. Gilmore and Dr G.W.A. Newton, for their contributions to the book, and for their co-operation and substantial endeavours on behalf of the Kahun Project.

Many people have contributed to the production of the book. For the illustrative material, I am indebted to Mr W. Thomas of the Manchester Museum for the photographs of the Kahun collection, and to Mr P.A. Clayton for the photographs of the Lahun treasure, the scenes in the tomb of Rekhmire, the Lahun pyramid, and the village of Deir el-Medina. I would like to thank Dr M. Saleh, Director of the Cairo Museum, for granting permission to include the photograph of the model of the weavers' shop from the tomb of Meket-Re^c, which has been kindly supplied by the Cairo Museum. I am grateful to Mr E.G. Yong Wong for enabling us to use his reconstruction drawings of Kahun town and the Kahun carpenter.

The publishers have given me every encouragement and support, and I am particularly grateful to Ms Elizabeth Fidlon for her enthusiastic reception of the idea of a book on this theme, to

Mr A. Wheatcroft who, as editor, has guided it through to its conclusion, and to Ms Victoria Peters for initiating this particular edition.

Finally, my special thanks and appreciation are due to Mrs Carole Higginbottom who typed the manuscript, and to my husband for his continuing support.

Introduction

South-west of Cairo, the modern capital of Egypt, on the west side of the Nile, there lies the province of Fayoum, the largest of the country's oases, which owes its remarkable fertility both to springs of water, and to the Bahr Yusef, a channel through which the waters of the Nile flow into the famous lake of the oasis, known today as the 'Birket El-Qarun'. In antiquity, as today, the area provided excellent hunting and fishing, and the kings and their courtiers visited the area regularly to enjoy these pastimes. The kings of the 12th Dynasty (1991–1786 BC) chose to build their capital city here, and to be buried in pyramids built nearby, on the edge of the desert. Their decision brought unprecedented activity and prosperity to the area; not only was a workforce employed to build and decorate each king's pyramid and associated temples, but officials and overseers were brought in to supervise the work. Subsequently, priests and other personnel were employed in the pyramid temples, where the king's mortuary cult was performed after his death and burial. Around this nucleus, the community soon developed and lawyers, doctors, scribes, craftsmen, tradesmen and all the other elements of a thriving society came together.

It was in the Fayoum, in the late nineteenth century, that the famous Egyptologist, Sir William Flinders Petrie, made one of his earliest and most significant discoveries. In 1888/9, he began his excavation of several sites in the area. These sites lay at the north and south ends of the great dyke of the Fayoum mouth. At the north was the pyramid of Illahun (or Lahun) built by King Sesostris II, and around it lay the cemetery which had been started in the 12th Dynasty, and then ransacked, before the tombs were re-used between the 21st and 26th Dynasties. A small temple adjoined the pyramid on the east, and half a mile distant on the edge of the desert lay another temple, also part of the original pyramid complex. North of the larger temple was situated the town of the pyramid workmen, known today as 'Kahun'. At the south end of the dyke, a later town, built in the 18th Dynasty, also attracted Petrie's attention. Egyptologists know it by the name of 'Gurob' or 'Medinet Gurob'.

An entry in his *Journal* for the period 24 February to 2 March 1889 clearly indicates Petrie's initial interest in the site of Kahun, and his accurate perception of its historical importance:

> The town beyond the temple (called Medinet Kahun I hear) I now suspect to be of the age of the temple, 12th Dynasty, and to be almost untouched since then. If so, it will be a prize to work for historical interest of dated objects. I cannot be certain yet as to its age, but the pottery is quite unlike any that I yet know, except some chips of 12th Dynasty that I got at Hawara: and the walls of the town run regardless of natural features, over a low hill and back again but square with the temple.

In the 1888/9 season, Petrie, anxious to prevent a German dealer Kruger from ransacking the sites, placed a small number of workmen at Kahun and Gurob. He visited them and supervised their work as frequently as possible from the nearby site of Hawara which he was currently working. According to an entry in his *Journal* (8–15 April 1889), he was finally able to start his excavation at Kahun:

> So at last, I felt justified in beginning the site I had been longing to try, the town adjoining the temple of Usertesen II (*Sesostris II*), which I had guessed might be of the 12th Dynasty.

After leaving Hawara, he divided his time between the two sites of Illahun and the associated town, Kahun, and Gurob.

> On my Illahun days, I have my wash before I go out, carry my breakfast tied up in a towel, look over this place on my way, and get to Illahun, about 10 or 11. . . After seeing the work

there, I have breakfast about noon; go over to Tell Gurob,
look over that and pay up, and then come back.

These sites, and Kahun in particular, were not to disappoint
Petrie. Kahun was built, c.1895 BC, to house the workmen
employed in building the pyramid and temples of King Sesostris
II. However, it was also occupied by officials who supervised the
pyramid building programme, and later, by priests and other
personnel who served in the temples. The kings of the 12th
Dynasty developed various irrigation projects in this area, and
Kahun would also have played a significant role in these concerns.
It undoubtedly became a prosperous and important centre, and it
would be wrong to regard it simply as a pyramid workmen's town.
In antiquity, both the town and the temple, which adjoined it and
was part of the pyramid complex, were known by the name of
'Hetep-Sesostris' – 'Sesostris is pleased, or satisfied'. However,
Petrie, on discovering the site in 1887, asked an old man what the
town was called. In his *Journal* (8–15 April 1889) he recalls:

> I only got this name (Medinet Kahun) from one man. No one
> else knows any name for it, and he only heard it from
> someone in his youth. It may be wrong, therefore, but it will
> be a name to know it by.

The discovery and excavation of Kahun was important for
several reasons. It was the first time that a complete plan of an
Egyptian town was uncovered. Petrie discovered that the houses
were still standing, and that many contained property left behind
by their owners. Laid out by a single architect on a regular plan,
the town was purpose-built and had not grown randomly. It could
be dated to two specific periods of occupation, and the objects
found at the site illustrated living conditions at these periods.
    Most of our knowledge of ancient Egypt is based on the evidence
of the tombs and temples – their painted and sculptured wall-
scenes, and the funerary goods which the Egyptians placed in the
tombs to provide a comfortable afterlife for the deceased. Tombs
and temples were intended to last 'for eternity' and were therefore
built of stone. The dwellings of the living, even the royal palaces,
were constructed mainly of sun-dried mud-brick, and have therefore usually succumbed to the ravages of time. 'Living' sites such
as towns and villages are therefore less well preserved and few

such sites have been discovered or excavated in Egypt. Our view of ancient Egyptian society is therefore coloured to some degree by the find-spots and types of artefacts which have been excavated, for even those towns or settlement sites which have been found have not revealed a wealth of objects used by the inhabitants in their daily pursuits.

However, at Kahun, the domestic wares, the workmen's tools, the agricultural equipment, weaving equipment, children's toys, the make-up and jewellery of the women, and the articles associated with their daily religious observances have all been discovered, lying as they were left, some 4,000 years ago, in the streets and rooms of the houses. In addition to the objects of daily use, a collection of papyri found at Kahun provides written records of civil and domestic life, and includes details of legal cases, medical treatments and veterinary practices. This material provides the historian with a unique opportunity to examine the living and working conditions of ordinary men and women.

The objects excavated from Kahun were ultimately distributed amongst various museums around the world, but the largest proportion of this material was divided more or less equally between Petrie's own collection, now held in the Department of Egyptology at University College London, and the Manchester Museum at the University of Manchester. Here in Manchester, the objects from Kahun, together with a substantial number from Petrie's excavations at Gurob, came to form the nucleus of an important Egyptology collection. The existence of such a collection was largely due to the generous patronage of a local textile manufacturer, Jesse Haworth, for his interest in the subject led him initially to support Petrie's excavations at Kahun and Gurob, and subsequently to establish the collection in Manchester.

Jesse Haworth, a partner in the Manchester firm of James Dilworth and Sons, yarn merchants, was a highly esteemed businessman, and one of the longest-established members of the Royal Exchange in the city. He collected Wedgwood china and paintings, but his great passion was Egyptology. This interest probably began around 1877, when the novelist Amelia B. Edwards published her best-selling book, *A 1000 Miles up the Nile*, in which she described her own journey. Jesse Haworth and his wife read this book together, and derived such pleasure from it that they decided to follow in Amelia Edwards's footsteps. They made the same Nile journey in 1882, and on their return, they never ceased to support and encourage Egyptology, especially in Manchester. Amelia Edwards was a remarkable woman who founded the Egypt Exploration Fund to further the aims of scientific excavation and publication, and to generate public support and enthusiasm for Egyptology. In her will, she bequeathed her library and valuable collection of Egyptian antiquities to University College London; she also left a sum of £2,400 to found the first chair of Egyptology in Britain, at University College London, expressing a wish that Petrie should be appointed. He held this post for forty years. It was a meeting with Amelia Edwards, shortly after his return from Egypt, that inspired Jesse Haworth to give financial support to the subject, and in 1887, he began to show his enthusiasm in a practical way when he secured the throne, chessboard and chessmen of the Egyptian queen Hatshepsut, which had been discovered in Egypt in the previous year. The throne was in pieces, but it was skilfully reassembled and exhibited at the Jubilee Exhibition in Manchester in 1887. When the exhibition closed, Haworth presented it to the British Museum.

His donations to the British Museum, the Ashmolean Museum in Oxford, and the Egypt Exploration Fund were generous, but it was his support of Petrie's excavations in the Fayoum which was particularly significant. Petrie had become Hon. Joint Secretary of the Egypt Exploration Fund in 1883, and excavated for the Fund in Egypt during 1884–6. However, he quarrelled with them, and decided to set up an archaeological body of his own, which would be independent. With his original source of funding for excavation no longer available, he faced considerable difficulties, but through the good offices of Amelia Edwards, Jesse Haworth was approached. Petrie received the welcome news that a new avenue of support for his excavations in Egypt had appeared. In his book *Seventy Years in Archaeology*, Petrie recalls this important turning point,

> While in England, I heard that the offer of help in excavating
> came from Jesse Haworth of Manchester, through the kind
> intervention of Miss Edwards. Just at the same time, I had
> an offer of assistance from Martyn Kennard, who had a
> family interest in Egypt. Nevertheless I did not wish to
> pledge my time to be entirely at the service of anyone. The
> plan, which worked very smoothly, was that I drew on my

two friends for all costs of workmen and transport, while I
paid all my own expenses. In return, we equally divided all
that came to England. Thus it was my interest to find as
much as I could.

In 1890, Jesse Haworth and Martyn Kennard presented to the
Manchester Museum the unique and valuable set of objects of
daily use from Petrie's excavations at Kahun, Illahun and Gurob.
These constituted one of the best collections of Egyptian antiquities in Britain. They were only the first of a succession of gifts
made by Haworth to the Museum, which he acquired from Petrie's excavations. For some nine years, he and Kennard were the
sole major supporters of his excavations.

His magnificent donations to the Manchester collection kindled
great interest in Egyptology in the area. The Museum's first
major Egyptian acquisition had been the gift of a mummy with its
coffins belonging to 'Asru, Chantress of Amun in the Temple of
Karnak'. These were presented to the Manchester Natural History Society (founders of the Museum) in 1825, when it was
claimed that this was 'one of the best preserved mummies in the
kingdom'. It was, however, Jesse Haworth who contributed most
to the Egyptian collection, and the year 1911 was an important
landmark in the Museum's history.

By now, public enthusiasm for Egyptology had been widely
fostered in Manchester. In 1906, Professor Petrie was invited to
lecture in Manchester, and before a large audience in the Chemical Theatre of the University, he addressed a rapt audience on the
subject of 'The Hyksos and Israelite Cities'. Contemporary news-
paper cuttings describe the reception of his account of this discovery, and his appeal for public support for the work of exploration
was received with enthusiasm. From then onwards, not only Jesse
Haworth, but also the people of Manchester, took up active
support of Egyptology. Petrie's suggestion for a local society,
operating on the lines of the Egyptian Research Students' Association in London, was put into effect, and the Manchester Egyptian Association was founded. This was intended to further the
study of Egyptology in the area in every possible way, and Jesse
Haworth was elected its first President. Regular meetings were
held at which lectures were given and discussions took place, and
it attracted important members, including famous anthropolo-
gists and anatomists such as Elliot Smith and Boyd Dawkins. Sir

Flinders Petrie continued to visit Manchester annually for many years, providing a continuing stimulus for the Association, by giving the first Museum lecture of the session. In later years, Lady Petrie continued this tradition, and the links between Manchester and the Petries flourished for many years.

By 1911, Haworth's generous and continuing donations to the Museum persuaded the University to consider a scheme to extend the Museum to provide suitable accommodation for the fine collection of Egyptian antiquities which the Museum now possessed but was unable to exhibit properly. The Manchester Egyptian Association opened a fund for subscriptions to assist this enterprise, but it was Jesse Haworth's generosity which finally enabled this scheme to be realised. The Jesse Haworth Building was opened in 1912 and the collections, with the Kahun and Gurob material as a central feature, were displayed to the public. In recognition of his generosity, and of his position as one of the first patrons of scientific excavation in Egypt, the University of Manchester conferred on him the honorary Degree of Doctor of Laws in 1913.

The collections, drawn from many of Petrie's most important sites, included such special features as the fine array of domestic articles; the excavated material from predynastic and early dynastic sites; the unique tomb group of the 'Two Brothers' from Rifeh; splendid examples of Old Kingdom craftsmanship; and the spectacular cartonnage masks and painted panel portraits which Petrie had excavated from the Graeco-Roman period sites in the Fayoum.

In 1919, Jesse Haworth donated a further £10,000 to the Museum, and under the terms of his Will, in 1921, he bequeathed to it £30,000 and his own private collection of Egyptian antiquities. Before his death in 1920, he approved plans for a third stage of the Museum building which was to give a further display area and much-needed workrooms and storage space for the Egyptian collections. This extension was opened by his widow in November 1927.

The story of the Kahun excavation and the development of Egyptology at the Manchester Museum are therefore closely interwoven. However, it is a series of events in the last few years which have led to the new, scientific study of the artefacts from Kahun which may help to answer some of the questions which Petrie himself posed.

In 1975, the Manchester Museum became widely known through the Press and the media, when one of the Egyptian mummies in the collection was unwrapped and subjected to intensive investigation by a team of Egyptologists and medical and scientific experts from Manchester and elsewhere. This was the first time since 1908 that an Egyptian mummy had been scientifically dissected in Britain. On the previous occasion, Dr Margaret Murray, the first curator of the Egyptian collection in Manchester, gathered together a team of scientists and unwrapped the mummies of the 'Two Brothers' in the University. The current project which was inaugurated in 1973 sought to use a wide range of the most recent medical and scientific techniques to examine all the human and animal mummies in the Manchester collection. A multi-disciplinary team was brought together, and, in addition to discovering information about the occurrence of disease, possible causes of death, dietary habits, living conditions and funerary beliefs and customs, the project planned to establish a methodology which other institutions could adopt and adapt for the examination of their own collections. Only one of the mummies was unwrapped. The rest were examined by means of other techniques, particularly radiology, which is non-destructive. Investigation of the mummified viscera was carried out, using various histo-pathological techniques. Since 1979, a new range of virtually non-destructive methods have been developed including endoscopy and serology, and these were employed to provide additional information.

An International Mummy Data Bank, using the University Computer, has been established at the Museum. This holds information on mummies in collections around the world. Eventually, it is hoped that it may be possible to determine patterns of disease and diet in mummies from different periods and sociological groups.

A logical development of this initial scientific study at the Museum, which still continues to pioneer new research, was to extend the principles involved to another major area of the Egyptian collection. The concept had been established that a group of specialists, experts in a wide range of scientific techniques, could work together with the Egyptologists in an attempt to extract new information from the artefacts, and to answer some of the questions which the excavations had produced. The material from Kahun was particularly appropriate. It formed a unique collection of objects which had not been studied since Petrie's day and had never been subjected to the sophisticated scientific scrutiny now available. The tools, weapons and other objects could provide unparalleled information about the ancient technology of the period and about the lifestyle of the town's inhabitants. In particular, analyses of the pottery and metal artefacts could be carried out, in an attempt to examine anew Petrie's theory that a significant proportion of foreign labour was resident at Kahun in the Middle Kingdom. The Kahun project was therefore established to 'rework' some of the material from the site.

This, then, is the story of a 'detective investigation', carried out on the artefacts which were handled and used by the inhabitants of Kahun some 4,000 years ago before the town was deserted. It shows how modern research can reveal new details about everyday existence in an ancient community like Kahun, although it can never present a complete picture. Nevertheless, by piecing together the evidence derived from these simple, utilitarian articles, we can learn much of the lifestyle of the period, and can share something of Petrie's enthusiasm which he expressed in his own words:

> . . . having examined hundreds of the rooms, and having discovered all the ordinary objects of daily life as they were last handled by their owners, I seem to have touched and realised much of the civilisation of that remote age; so that it is hard to realise that over 4,000 years have glided by since those houses last echoed to the voices of their occupants.

PART I

THE BACKGROUND

CHAPTER 1

The Geography and Historical Background

The geography of Egypt

Every civilisation reflects, to some degree, the influence of its environment. Egypt is a country where, perhaps more than most, the physical and natural features provide a dramatic and contrasting setting for human events. It would be difficult to reside in Egypt and remain unaffected by the natural forces and their cycles. In antiquity, as now, the two great life-giving forces were the Nile and the sun, and in their religious beliefs the Egyptians recognised the omnipotence of these, as well as the existence of the other natural elements which shaped their world.

In the words of a Classical writer, Egypt is the 'gift of the Nile'. The existence of the fertile areas has always been due to the natural phenomenon of the regular inundation of the river, for Egypt's scanty and irregular rainfall would never have supplied sufficient water to support crops and animals. The Nile, Africa's longest river, rises far to the south of Egypt, in the region of the Great Lakes near the equator. Known as Bahr el-Jebel (Mountain Nile) in its upper course, after its junction with the Bahr el-Ghazel it becomes the White Nile. In the highlands of Ethiopia, another river, the Blue Nile, rises in Lake Tana, and the Blue and White Niles join at Khartoum. From Khartoum to Aswan the river is now interrupted by a series of six cataracts. These are not waterfalls, but appear as scattered groups of rocks across the river which obstruct the stream, and at the Fourth, Second and First cataracts, interfere with navigation. Egypt begins at the First Cataract, and comprises the area between this natural barrier and the Mediterranean, some 965 km to the north. It was in the region of the northernmost cataracts that the Egyptians, from early times, subdued the local population, to gain access to the hard stone and gold supplies of Nubia.

Within Egypt, the Nile follows a course which divides into two regions. The Nile Valley, a passage which the river has forced through the desert, runs from Aswan to just below modern Cairo, a distance of some 804 km. The scenery along this valley varies from steep rocky cliffs which rise up on either side of the river, and then give way to the encroaching deserts, to flat, cultivated plains, with lush vegetation which, again, in the far distance, succumb to the desert. This cultivated area, wrung from the desert by the irrigation of the land with the Nile floods, varies in width; in parts, the Nile Valley is between twelve and six miles wide, but elsewhere, the cliffs hug the edges of the river and there is no cultivatable land. Nowhere in Egypt is the traveller more aware of the significance of the river's life-force, for here there is virtually no rainfall. The sun is always present, and without the Nile, this region would be desert, like the surrounding area.

The ancient Egyptians recognised the geographical facts and divided their country into two regions. In earliest times, this was a political as well as a geographical reality, but even after the unification of the country, the concept of 'Two Lands' was still present. To them, the Nile Valley was 'Upper Egypt', whereas the northern area, the Delta, was 'Lower Egypt'.

Today, the modern capital of Egypt, Cairo, stands at the apex of the Delta. In antiquity, the ancient capital of Memphis lay a few miles south, and from here there was a marked change in the Nile and its surrounding countryside. Here, the river fans out into a delta nearly one hundred miles long; through the two main branches at Rosetta in the west and Damietta in the east, it finally flows into the Mediterranean. The Delta forms a flat, low-lying plain, scored by the Nile's main and lesser branches; at its widest, northern perimeter, it spreads out over some two hundred miles. However, despite the considerable area of watered land in this region, much of the Delta is marshy or water-logged and cannot be cultivated. Here in antiquity, the nobility and courtiers enjoyed favourite outdoor pastimes of fishing and fowling in the marshes. The climate in the north also differs from that of Upper Egypt, for the temperatures are more moderate and there is some rainfall.

The 'Two Lands' were therefore distinct regions, but were nevertheless interdependent, joined together by the unifying force of the Nile. However, their geographical features imposed

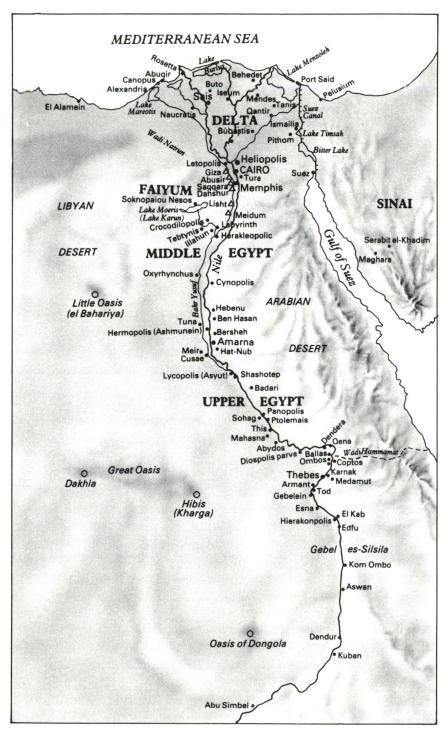

MEDITERRANEAN SEA

Rosetta
Lake Burlus
Behedet
Lake Menzoleh
Abuqir
Canopus
Alexandria
Buto
Iseum
Port Said
Pelusium
Sais
Mendes
Tanis
El Alamein
Lake Mareotis
Naucratis
Qantir
Suez Canal
DELTA
Bubastis
Ismailia
Lake Timsah
Wadi Natrun
Pithom
Bitter Lake
Letopolis
Heliopolis
Giza
CAIRO
Abusir
Tura
Saqqara
Memphis
Suez
SINAI
FAIYUM
Dahshur
Soknopaiou Nesos
Lisht
Lake Moeris
(Lake Karun)
Meidum
LIBYAN
Crocodilopolis
Labyrinth
Tebtynis
Illahun
Herakleopolis
DESERT
MIDDLE EGYPT
Gulf of Suez
Serabit el-Khadim
Oxyrhynchus
Nile
Maghara
Little Oasis
(el Bahariya)
Cynopolis
Bahr Yusuf
ARABIAN
Hebenu
Ben Hasan
Tuna
Bersheh
Hermopolis (Ashmunein)
Amarna
Hat-Nub
DESERT
Meir
Cusae
Shashotep
Lycopolis (Asyut)
Badari
UPPER EGYPT
Panopolis
Sohag
Ptolemais
This
Dendera
Mahasna
Qena
Abydos
Wadi Hammamat
Diospolis parva
Ballas
Ombos
Coptos
Great Oasis
Karnak
Dakhla
Thebes
Medamut
Armant
Tod
Gebelein
Hibis
(Kharga)
Esna
El Kab
Hierakonpolis
Edfu
Gebel es-Silsila
Kom Ombo
Aswan
Oasis of Dongola
Dendur
Kuban
Abu Simbel

FIGURE 1   Map of Egypt (Taken from G. Posener (ed.), *A Dictionary of Egyptian Civilisation.*

different attitudes on their inhabitants. Lower Egypt, closest to the Mediterranean, looked towards the other countries to the north, and was more readily receptive of influences from outside, becoming a centre for the cross-currents of the politics and culture of the ancient world. Upper Egypt, encapsulated by the deserts and bordered on the south by the land of Nubia, was more isolated from new ideas and influences. The contrast between the Two Lands can be seen not only in the geographical and environmental features, but in the distinctive art schools which emerged and even in the physique of the people. The northerners tended to be more stockily built, with lighter skins, while the southerners displayed something of the angularity evident in the southern school of art. However, these are broad generalisations, for Egypt remained a strongly unified country; at different periods, the capital moved from one region to another, and with it, the courtiers, officials, craftsmen, and workforce associated with the requirements of a great city; and the art followed the same broad traditional principles in both north and south, so that today only an experienced eye can detect differences in the ancient regional art styles.

It was the Nile however which enabled the Egyptians to cultivate crops and to rear animals, and indeed to develop their remarkable civilisation. Rain in Upper Egypt was the exception, and the infrequent, short and violent rainbursts could often bring damage; these were regarded as evil rather than beneficent events. In the Delta also, only the northernmost area benefited from the wintry rains of the Mediterranean. It was the annual inundation of the Nile which brought life to the parched land.

This was the most important natural event of the year, and inevitably became the focus of religious attention. The annual rains in tropical Africa caused the waters of the Blue Nile to swell; in Egypt, this eventually had the effect of causing the river to flood its banks, and spread out over the fields, carrying with it the rich, black mud which was deposited on the land. It was this silt and the people's management of the water which enabled the Egyptians to grow and cultivate crops. The rise of the river was first noticeable at Aswan in late June; by July, the muddy silt began to arrive. The swelling flood would cover the surrounding fields, and if it breached the dykes, would submerge the fields and villages to a depth of several feet. The flood finally reached the area near Cairo at the end of September, and the waters would then gradually recede, with the river contained within its banks by October and reaching its lowest level in the following April. Thus, the countryside presented great extremes – for part of the year, the villages and palm trees could be marooned like islands in the expanse of floodwater; by the end of the cycle, the earth would be parched and cracked, awaiting the new, life-giving waters of the next inundation.

However, the Nile's gift was variable and although it rose unfailingly, the height of the inundation fluctuated. A Nile which was too high would flood the land and bring devastation and the ruination of the crops; towns, villages and houses could also be destroyed, with the consequent and considerable loss of life. On the other hand, a low Nile would bring famine. The erratic nature of the inundation was a constant threat to the safety and prosperity of the people, and although the Egyptians showed great awareness of their dependence on the inundation in their religious literature, they were also constantly concerned that the inundation should not be exceptional. Indeed, it is not surprising that moderation and balance were amongst their most highly valued concepts.

In addition to their religious observances, from earliest times, they took practical measures to control and regulate the Nile waters. Started in the predynastic period, their irrigation system evolved a pattern whereby the land was divided up into sections of varying sizes, each being enclosed by strong earth banks. These banks were arranged on a chequerboard system, with long banks running parallel to the river, and another series running across them, from the river to the desert edge. At the inundation, the water was let into the banked sections through canals, and was held there while the silt settled. Once the river had fallen, the water was drained off, and the ploughing and sowing began. This system provided Egypt with rich agricultural land, and the need for such a system was also probably responsible for the early centralisation and organisation of the country.

The interdependence of physically isolated village communities on the all-important joint project of constructing, extending and maintaining an irrigation system gave the people an awareness of the need to co-operate and an acceptance of a strong centralised state. Dykes and dams were built, canals were dug and the system was maintained with the active support of the first kings. Today, the advent of a successful harvest is no longer dependent on nature, and on the petitions addressed to the Nile god, Hapy, and to Osiris, the god of vegetation and rebirth. Modern technology has led to the building of dams at certain points on the river, enabling the volume of water to be held back and supplied for irrigation as required, through a series of canals.

The physical division of Egypt into northern and southern regions is not the only geographical distinction which the Egyptians recognised. It is still possible today to stand with one foot in the desert and one in the cultivation, along the clearly defined line of demarcation between these two areas. For the Egyptians, the cultivated area represented life, fertility and safety; here, with assiduous husbandry, they could grow ample crops, and establish their communities. The name they gave to their whole country was 'Kemet', which means the 'Black Land'. This referred to the cultivation, fertilised for countless years by the black mud of the inundation. Beyond this strip, however, lay the desert, stretching away to the horizon under the glaring sun, a place of death and terror to the Egyptians. They gave this the name of 'Deshret', meaning 'Red Land', because of the colour of the rocks and the sand. These two regions symbolised life and death, and probably influenced some of their most basic religious ideas.

The other most important natural life-force was of course the sun. The Egyptians acknowledged this as the creative force and sustainer of life, and worshipped it under several names as a god; however, Rec was the name by which the solar deity was continuously and most frequently known.

The two great life-forces of sun and Nile had much in common. Both expressed, in their natural cycles, patterns of life, death and rebirth. The sun rose every morning and set at night, to reappear unfailingly on the horizon; the Nile annually imparted its gift of water, so that the life, death and rebirth of the countryside was vividly experienced. It has been suggested that this regular environmental pattern impressed itself so clearly on the Egyptian consciousness that they transferred the concept of life, death and rebirth, seen in natural cycles, to the human experience. From their earliest development, it seems that they believed in the continued existence of the individual – his rebirth – after death, and the concept of eternity remained a constant feature of their religious and funerary ideas. Although the supposed exact location of this continued existence varied in the different historical periods and according to the individual's social status, all Egyptians believed in some kind of afterlife and, for those who could afford it, elaborate preparations of the tomb and associated funerary equipment were made, to facilitate the deceased's journey into the next world. Both the gods associated with these life-forces –

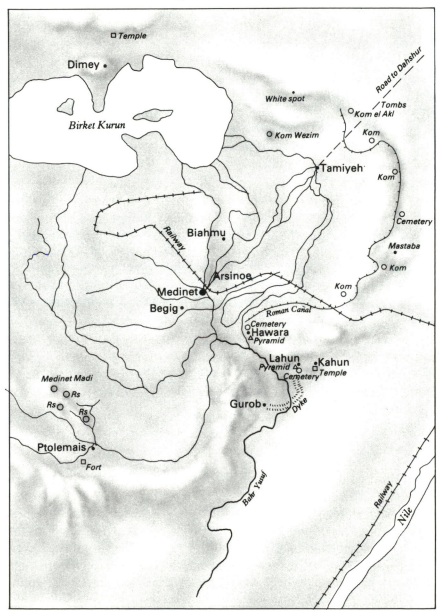

FIGURE 2   Map of the Fayoum oasis, showing location of Kahun, Lahun pyramid and Gurob. (From W.M.F. Petrie, *Illahun, Kahun & Gurob*, pl. XXX).

Re^c as the solar god, and Osiris, the god who symbolised vegetation and was king of the underworld by virtue of his own resurrection from the dead – promised regeneration and eternity to their followers.

It was possible for the often unique ideas which distinguished the Egyptian civilisation to flourish over many centuries and to develop largely unaffected by outside influences, because of the geographical situation of the country. A glance at a map of Egypt will immediately reveal the importance of its natural barriers. In antiquity, these were of more significance than they are today, for they encapsulated Egypt and buffered it against all invaders, so that, unlike many other areas, in the earlier times at least, Egypt was not subjected to continuous waves of conquerors. To the north, there lies the Mediterranean and to the south, the African hinterland; on the east there is the eastern desert and the Red Sea, while to the west, with its seemingly endless desolate hills, the Libyan desert stretches out. Here, in an otherwise waterless expanse, there runs an irregular chain of oases, scattered roughly parallel to the river. The largest 'oasis' (although, strictly speaking, it is not a true oasis) is the Fayoum, a depression in the desert, into which runs a minor channel, some 321 km long, known as the 'Bahr Yusef' (Joseph's river). This channel leaves the main stream of the Nile west of the river near the modern town of Assiut. It was here, in the Fayoum, that the community of Kahun lived some 4,000 years ago. But before returning to consider this area in more detail, it is necessary to examine the historical events which led the kings of the 12th Dynasty to select the Fayoum as their centre.

The historical background

Most studies of ancient Egyptian history cover the period from c. 3100 BC down to the conquest of the country by the Macedonian king, Alexander the Great, in 332 BC. However, the so-called Predynastic Period (5000 BC – c. 3100 BC) laid the foundations for much of the subsequent history, and the Graeco-Roman Period (332 BC – AD 641) illustrated the final decline and disappearance of many of those beliefs and representations that we would describe as 'ancient Egyptian'.

In the Palaeolithic Period, the Nile valley was virtually uninhabitable either because for three months of every year it was under water, or because it was otherwise covered with thick vegetation and supported teeming wildlife. The earliest inhabitants were hunters who lived on the desert spurs and made forays into the valley to pursue their game.

However, as the floor of the valley became drier, the people began to move down and to live together in settlements. Some time between 5200 BC and 4000 BC farming developed, and the people began to support themselves by growing grain, domesticating animals, and continuing to pursue, increasingly infrequently, the wild animals. Although these peoples fall into two broad geographical groups – one in the Delta and one in the Nile Valley – there are general features and patterns of development which, as Neolithic communities, they have in common. Much of our present knowledge of this era has been obtained from the remarkable discoveries and pioneering studies of William Flinders Petrie, the excavator of Kahun, and, with subsequent research, it has been possible to establish, for Upper Egypt, a well-established chronological sequence of divisions within the Predynastic Period, which lead up to the 1st Dynasty (c. 3100 BC). These are known as the Tasian, Badarian, Nagada I and Nagada II periods. In the Tasian and Badarian periods, the people practised mixed farming but still lived mainly on the desert spurs overlooking the Valley. However, in the Nagada I period, they settled along the Valley in fairly isolated communities. By the Nagada II period, there was increased contact with other parts of the Near East, and gradually, villages and towns in the north and south of Egypt developed into two distinct kingdoms, one in the Delta, known as the 'Red Land', and one in Upper Egypt, known as the 'White Land'. Each had its own king, who was the most powerful of the local chieftains in the area. It was the unification by a southern ruler of these two kingdoms – the 'Two Lands' – in c. 3100 BC that ushered in the historical period, with the establishment of the 1st Dynasty. The growing political awareness and development in these predynastic times was mirrored in a major advancement in the technological, artistic and religious spheres, and the artefacts, especially the painted pottery and metalwork, show an increasing ability to handle materials.

However, it was the unification of Egypt by King Menes who became the first king of the 1st Dynasty that marks the beginning of Egyptian history. The basis of our chronology for the historical period (c. 3100–332 BC) rests upon the work of Manetho, a learned priest who lived in the reigns of the first two Ptolemaic rulers of Egypt (323–245 BC). He wrote a history of Egypt (in Greek) around 250 BC and prepared a chronicle of Egyptian rulers, dividing them into thirty-one dynasties. There seems to be no clear-cut definition of a dynasty. Although some contain rulers related to each other by family ties, and the end of a dynasty can be marked by a change of family (brought about by the end of one line, or by wilful seizure of power by another faction), in other cases, family groups span more than one dynasty and the change of dynasty was brought about peacefully.

Modern research has shown that Manetho's record (preserved imperfectly in the writings of the Jewish historian Josephus (AD 79) and of a Christian chronographer, Sextus Julius Africanus (early third century AD) is not always entirely accurate. However, as a member of the priesthood, he undoubtedly had access to original source material in the ancient King Lists and records kept in the temples, and his work remains the basis of our chronology. Today, his dynasties are usually grouped together by Egyptologists into a number of major periods, distinguished by political, social and religious developments. Thus, we find that the Archaic Period (1st and 2nd Dynasties) is followed by the Old Kingdom (3rd to 6th Dynasties). This is followed by the First Intermediate Period (7th to 11th Dynasties), and then the Middle Kingdom (12th Dynasty). The Second Intermediate Period (13th to 17th Dynasties) leads on to the New Kingdom (18th to 20th Dynasties), which in turn gives way to the Third Intermediate Period (21st to 25th Dynasties). The Late Period (26th to 31st Dynasties) is followed by the Graeco-Roman Period. The three greatest periods were the Old, Middle and New Kingdoms, which were interspersed by times of internal dissension. The story of Kahun falls into the Middle Kingdom (1991–1786 BC), although some of the threads must be traced to the preceding and subsequent periods.

King Menes and his immediate successors established the foundations of a stable and unified kingdom. Untroubled by any major internal or external conflicts, Egypt, during the Archaic Period, was able to develop technological skills which were to lead to the great advances of the Old Kingdom. Central to their beliefs was the idea that the dead, in preparation for an afterlife, needed a tomb (a 'house' for eternity), and food, clothing, furniture, and other essential equipment. It was also necessary for the body of the deceased to be preserved in as lifelike a state as possible, to enable his spirit to re-enter the body and to partake of the essence of the food offerings either placed in the tomb or subsequently brought to the associated funerary chapel by the dead person's relatives.

At first, such elaborate funerary preparations were only made for the king, and his great courtiers. Other people were simply buried in the sand in shallow graves, surrounded by their few personal possessions. However, the funerary preparations of the few, and especially of the king, were so important that considerable resources were devoted to achieving secure and increasingly elaborate burial places. The technical advances made in Egypt at this early period were primarily directed to this end, and only gradually filtered through to benefit the burials at other levels of society, and also the general conditions of daily existence.

Thus in the earliest dynasties, we see the development of a type of tomb which is known today as a 'mastaba', because its superstructure resembles the shape of a bench, for which 'mastaba' is the modern Arabic word. From the 1st Dynasty onwards, kings and nobles were buried in mastabas, in the substructure below ground. Built of mud-brick, the superstructure was rectangular and divided internally into many cells or chambers, in which the domestic and other equipment for the next life was stored. This structure was almost certainly regarded as a house, embodying the same elements as a dwelling for the living, but to be occupied by the dead owner's spirit. The substructure incorporated the burial pit and was theoretically protected from robbers and animals by the superstructure. However, the mastaba afforded only ineffectual protection for the body, and in the 2nd and 3rd Dynasties the storage area was transferred below ground, and the superstructure was built of stone rubble, faced with brick. This again failed to defeat the tomb-robbers, but although the mastaba continued to be used for nobles, by the beginning of the Old Kingdom, the Egyptians had developed for the king the most spectacular place of burial – the pyramid.

The pyramid, as an architectural concept, seems to have developed out of the mastaba, and although pyramids were also built in later periods, they most perfectly signify the wealth, single-mindedness and religious beliefs of the period of their creation – the Old Kingdom.

For some, the Old Kingdom symbolises the Egyptian civilisation at its zenith, when many artistic and architectural forms are seen in their first flowering. It is certainly true that, in this period, the Egyptians perhaps held the clearest idea of their collective destiny and focussed upon one main objective – the building and completion of a monumental burial place for their king, which would withstand the ravages of time and robbery, which would facilitate the god-king's safe passage into eternity, and thus, vicariously, would ensure survival beyond death for all his subjects.

This common goal welded together, in religious and political unity, a country which, geographically, was difficult to rule. It also inspired great advances in technology and artistic expression, and indeed, few if any of the later periods produced such originality. King Zoser of the 3rd Dynasty was the first ruler to be buried in a pyramid. Apparently designed by his architect, Imhotep, it took the form of a stepped structure in six stages, representing, it has been argued, a series of mastabas of decreasing size, piled upon each other. This pyramid was only the central feature of a large funerary complex, with temples and other buildings where the king's cult could be performed after the burial.

Zoser's Step Pyramid, the first large-scale stone building in the world, introduced a series of pyramids which continued to be raised during the Old and Middle Kingdoms. Altogether, about 80 were built in the Nile Valley, mainly in the north and, in the Middle Kingdom, in the Fayoum. From the Step Pyramid, the builders attempted to create a true pyramid, and although some of their less successful attempts can still be seen in the transitional pyramids at Medum and Dahshur, by the 4th Dynasty, they had mastered the necessary techniques.

At Giza, strung along the plateau, are the three most celebrated pyramids, built for the rulers Cheops, Chephren and Mycerinus. The famous Sphinx stands closely associated with the Pyramid of Chephren, and, surrounded by a vast cemetery of mastabas once occupied by the families and courtiers of these kings, the pyramids form the centre of an extensive mortuary area.

However, the drain on the resources of the country was considerable. Not only did the pyramids and their complexes have to be built, but the altars in the mortuary temples of the kings had to be continuously replenished with food and other offerings, in perpetuity. The king's bounty also extended to his favoured courtiers; he gave them their tombs and an 'eternal' food supply for their associated chapels, to ensure the satisfaction of their souls. Before long, the royal coffers were depleted.

Because of this, and also because of the rising importance of the sun-god, Re^c, to whose priesthood the impoverished kings were becoming increasingly subordinate, the pyramids of the 5th and 6th Dynasties suffered a lessening of standards. Although they conform to the same regular pattern, these pyramids were constructed of inferior materials, with brick or rubble cores instead of stone. It was the new solar temples of the 5th Dynasty which now benefited from the major direction of royal resources. Indeed the method of construction of the pyramids provides a fair indication of the economic prosperity of Egypt and of the power of the king.

By the end of the 6th Dynasty, the stable society of the Old Kingdom, which must have appeared unassailable, began to disintegrate. The seeds of destruction – the withering away of royal resources with the king's gifts to the nobility and the priesthoods; the gradual lessening of the king's power at the expense of the nobles (who now built increasingly fine tombs) and the priests (especially of Re^c, who probably supported the succession of the 5th Dynasty kings); and, with his marriage to commoners, the abandonment of the myth that the king was half-divine, born of the Great Queen and the chief state-god – had long been present. Economic and political pressures weakened the king's hold. The governors of distant provinces at one time held their posts on a non-hereditary basis and were therefore anxious to remain loyal to the king. However, since these became hereditary, passing from father to son without the need of the king's consent, the local governors became increasingly independent in their attitude towards the centralised government at Memphis. They often no longer elected to be buried in mastabas near the king's pyramid, but were buried in rock-cut tombs in the cliffs of their own localities. In effect, they became minor princelings, and Egypt was soon to revert to the decentralisation of the Predynastic Period, when many chieftains had held sway in their own districts.

With the long reign of Pepy II at the end of the 6th Dynasty, and possibly exacerbated by incursions of Beduin on Egypt's northeastern border, the kingdom finally succumbed to the many internal and external pressures. During the First Intermediate Period, there was anarchy for nearly a century and a half. Centralised government broke down, and the country was split once again into warring factions which fought each other, sometimes in loose alliances, to gain control of various areas. Consequently, the irrigation system, dependent upon centralised order and control, broke down, and famine and despair became commonplace. We are fortunate that a number of manuscripts have been discovered which describe events during this period, and provide a vivid picture of the horrors which afflicted the Egyptians.

One manuscript, the so-called 'Admonitions of a Prophet', tells how a terrible calamity overtakes Egypt. People rebel against the officials, the foreign mercenary troops are in revolt, and Asiatics threaten the eastern frontier. However, the aged king is oblivious of the state of his country, living in his palace, and protected by the lies of his courtiers. At this point, a sage or prophet, Ipuwer, comes to the court and describes the state of the country and of its people, and also predicts the misery yet to come. It has been convincingly argued that this story reflects conditions at the end of the Old Kingdom, and that the aged king is Pepy II.

Another poem, known as the 'Dispute with his Soul of One who is Tired of Life', reflects the individual misery of the same period. A man, impoverished and disillusioned with the conditions of his life, argues with his soul. The man wishes to kill himself, and compares the joys of death with the agonies of his present existence. However, the soul, anxious that, if the man dies without adequate funerary provision of tomb and goods, the soul will be threatened with hunger and discomfort, tries to persuade him not to follow this course. We are told of the general social evils – men's covetousness, theft, and the lack of trust even amongst brothers and friends. In the account which Ipuwer gives, the irrigation system has broken down, the poor have seized the riches of their former masters, plague and famine are rife, and bodies remain unburied. His own words paint a dismal picture –

> Nay, but the Nile is in flood, yet none plougheth for him.
> Every man saith: 'We know not what hath happened throughout the land.'

and

> Nay, but poor men now possess fine things. He who once made for himself sandals now possesseth riches.

In time, however, the grief and destruction passed. Egypt, in the second half of the 11th Dynasty, was once again united. There was a return to more settled conditions under three kings, all named Mentuhotep, who had been princes of the city of Thebes which would one day become the great capital of Egypt in the New Kingdom. The widespread destruction of the monuments and the ravages of the countryside became memories, but the events could never be completely erased and the Egyptians' perception of themselves was changed. The simple concepts of the Old Kingdom, rooted in the stability of the society and the invulnerability of the king, no longer held sway. New beliefs were required to meet the emotional and religious needs of the people, and these, together with a political maturity, were to develop and flourish during the Middle Kingdom.

The first Mentuhotep – Nebhepetre-Mentuhotep – brought the country together, and he is also remembered for the unique funerary monument which he built at Deir el-Bahri on the west bank opposite Thebes. This incorporated a small pyramid, a rock-cut burial chamber beneath the cliff, and a mortuary temple. One of his successors, Mentuhotep III, had in his employ a powerful official named Amenemmes. He was the vizier and governor of all Upper Egypt and 'overseer of everything in the entire land', but his loyalty to his king was apparently non-existent, and he usurped the throne, making himself King Sehetepibre Amenemmes I, founder of the 12th Dynasty.

The details of this *coup d'état* are still incomplete, but it is obvious that there was widespread conflict and disorder and that the supporters of the 'legitimate' rulers of the 11th Dynasty opposed the usurper. Amenemmes I consciously adopted the title of 'Repeater of Births', indicating his view of himself as an inaugurator of a new era, but his successors went to some lengths to ensure that they were regarded as legitimate successors to the Mentuhoteps.

Propagandist literature from Amenemmes I's own reign, or soon afterwards, is preserved for us in the so-called 'Prophecy of Neferty'. This work is known from later copies found on a papyrus, two writing-boards, and three ostraca, which date to the New Kingdom. It describes fictitious events by which it attempts to justify Amenemmes I's reign, and to win support for him by discrediting his predecessors. A lector-priest, Neferty of Bubastis, a supporter of the king, is supposed to have composed the piece. The work, however, is set in the reign of Sneferu, a revered king of

the Old Kingdom, with Neferty as his contemporary. Brought to
court, he is asked by the king to foretell the future. He prophesies
that a great upheaval will come to pass in the eastern Delta,
where Asiatic incursions will occur. It is implied that this picture
represents the last years of the 11th Dynasty, although in fact
this period was probably relatively peaceful. However, such conditions are doubtless described to justify the actions of Amenemmes
I, who the prophecy now introduces, to found the 12th Dynasty
and to bring salvation to the country. As a usurper, such literature probably assisted his cause and was aimed at making his
coup more acceptable. The prophecy, however, also supplies some
detail about his background:

> A King shall arise in the South, called Ameny, the son of a
> woman of Ta-Sti, born in Upper Egypt. He shall receive the
> White Crown and wear the Red Crown. . . .

We know, therefore, that Amenemmes I was of non-royal birth;
his father was a commoner, Sesostris, and his mother, Nefert, was
a native of Elephantine, near the First Cataract. He was born in
Upper Egypt. However, despite the inauspicious beginning of his
reign, Amenemmes I succeeded in reorganising the country, and
in inaugurating the second great and prosperous era of Egyptian
history.

The first two decades of his reign were taken up with the
consolidation of his position. He had relied heavily upon the
hereditary local governors (often referred to as 'nomarchs') to
assist him in seizing the throne. Although they still posed a
considerable threat to any ruler, as they had done in the Old
Kingdom, Amenemmes I decided to foster their support. He
restored to them many of their ancient dignities and privileges
and installed new families of governors at Beni Hasan, Elephantine, Assiut, Cusae and elsewhere, to replace those who had
disappeared under the 11th Dynasty rulers who had tried to
remove their power. However, Amenemmes set limits to their
scheming, by firmly establishing the boundaries of their nomes
(the ancient land divisions of Egypt), and restricting each district's supply of Nile water for irrigation. He could also demand
the nomarchs to supply fleets of ships, levy troops, and to provide
other supplies to support the king's campaigns in Egypt and
abroad. Nevertheless, the problem posed by these governors

remained, and it was a direct descendant of this king who finally brought about a solution.

Amenemmes I chose to move the capital city to a new area. The 11th Dynasty had ruled Egypt from Thebes, but this southern centre was far removed from Egypt's northern borders where problems were occurring, and Amenemmes set up his new capital some 18 miles south of Memphis. Here, he built a fortified town called It-towy ('Seizer-of-the-Two-Lands'), as his Residence. In the twentieth year of his reign, he introduced the policy of co-regency, taking his son, Sesostris I, as his co-ruler. They ruled jointly for ten years, and this move, to ensure a smooth and peaceful succession in a dynasty which still felt unsure of its stability, was obviously wise. Indeed, the practice of co-regencies was followed by all the subsequent rulers of the 12th Dynasty.

Literary sources indicate that Amenemmes I was assassinated. In the *Instruction of King Amenemhet*, a book preserved in the later writing exercises of schoolboys of the 19th Dynasty, the words of wisdom and instruction are put into the mouth of the dead king as he addresses his son and co-regent, Sesostris I. This is another example of propagandist literature, for its aim was primarily political, to exalt the achievements of Amenemmes I and to affirm his son's claim to rule. Apparently composed by a scribe, Achthoes, for Sesostris I, it recalls Amenemmes I's own death at the hands of assassins who visit the palace in the night, while Sesostris is away fighting in Libya. Another literary account is given in the famous Middle Kingdom 'Story of Sinuhe'. Sinuhe tells how, as an official of the royal household, he returned from Libya with Sesostris I, after news of Amenemmes I's death. However, fearing civil war, Sinuhe deserts his royal master and flees to Syria where he spends many years in exile. Wishing, however, to return to die in Egypt, he finally sends a humble plea to Sesostris I to receive him again, and the king pardons him when he returns to It-towy.

It was Amenemmes I who re-introduced the traditional royal burial within a pyramid complex, choosing a new site, near the modern village of el-Lisht, and here the king's pyramid was once again surrounded by the mastabas of his courtiers and officials, after the pattern of the Old Kingdom.

The dynasty was now firmly established, and certain policies, especially relating to foreign affairs, can be determined. Egypt's relations with Nubia in the south had been pursued with some vigour in the Old Kingdom, because of her need to gain access to supplies of hard stone. In the intervening years, internal affairs had caused Egypt to cease activity there, and a new and more aggressive people, known as 'C-group', had now obtained a foothold in Lower Nubia. By the 12th Dynasty, there was an additional spur. Perhaps because the old workings in the Eastern Desert were exhausted, the need for Nubian gold became pressing, and the Egyptians now adopted a more aggressive policy towards the region. Indeed, from the Middle Kingdom onwards, Nubia became Egypt's main source of gold.

Amenemmes I began the subjugation of Lower Nubia but it was Sesostris I who completed the conquest and military occupation of the region. Fortresses were now built along the river in the region, most of which have been identified and planned. These substantial brick structures were garrisoned by Egyptian troops, and some control was even exerted as far as the 3rd Cataract. However, constant vigilance was required, and during the peaceful years of Amenemmes II and Sesostris II, tribesmen again began to threaten the area between the First and Second Cataracts. Sesostris III therefore led a series of new campaigns and in his 8th year established a new southern boundary at Semna. Further fortresses were founded or extensively rebuilt, and dispatches between their commandants, dating to the reign of Amenemmes III, have provided a vivid picture of the life which developed in these communities.

The lands to the north of Egypt seem to have received different treatment. Here, the main aim was to defend Egypt's boundaries. Amenemmes I is known to have built walls to repel the Asiatic incursions on the north-eastern frontier, although their exact location is uncertain. It seems that at this time Syria and Palestine were comprised of a number of minor states, ruled by princelings. Egypt apparently maintained diplomatic relations with these rulers, and indeed, there is evidence of perhaps considerable trade and contact between the two areas. Merchants and couriers from Egypt and Byblos (on the coast of Syria/Palestine) passed between the two lands, and several objects of Egyptian design have been found in Syria. Amongst these were a collar bearing the cartouche of Sesostris I which was found at Ras Shamra (Ugarit), and there is abundant evidence of contact in the reign of his son and successor, Amenemmes II. At Ras Shamra in Syria, a statuette of a daughter of Amenemmes II was found, as well as part of a figure of the vizier Senwosretankh; a sphinx with the name of another of his daughters was discovered at Katna, north of Homs. At Megiddo, there were four fragmentary statuettes of Thuthotep, a nomarch of Hermopolis, while Byblos, which had enjoyed close relations with Egypt from early times, in the Middle Kingdom was governed by local rulers who adopted the Egyptian title of 'prince', and wrote their names in hieroglyphs. They also wore Egyptian jewellery, and possessed other objects which were Egyptian in style and often in manufacture.

However, one of the most spectacular finds which may date to the 12th Dynasty was the rich treasure found in the foundations of the Temple of Montu at Tod in Upper Egypt. It consisted of four copper caskets inscribed with the name of Amenemmes II. These contained ingots of gold and silver, silver vessels, amulets of lapis lazuli and cylinder seals. At least one vessel was of the Aegean type, and other items were of Mesopotamian origin. It is believed that this treasure may represent either a gift or tribute to the Egyptian king from a Syrian ruler.

Egypt also had contacts with Crete and other areas of the Aegean; some Egyptian objects have been discovered in Crete, and the polychrome decorated pottery of Cretan manufacture, known as 'Kamares Ware', has turned up at various sites in Egypt, including Kahun. A particularly striking example of this ware was found at Abydos.

Other sources which suggest considerable links between Egypt and her northern neighbours include stelae and papyri in which Asiatic slaves are mentioned as being present in Egypt during the 12th and 13th Dynasties. Two series of Execration Texts from the reign of Sesostris III and the succeeding years also leave little doubt that the Egyptians had a detailed knowledge of the princes of Syria and Palestine in the 12th Dynasty. It was believed that if the names of the king's potential and known enemies were thus written on sherds and ceremonially smashed, they would, by means of sympathetic magic, be rendered harmless, and these Texts give lists of names of foreign princes.

Altogether, there can be little doubt that, in the Middle Kingdom, Egypt had continuous contact with these areas, and that numbers of foreigners came to reside in Egypt, although whether they arrived of their own accord or came as prisoners-of-war is unclear. This background of foreign influence will play an important part when the population and workforce at Kahun are considered. It can, however, be claimed that the rulers of the 12th Dynasty were considerably more aware of the need to deal with their neighbours than any previous Egyptian kings. Not only were the links with the northern area established, but trading expeditions were sent to Punt on the Red Sea coast (probably present-day Somalia), to bring back incense trees for use in temple and funerary rituals, and working parties were sent to the turquoise mines at Serabit al-Khadim in Sinai where their labour was augmented by that of the local inhabitants. Their camp-sites were transformed into permanent settlements, fortified against the Beduin raiders, and housed officials as well as workmen. Here, also, the Egyptian goddess Hathor, 'Mistress of Turquoise', was worshipped with a special cult.

Thus, the rulers developed wise foreign policies, and ensured access to raw materials which were increasingly required for the fine works of art which the craftsmen produced. Before considering these, we should, however, return briefly to the domestic policies of the kings which laid the foundations for an era of prosperity. Sesostris III perhaps contributed most to the internal security of the country, when, by methods which are still unknown to us, he brought to an end the privileges and power of the hereditary nomarchs, reduced them forever to the status of local nonentities, and ensured that the great provincial tombs were never built again. He thus removed one of the greatest threats to the position of the king, and consequently, to the stability of the country. The provinces of Lower Egypt, Middle Egypt and Upper Egypt were now administered from It-towy by three separate departments of central government which came under the overall supervision of the vizier (prime minister) who was himself responsible to the king. With the disappearance of the nobility, a new middle class emerged, made up of craftsmen, tradesmen and small farmers, who felt a debt of allegiance to the king. In the reign of Amenemmes III, the prosperity of the 12th Dynasty reached its peak; both internal and external threats had been brought under control and by his death, Egypt had become a renowned world power. However, his co-regent, Amenemmes IV, succeeded to the throne as an old man, and was soon replaced by the last ruler of the dynasty, a queen regnant, Sebekneferu, who was probably the daughter of Amenemmes III, and sister of Amenemmes IV. Her accession as ruler was probably due to the lack of a male heir, and her short reign marked the end of the dynasty.

The Middle Kingdom saw major developments in art and architecture, in religious and funerary beliefs and in literature. The kings of the 12th Dynasty once again established the supremacy of a state cult. This had existed in the Old Kingdom, exemplified by the cult of the solar deity, Re^c, but in the First Intermediate Period, political upheaval and decentralisation had led to a reversion to the worship of many local deities. This resembled the situation in the Predynastic Period, when communities had worshipped many tribal gods. However, the Mentuhoteps of the 11th Dynasty introduced a new state-god, Montu, the god of war, who came originally from Hermonthis, and now the 12th Dynasty rulers re-established a unifying, centralised cult. Not wishing to associate themselves with Re^c, the patron of kings in the Old Kingdom, they promoted Amun, who had previously appeared in one of the Old Kingdom creation myths as a member of the Ogdoad (group of eight gods) at Hermopolis. However, at some time in the First Intermediate Period, his cult had been established at Thebes, where he became associated with Min, a local fertility god, represented as an ithyphallic male. To establish his right to supremacy, the kings now also associated him with Re^c, and built him a great temple at Karnak, Thebes, where he acquired a consort. She was the vulture-headed goddess Mut, and their son was the falcon-headed lunar god, Khonsu. Amun was generally represented in human form, wearing a tall, plumed headdress, and the animal specially associated with his cult was the ram. The original concept of his role as a god of the air developed into the idea that he was the king of all the gods, and the creator of the universe. By the New Kingdom, as Amen-Re^c, he would become the great state god of the Egyptian Empire, with universal creative powers, features which paved the way for the later solar monotheistic cult of the Aten at the end of the 18th Dynasty. However, Amun's first elevation as a royal patron was due to the 12th Dynasty kings.

Whereas Amun reigned supreme in the world of the living during the Middle Kingdom, for comfort and support in death, the Egyptians turned increasingly to Osiris. Originally a god of vegetation, Osiris soon took on the role of king and judge of the underworld, associating his powers as a regenerative force of nature with an ability to promise his followers a chance of individual eternity. He had been worshipped during the Old Kingdom, but then his importance had centred around his ability to ensure the king's resurrection and safe passage to the next world. The mythology of Heliopolis, the centre of the sun cult, had dominated the Old Kingdom, and the king, as Re°'s son, had hoped to achieve a solar hereafter, sailing with the sun and other gods in the sacred barque across the heavens. However, the mythology of Osiris promised an additional assurance of this eternity. According to the myth, which is preserved in a complete form only in the much later account of the Classical writer, Plutarch, Osiris was originally a human king who brought civilisation and agricultural knowledge to the Egyptians. The envy of his brother Seth caused Seth to murder Osiris, but Isis, devoted wife of Osiris, gathered together Osiris' dismembered body, and by her magical skills, reunited his limbs. Posthumously, she conceived Osiris' son, Horus, whom she reared in the Delta marshes, away from the hatred of Seth. When he was grown, Horus wished to avenge his father's death, and fought Seth in a vicious and bloody conflict. Their dispute was brought before the tribunal of divine judges, and the gods found in favour of Osiris and Horus. Osiris was declared 'pure' or 'justified' and was resurrected as a god and king, not of the living, but of the dead in the underworld, while Horus became king of the living. Seth, the embodiment of evil, was banished. Every living king of Egypt was therefore regarded as an incarnation of Horus, and at death, was believed to become Osiris.

Gradually, with the fall of the Old Kingdom, and the rise of the great provincial nobles, the funerary rites and privileges originally reserved exclusively for the king to ensure his individual resurrection were sought by the nobles. A democratisation of the afterlife was brought about, and increasingly, the tombs, coffins, spells and other royal funerary paraphernalia were taken over at first by the nobility, and then by all Egyptians who could afford them. The Pyramid Texts, magical spells based on solar and Osirian beliefs, had been inscribed on the internal walls of some of the later Old Kingdom pyramids, to protect the king on his last journey, and to ensure his safe passage into the afterlife. These texts were now amended, and in the First Intermediate Period and the Middle Kingdom, were painted on coffins to provide the same protection for non-royal individuals. As such, we know them as 'Coffin Texts', and they were later developed into the 'Book of the Dead' which was used in the New Kingdom. The cult of Osiris was central to this democratisation of funerary beliefs and the afterlife, and the 12th Dynasty kings encouraged the god's worship at the expense of Re^c, supreme deity of their predecessors. Osiris came to have an almost universal appeal, promising eternity to all those, rich or poor, who fulfilled the requirements – to have led a blameless life and to be a follower of his cult. Any man or woman who, at death, satisfactorily faced the mythical Day of Judgement (when an individual was judged by the gods according to his good or evil deeds in this world) could expect to pass on to the Osirian netherworld. This was believed to be situated on islands in the west, below the horizon, where there was eternal springtime; here all were equal, receiving identical plots of land to till throughout eternity. Pleasing as this idea was to the humbler worshippers, the wealthier sought to bring additional comfort to their hereafter, and equipped their tombs with increasingly fine funerary goods and models of brewers, bakers, and craftsmen, which it was believed would be magically 'brought to life' to work for the deceased. These people hoped to spend at least part of their eternity in the comfortable surroundings of their tombs. Nevertheless, every man at death could now expect to become an 'Osiris' and to experience an individual resurrection.

The appeal of this cult was far-reaching, and many people made annual pilgrimages to the god's cult centre at Abydos, instead of to the old religious city at Heliopolis. Here, they would participate in the great annual festival of the god which coincided with the renewal of the vegetation after the inundation. The wealthier tried to be buried at Abydos, or to have their mummies transported there and then returned to their own locality for burial. Any association with Osiris, and with Abydos, the supposed place of his own burial, was believed to confer blessedness and an increased assurance of resurrection. Therefore the two great gods of the Middle Kingdom were Amun and Osiris. The fact that the 12th Dynasty rulers returned north to establish their capital at It-towy, and revived the Old Kingdom custom of royal burials in pyramids (originally a practice symbolic of the solar cult), in no way undermined the power of these two gods, for these were merely political moves.

However, other gods also achieved importance in the 12th and 13th Dynasties. In particular, the crocodile god Sobek became a patron of the kings and was associated with both Osiris and with Re^c, and was sometimes known as Sobek-Re^c. He was resident in the Fayoum and had temples there at Shedet (Crocodilopolis) and Dja (Medinet el-Ma^{c}adi), but the cult was widely established at centres from the Delta to the 1st Cataract. He was a deity of water and vegetation, and was worshipped sometimes with Renenutet, the cobra-goddess. The kings' interest in developing the Fayoum undoubtedly influenced their promotion of his cult.

Religion permeated almost every aspect of life in ancient Egypt, and the influence of these new beliefs can be seen in the art, architecture and literature of this period. During the Old Kingdom, a distinctive school of art had grown up at Memphis. Craftsmen were attracted to the capital by the need for sculptors, carpenters, goldsmiths, and other skilled workers to produce fine artefacts, particularly for the tombs. The Memphite school developed a style of tomb decoration and certain types of statuary and other funerary goods which formed the basis for all future funerary art in Egypt. However, with the collapse of the Old Kingdom, and the decline of Memphis as a centre, during the First Intermediate Period there was a growth of provincial schools of painting and sculpture. These still followed the traditional principles of Memphis, but developed their own peculiarities. With the democratisation of funerary beliefs, many more people now required burial goods and there was an increased demand for the craftsmen's skills. In the First Intermediate Period, their work is most evident in the painted wooden coffins and small wooden statuettes and models found in non-royal tombs. However, the political situation is reflected in the paucity of royal monuments or large statuary. The sophistication of the Memphite school was replaced, in these provincial paintings and sculptures, with a fresh, spontaneous and naive approach; the figures have an angularity and a crude vigour, while great attention is given to detail.

With the re-establishment of some kind of central power with the emergence of the 11th Dynasty rulers at Thebes, we see the development of a distinctive southern style of art at Thebes. This preserved many of the characteristics of the earlier provincial art forms, but added considerable advances in technical skills, and it became the basis on which all Middle Kingdom art was founded. When Amenemmes I moved his capital north, he brought with him the best of the Theban artists. Contact with the old Memphite tomb sculptures and paintings now had a marked effect on them which can be seen in the quality of work produced in the 12th Dynasty. The major building projects, to which we shall return, are the pyramids, but the other surviving monuments also indi-

cate the elegance of the period. A solitary obelisk remains of
Sesostris I's once-magnificent temple at Heliopolis, but an early
example of a cultus temple survives at Medinet el-Maᶜadi in the
Fayoum. It is also apparent that these kings added to existing
structures, and generally promoted building projects. One of the
most exquisite monuments of the age is the small jubilee chapel of
Sesostris I which has now been reassembled; its blocks had been
used in the later construction of the 3rd pylon in Amun's temple at
Karnak. At Hawara in the Fayoum Amenemmes III built his
fabled 'Labyrinth' which was greatly admired and described
variously by travellers as a labyrinth, a palace, a temple and an
administrative centre. Its exact purpose is still uncertain,
although it probably combined all these functions. In the 12th
Dynasty tombs, as well as on the coffins, the artists expressed
their skills in lively wall paintings, and colourful decoration. Some
of the best examples were found in the tombs at Beni Hasan and at
Bersheh, in Middle Egypt.

However, it was perhaps in the smaller items that the Middle
Kingdom craftsmen excelled. Most important are the realistic
royal sculptures, which show the artist's ability to master his
materials and to combine the realism of the Theban school with
the older Memphite traditions. The portrait heads of Amenemmes
III which have survived are particularly fine. These skills were
also applied to the production of large numbers of private, or
non-royal, statuettes which were placed either in tombs, or as
votive figures in temples. For this, a particular type of statue,
known as a 'block-statue', was developed. In another field, excellence was also achieved – Middle Kingdom jewellery was never
surpassed in other periods, and demonstrates the standards of
technical ability which had now been reached.

With regard to non-religious architecture, we shall see how
towns and houses were designed and constructed at Kahun.
Elsewhere, in Nubia, great brick military fortresses were erected
to subdue the local population.

Although the Middle Kingdom was a time of excellence in art, it
is generally remembered for its major contribution to the literature of Egypt. The troubles of the First Intermediate Period had
forced the Egyptians to reconsider their accepted values, and this
self-questioning ultimately led to the literary flourishing of the
Middle Kingdom. It is evident that the Egyptians themselves
regarded this as a 'golden age', for the language used in the

compositions, known today as 'Middle Egyptian', was later re-garded as its classical stage. Middle Kingdom literary texts were copied by later generations of schoolboys as exercises not only in composition but also in the use of their language. Indeed, most of the Middle Kingdom literature has only survived in these later model compositions, preserved on papyri, writing boards and ostraca (sherds used for writing).

The works include wisdom teachings, which were probably first introduced in the Old Kingdom. These sought to instruct young men in the attitudes and skills necessary to live in that society – although some, such as the Instruction of King Amenemmes I, were composed to strengthen the dynastic succession. Even the stories of this era often incorporate a moral or propagandist message, such as the famous 'Story of Sinuhe', where the king's benevolence is stressed. The so-called 'Pessimistic Literature' of this period incorporates elements of history from the earlier periods, and reflects the total disillusionment which followed the collapse of the Old Kingdom. Important examples of this genre include the 'Admonitions of a Prophet', 'The Prophecy of Neferty' and 'The Dispute with his Soul of One who is Tired of Life'.

Other religious writings illustrate the development of the concept of 'sacred drama'. Some were designed for special occasions, such as the 'Memphite Drama', and the 'Coronation Drama', used for the coronation of Sesostris I. Others took the form of 'Mystery Plays' which were enacted at the great seasonal religious festivals. Details of one of these are given in an inscription on a stela belonging to a man named Ikhernofret. He was an official who was sent to Abydos to oversee the refurbishment of the temple, and he describes how he participated in a 'Mystery Play' which was held annually at Abydos, re-enacting events in the life, death and resurrection of Osiris.

Many of the technical treatises, composed before or during the Middle Kingdom, have also come down to us, although they are mainly preserved on later papyri. The medical papyri, including the famous Kahun gynaecological papyrus, will be considered later, together with the legal and business documents, the temple journals, the fragmentary mathematical and veterinary papyri and the hymn to Sesostris III, which were all found at Kahun.

Two of the most important undertakings of the 12th Dynasty kings were their renewal of pyramid-building and the development of a major land reclamation project in the Fayoum. It was these schemes which provided the background and *raison d'être* for the town of Kahun, and they will now be considered.

CHAPTER 2

The Lahun Pyramid

Scattered across the great plateau of the Libyan desert, which rises 91–121 m above sea level, are the Egyptian oases. The first of these, usually considered to be part of the Nile Valley, takes the shape of an oval basin on the west of the valley and is surrounded by the Libyan hills. It lies some 64 km south of the old capital of Memphis, and today is known as the province of Fayoum. In antiquity, it was praised for its scenery, its fertility, and its cultivation, for it had an abundance of trees and plants. In Classical times, Strabo noted that richly productive olive trees grew there. The cause of this fertility was two-fold; first a number of springs of water fed the oasis and secondly, the Bahr Yusef, an arm of the Nile, flows into the Fayoum basin from the south-east through a narrow opening in the desert hills, near Lahun. It then branches out into numerous channels, providing abundant water for the area. The Bahr Yusef also feeds the great lake of the oasis which was of such importance in antiquity.

Known today as the Birket el-Qarun, the lake is now much smaller than it was in antiquity and there has been controversy over the original exact extent and position of the lake. It has been argued that in the remote past the lake occupied almost the entire Fayoum basin, but that in historical times it began to shrink. It seems that by the 12th Dynasty, the lake lay 2 metres below sea level.

A triangle of fertile land, deposited by the silt brought down by the Bahr Yusef, gradually built up in the middle of the lake. Here, probably protected by embankments against the inundation, the town of Shedet (Crocodilopolis) was built. As early as the Old Kingdom, this became a cult-centre of the crocodile god, Sobek. However, it was the 12th Dynasty rulers, seeking to enlarge the inhabitable and cultivable land area, who initiated major land reclamation projects here. By artificially reducing and regulating the inflow of water to the Fayoum basin, a natural rapid evaporation of the lake surface would have been achieved with the result that additional land was made available. This land was then protected from re-flooding by a system of dykes and drainage canals. Sesostris II was probably the first king to concern himself with this project and ordered the construction of a barrage across the mouth of the Hawara Channel, near Lahun. However, it was his successor, Amenemmes III, who completed the reclamation, gaining more than 17,000 acres of additional land around Crocodilopolis (the modern Medinet el-Fayoum). He enclosed this land within a vast semi-circular embankment. Indeed, Classical writers credit him with the creation of Lake Moeris, to accommodate the superfluous water so that the land would not be flooded by the rising water level of the river. However, this is almost certainly an exaggeration of his project, although his major works in the Fayoum were significant. In the Ptolemaic period, chiefly under Ptolemy II Philadelphus, the area of the lake was further reduced by means of embankments to approximately its present size, and the land thus reclaimed for agricultural purposes was successfully used.

Fishing and hunting were always favourite royal pastimes, and the area was noted for its ample supply of fish and game. In a later period, the Greek writer Herodotus (*The Histories*, Bk II, 49) mentions the large annual produce of the lake:

> During six months, the water of the river flows into it, and during the remaining half of the year, it returns from the lake into the Nile. At this time, while the water is retiring, the profits derived from the fisheries, and paid daily into the royal treasuries, amount to a talent of silver.

Another Classical writer, Diodorus (Bk I, 52), also enthuses about the lake:

> They say that twenty-two kinds of fish are found in it, and so large a number is caught that the numerous salters who are constantly employed there can with difficulty get through the work imposed on them.

Even today the fish from the lake, although of the same species as

Nile fish, are said to be superior in flavour to them, and fishing is still a major occupation here.

It is therefore not surprising that the kings of the Middle Kingdom chose to establish a residence in the area, and to set up a harem at Lahun where the king could stay when hunting in the area. Later, in the New Kingdom, the kings continued to frequent the Fayoum, but a new harem had by then been established at Gurob.

Greek travellers and geographers later gave the lake the name of 'Lake Moeris', which was assumed to be derived from the Egyptian 'Mi-wer' but this name has itself been the subject of scholarly debate. It was thought that perhaps 'Mi-wer' was the name of a branch of the Bahr Yusef, the canal that fed the lake. However, archaeological and literary evidence have shown that Mi-wer was actually most used as the name of the town known today as Gurob; this was in fact probably derived from the nearby stretch of the Bahr Yusef, similarly named. The ancient Egyptian name for the lake seems to have been 'The Lake of Mi-wer' (*Ta-henet en Merwer*), and not 'Mi-wer'.

Therefore, royal recognition and a favourable environment soon led to the establishment and development of some major towns in the area. Every king had several harems or residences scattered around Egypt and these were major institutions, possessing fields and herds and employing many people. The ladies of each harem, who presumably lived permanently at these residences, were placed in the charge of an 'Overseer of the Harem'. A harem town quickly grew up around the Residence, to supply the needs of the Court. These were always busy places, and the harem itself was a centre of industrious activity.

A scrap of papyrus from Gurob mentions garments or cloth which were owned by or destined for a foreign princess who was to marry Ramesses II, a later king of the 19th Dynasty. Fragmentary documentary evidence also suggests that here the harem ladies were either personally occupied with spinning or weaving, or were expected to train others, sometimes foreign slaves, who had perhaps previously worked as ordinary servants in well-to-do houses. The manufacture of textiles seems to have been continued in the area for thousands of years, for when the anthropologist, Miss W.S. Blackman, stayed for three months in 1924 at the modern village of Lahun, weaving was still the chief local industry.

It was here at Lahun, overlooking the mouth of the channel leading from the Nile Valley into the Fayoum, where Sesostris II had doubtless spent some of his happiest hours, that he chose to be buried, in the manner of the 12th Dynasty rulers, in a traditional pyramid.

The pyramid complex had been developed by the rulers of the Old Kingdom as the customary burial place for kings, and it appeared in its earliest form as the Step Pyramid at Saqqara. From this design, perhaps intended to represent a ramp or 'stairway' to enable the deceased ruler to ascend and to join the gods in the sky, the Egyptians developed the true pyramid form, best exemplified by the famous three pyramids of Cheops, Chephren and Mycerinus at Giza. The true pyramid may be an attempt to represent in stone the form and appearance of a sun's ray and again to provide the king, whose body rested within the pyramid, with a means of access to the sky. There are various indications that the development of the true pyramid was closely associated with the increased importance of the Solar cult, centred around the worship of Re^c, the Sun-god. This cult, particularly linked to the kingship in the Old Kingdom, promoted the belief of the king's divinity as the Sun-god's son. It was envisaged that the king upon death would join Re^c in his barque, journeying across the skies, and that he therefore needed a means of ascent. However, he was also believed to descend to re-occupy his mummified body which was placed in the pyramid, and to partake of the essence of the food offerings presented to the dead king through the medium of his mortuary ritual.

The pyramid itself was only one element in a complex of buildings, designed to ensure the king's resurrection and the continuation of his power as a ruler in the hereafter. In the Old Kingdom it was believed that the king alone enjoyed an individual afterlife, and all his subjects experienced eternity only through him. Later, in the Middle Kingdom, when a process of democratisation occurred in funerary and religious beliefs, every individual might expect a chance of eternity. The idea of a pyramid had been fully developed by the early 4th Dynasty, and indeed the second pyramid at Giza, built for Chephren, is the best-preserved example of this type which later became the standard layout. It consisted of a Valley Building, a covered Causeway, a Mortuary Temple, and the pyramid itself.

The pyramids were built on the edge of the desert and each

Valley Building, situated on the river bank, was the place where the funerary goods, the king's body, and later, the ritual food offerings were first received. According to one theory, the actual mummification of the king's body was carried out here. From the Valley Building, a covered causeway led across the cultivation to the Mortuary Temple which adjoined the pyramid. The Causeway was used to transport the king's funerary procession and his body from the river to the burial place within the pyramid. Since it was covered by a roof, the body was protected from the gaze of all onlookers except the chosen priests and members of the royal family and entourage. In the Mortuary Temple, the final funerary rituals were performed, including the ceremony of 'Opening of the Mouth', in which rites performed on the king's mummified body and funerary statues were believed to restore them to life. Here, in the Mortuary Temple, after the king was buried in a special chamber in the pyramid, the priests continued to perform daily rituals to ensure an eternal supply of food and strength for the deceased ruler.

Around each royal pyramid complex, there grew up a large number of other buildings – the mastaba tombs belonging to the king's family and courtiers, and the dwellings of the necropolis officials and workmen. All the subsidiary tombs had to be provisioned and the priests who attended to them had to be paid, an expense borne by the king as a mark of esteem for his favoured courtiers and officials. Thus, in addition to building and equipping and provisioning his own pyramid and funerary priesthood, each king had continuing obligations to the pyramid complexes and priesthoods of previous rulers, and to the courtiers and their tombs. After a few generations, this became an onerous burden, and the depletion of royal resources as a result of pyramid-building was one of the main reasons for the eventual decline and disintegration of centralised power at the end of the Old Kingdom. The gradual but steady loss of economic power is reflected in the material structures of the later pyramids of the 5th and 6th Dynasties when a core of rubble now replaced the original stone construction inside the pyramid.

During the 1st Intermediate Period, pyramid-building disappeared, although Mentuhotep of the 11th Dynasty erected a unique structure at Thebes which incorporated a pyramid. Amenemmes I, however, returned to the north and re-introduced the traditional pyramid complex based on the Old Kingdom design. He chose a site at Lisht, near his new capital of It-towy, as his burial place. It had the main features of a standard pyramid complex, but it was built on rising ground, with the buildings on two different levels. The pyramid was situated on the upper terrace, surrounded by a stone wall, whereas the Mortuary Temple stood on the lower terrace, to the east of the pyramid. Another feature of earlier pyramid burials had also returned. The tombs of courtiers once again clustered around the king's pyramid, some to the north and south of the Mortuary Temple, and others – about 100 belonging to nobles and officials – outside a rectangular brick wall which enclosed the main complex.

Sesostris I followed this revival and constructed a pyramid about 1.61 km to the south of Amenemmes I's complex. Amenemmes II built a similar pyramid at Dahshur (where a remarkable discovery of jewellery has been made; this belonged to the royal princesses). Sesostris II built his pyramid at Lahun, just north of the place where the Bahr Yusef turns westward to enter the Fayoum oasis. Here, Petrie also made a major discovery of royal jewellery. Successive rulers, Sesostris III and Amenemmes III, built pyramids at Dahshur. The archaeologist De Morgan also found splendid jewellery in the shaft tombs within the enclosure walls of these pyramids. Amenemmes III, famed for his irrigation and land reclamation schemes in the Fayoum, built a second pyramid at Hawara, which was probably intended as an elaborate replacement for the Dahshur pyramid. At Hawara, the Mortuary Temple was the famous 'Labyrinth' which was described in the writings of Herodotus, Strabo and Diodorus Siculus.

For Amenemmes IV and Sebekneferu, last rulers of the 12th Dynasty, there is no literary evidence of pyramids, but two ruined pyramids which were discovered at Mazghuna in 1910–11, some 4.83 km to the south of Dahshur, have been tentatively assigned to them, since the structures bear a close resemblance to the pyramid of Amenemmes III at Hawara.

During the 13th Dynasty, royal funerary monuments are more rare, but the ruined remains of a number of pyramids indicate that this form of burial was still used. By the New Kingdom, following the troubled years of Hyksos domination in the 2nd Intermediate Period, pyramid-building was abandoned, after the reign of the early 18th Dynasty king, Amosis I. Thereafter, in the New Kingdom, the kings elected to be buried in rock-cut tombs in the Valley of the Kings at Thebes.

The 12th Dynasty rulers sought to make their pyramids im-
pregnable. Generally, their pyramids at Lisht, Dahshur, Lahun
and Hawara followed the Old Kingdom type of construction, but
they were smaller and of an inferior construction. Only
Amenemmes I built his pyramid entirely of stone. The others
resembled the later constructions of the Old Kingdom, with either
a core of rubble-filled cellular construction, or of mud-brick. They
were all cased with limestone, and an extensive cemetery of
mastaba and pit tombs for the families and courtiers of each king
surrounded each pyramid.

The pyramid of Sesostris II at Lahun can be regarded as
innovatory in several respects, in terms of general pyramid development in the 12th Dynasty. The normal entrance position for
a pyramid had previously been on the north side, so that the
entrance corridor was orientated towards the circumpolar stars.
However, this fact was so well known that it greatly facilitated
tomb robbery. Therefore, more influenced by the need for increased security than by traditional beliefs, Sesostris II's architect
moved the entrance outside his pyramid. Petrie searched for the
entrance for several months in 1887–8, and finally located a shaft
to the south of the pyramid which descended vertically to a
passage which had been tunnelled 40 feet below ground. This
eventually led to a granite burial chamber in the interior of the
pyramid. However, the burial had been plundered in antiquity,
and only the red granite sarcophagus and an alabaster offering
table remained. There were also differences in the superstructure, and this pyramid strongly influenced the pyramids of Sesostris III and Amenemmes III at Dahshur, where brick was again
used for the inner core of the superstructure, and a maze of
chambers and corridors was incorporated in the superstructure to
confuse the robbers. Also, the innovation of placing the entrance
to the pyramid not on the northern side, but elsewhere outside the
pyramid, was retained.

Petrie's work at the pyramid of Sesostris II at Lahun began on
6 December 1913. Previous work in 1889–90 had revealed that
Sesostris II was the builder, and had disclosed that the pyramid
entrance lay on the south-east. Petrie therefore decided that he
would make a thorough study of the site, searching every foot of
the rock surface within the pyramid enclosure wall for possible
royal tombs, as well as planning the pyramid and all its surrounding constructions. The clearing of the site lasted until March 1914.

Originally, the site of the pyramid had been a rocky slope. The core of the pyramid was cut out from this solid rock, rising about 12.19 m from the ground. Above this natural rock mass, a framework of retaining walls was built of mud-bricks. In the lower part was a gridiron of massive walls of limestone to give firm support to the stone casing and to prevent its being shifted by settlement of the brickwork. This core was cased with fine limestone blocks, and the lowest were embedded in the natural rock, so that the structure could be secured. The external structure of the pyramid is therefore unlike any other in Egypt.

The base of the pyramid was surrounded on all sides by a shallow sand-filled trench which was intended to absorb the rain-water flowing off the face of the pyramid. Indeed, the nature of the site led the architect to take various precautions against subsidence. Despite the knoll of hard limestone, the pyramid rested at the south and west on marl which could easily turn into mud, and therefore several features were incorporated to absorb the heaviest downpour. This trench was encompassed by a stone wall, outside which was a thick brick wall. Beyond this, a single line of trees had been planted in circular pits sunk in the rock and filled with soil. There were 42 on the south, 42 on the east and 12 on the west, perhaps planted by the 42 nomes or geographical divisions of Egypt. Examination of the roots did not enable an identification of the trees to be made. Between the stone and brick enclosure walls, on the south side of the pyramid, four shaft tombs were discovered, belonging to members of the royal family. In one of these, Petrie found the magnficent jewellery belonging to Princess Sit-Hathor-Iunut, placed originally in three ebony caskets, and now in museums in New York and Cairo.

One of Petrie's main aims at Lahun was to discover the entrance to the pyramid. He found that much ancient tunnelling had been carried out in search of chambers, but success eluded him, until finally he uncovered a possible entrance. This led ultimately, by a devious route, to a burial chamber lined with fine white limestone. A light red granite sarcophagus, unique in form, was also discovered there, of which he says, it was '. . . perhaps the finest piece of mechanical work ever executed in such a hard and difficult material'. In front of the sarcophagus lay a white alabaster offering table of the usual 12th Dynasty style. There was also some broken pottery and bones from the funerary offerings, but everything else had been plundered and removed.

Outside the pyramid, other discoveries were made. Several pits cut into the rock contained foundation deposits, including pottery, model mud-bricks, beads, and the bones of a sacrificial animal. On the north side of the southern sand trench which ran around the pyramid, a plain wooden box was found inside a rectangular pit. This contained the bones of a child of less than 5 months of age, sealed with the official seal of the Treasury and therefore not a chance burial. Petrie was led to speculate about the origin of this burial and whether it represented a foundation sacrifice.

To the east side of the pyramid were the remains of the pyramid temple, from which many blocks were recovered. It had been adorned with lintels and jambs of red granite, carved with hieroglyphs coloured in green. Here, also, two foundation deposits were found, consisting simply of several little pottery saucers laid in the sand. Many pieces of sculpture were recovered, some bearing the names of Sesostris II and others showing some of the offerings. The fine workmanship which was evident in these pieces indicated the original quality of the work, before the building was destroyed by the workmen of the 19th Dynasty king, Ramesses II, who stripped the complex for building stone to use in nearby Ramesside constructions.

Petrie also discovered other associated buildings outside the complex of Sesostris II. These included, on the north-east, a lesser pyramid which probably belonged to a queen. Petrie believed that the queen who may have owned the pyramid had also been worshipped in the temple at Kahun. However, he sought in vain for its concealed entrance.

Along the north side, Petrie discovered eight rock mastabas in 1888 and 1914, but no burial was found in them although they were evidently intended for royalty. Just outside the northern brick wall, he uncovered a fine tomb – No. 621 – which was obviously intended for a senior royal person. It was probably built for a queen and was prepared for use, although the interment was never made. A fine red granite sarcophagus, a canopic chest to contain the jars holding the queen's eviscerated organs, and a large quantity of 12th Dynasty pottery comprised the total finds in this tomb.

An extensive re-examination of the debris in the pyramid chambers and in the vicinity of the complex revealed further artefacts. From the king's pyramid came the uraeus from his crown, made of solid gold and inlaid with lapis lazuli and garnet.

Beads were also found, and a few human bones of an adult male, perhaps belonging to the king himself. Pottery and lamps were also discovered. In the sand around the pyramid, several objects were revealed which probably belonged to the workmen – wooden mallets and some crudely worked limestone bowls, which may have been attempts by the workmen to fashion vessels out of builders' waste. Rollers were also found here. On the ground leading to the quarry, there were many logs of wood, laid level in the rock floor, and thus arranged to aid the dragging of stones from the quarry. The logs were apparently all old timbers from ships. In general, it was the transportation of quarried blocks (many of which weighed several tons) from the quarry to the site which caused considerable difficulty. For longer distances, the stones were transported by barge on the river, but there was always some distance to cover between the river and the pyramid site. Wheeled vehicles were never popular in Egypt until later times, and sledges and rollers were preferred. Occasionally, sledges were pulled over rollers, but it was more usual for sledges to be pulled by men with tow-ropes, along a carefully lubricated route.

The stone blocks were cut out from the quarries by a simple method. Holes were made in the rock using a chisel, along a required line, and very dry wooden wedges were inserted into the prepared holes. The wedges were then saturated with water so that they expanded and split the stone into the desired shape and size.

Once at the pyramid site, the sledge carrying the stone was probably dragged up a ramp, built against the side of the pyramid, and the stone would finally be levered into position. It would be carefully trimmed before it was lowered into place, to fit closely with the neighbouring block. As the height of the pyramid grew, so the ramps were extended in length; these were eventually removed when the building was completed. The face-trimming of the stones would have been carried out once the blocks were all in place. Tools included diorite picks, bronze and copper tools, and sandstone blocks to finely rub down the surfaces.

At Lahun, Petrie even found evidence of the workmen's daily food ration. Outside the pyramid walls, on the south-western side, he discovered the remains of the workmen's dinners – nuts in a little pottery saucer of the usual 12th Dynasty type, date-stones, small bones, pieces of fish skin, and part of a melon rind.

To the south of the pyramid, Petrie made one of his most spectacular discoveries. Here he found four shaft tombs, the most easterly of which, Tomb 8, contained the magnificent Lahun treasure. The mouth of the pit was discovered on 5 February 1914, and clearance of the area took the best part of five days. He uncovered an antechamber which gave on to the burial chamber, where a red granite sarcophagus was found which showed evidence of the work of ancient robbers. A white limestone canopic chest, containing wooden boxes to hold the canopic jars, lay nearby. Inside were the canopic jars, made of banded alabaster, which, although they were in perfect condition, contained not viscera but resinated bundles mixed with mud. The burial had obviously been plundered in antiquity and the body broken up. A small piece of black granite, perhaps from a statue, was found, inscribed with the words '(King's) daughter, King's wife, great consort', and although the name was broken away, it probably belonged to the tomb's owner, Princess Sit-Hathor-Iunut. However, despite the devastation of the tomb, the thieves had overlooked a recess in the west wall of the antechamber, and there the princess's jewellery was found, together with her caskets, wig-chest and toilet boxes.

The removal of the artefacts from the recess was time-consuming and difficult. The objects had to be loosened from hard and sticky mud; it seems that the jewellery was placed on a bed of mud in the recess at the time of the funeral, but later storms brought in floods which broke the roof of the shaft, and poured down into the tomb, washing the items around in the recess so that they were in a state of some confusion. The account of clearing the recess relates that:

> The whole of the mud from the recess was finally taken to the huts and washed, the mud remaining in suspension, and the beads, being heavier, fell to the bottom of the basins. In this way, we can be certain that not a single bead, however minute, can have been overlooked. Professor Petrie and Mr. Campion did this work, which was spread over some weeks.

The Lahun jewellery was a significant discovery, not only because it provided an outstanding testimony to the skill of the craftsmen who had made it, but also because Petrie's excavation techniques and methods at Lahun provided sufficient evidence to enable Egyptologists to more accurately reassemble a contemporary treasure discovered at Dahshur. Here, in 1894 and 1895, the archaeologist De Morgan had found, in the precincts of the pyramids of Amenemmes II and of Sesostris III, the tombs and jewellery of six royal women. This jewellery was again found hidden in the tombs and not placed on the mummies, probably to confuse the tomb robbers, although it is possible that an inferior set of jewellery was placed on the mummy. However, De Morgan's methods of removing the jewellery had been less painstaking, and the Lahun treasure, which closely resembled it, proved invaluable in reconstructing the design of the Dahshur jewellery.

A survey of the 12th Dynasty royal jewellery indicates that there was no standard set for a princess, although the ornaments owned by princesses who were almost contemporaries were frequently similar. At Dahshur, it was the Princess Merit whose jewellery most closely resembled that of Sit-Hathor-Iunut at Lahun, and they possessed pectorals of a similar design. Sit-Hathor-Iunut's treasure itself contained jewellery and other objects of different dates. She was the daughter of Sesostris II, from whom she received some of her ornaments. As the daughter of his old age, she was many years younger than her brother, Sesostris III, and her husband, Amenemmes III, was probably her nephew. Her second group of jewellery, from Amenemmes III, may have been given to her when he ascended the throne. However, she chose to be buried not with her husband at Hawara, but in her father's pyramid complex at Lahun, perhaps because the Hawara site was unfinished when she died.

Because the Lahun treasure appeared to duplicate much of the Dahshur hoard, Petrie was allowed to keep the jewellery, with the exception of three unique items – the crown, pectoral and mirror – which remained in Cairo. He sold the rest to the Metropolitan Museum in New York, who made a large grant available for future work.

The crown was an outstanding example of 12th Dynasty craftsmanship. A plain band of gold, with fifteen rosettes, a uraeus, representations of feathers, and a pair of streamers, it introduced a new design and seemed to be a ceremonial head-dress, to be worn over a wig. It differed from lighter crowns found at Dahshur, but was obviously worn and used in life, and was not designed for funerary purposes. Indeed, all this jewellery was for personal, lifetime adornment and showed evidence of wear.

One pectoral, the gift of Amenemmes III, remained in Cairo; the
other, presented by Sesostris II, was possibly the finest example of
Egyptian inlay ever discovered, with cut stones of lapis lazuli,
turquoise, carnelian and garnet set in gold, on to a backing of
white plaster. In the centre was the king's cartouche. The mirror,
made of silver, was set into an obsidian handle which represented
the head of Hathor, the cow-headed goddess, surmounted on a
lotus base; electrum, gold, lapis lazuli, crystal and carnelian were
also used to fashion this exquisite handle. Although the mirror
was of a type well-known at Dahshur, where the princess Merit
possessed five, the Dahshur mirrors had wooden handles, whereas the Lahun one, with its inlaid obsidian handle, was unique.
However, it is interesting to note that a much humbler version,
also with a wooden handle, was discovered in one of the houses at
the workmen's village of Kahun. In addition, the royal treasure
included a variety of beads of different types and materials;
tubular beads of thin sheet gold were perhaps worn on the plaits of
a wig; others were worn as necklaces, or threaded in panels for
belts, anklets or bracelets. One necklace was made of gold cowry
shells, and another incorporated representations of lion-heads.
Two lapis lazuli scarabs, one engraved with the name of
Amenemmes III, were found with the crown.

Other toilette articles included three gold-mounted obsidian
perfume jars and one kohl pot, which were the princess's personal
possessions; a set of eight alabaster ointment vases; copper knives
and copper razors with gold handles, together with two whetstones to sharpen the razors; caskets to contain the jewels; and the
alabaster vases. A plain wooden box, perhaps to contain a wig or
linen, was also found.

This treasure of the 12th Dynasty perhaps represents the acme
of the jeweller's craft in Egypt. It is also important because these
are items of personal royal adornment, rather than funerary
jewellery. At the other scientific excavations in Egypt which have
revealed royal jewellery, it has been mainly funerary items which
have been found. However, from other sources, such as tomb
wall-scenes and temple wall reliefs, it is evident that, although the
12th Dynasty jewellery from Lahun has certain features peculiar
to that period and exhibits a specially high standard of craftsmanship, it nevertheless follows the broad pattern of traditional
Egyptian jewellery.

The Egyptians used jewellery for a number of purposes. The

gods, the dead and the living received items of personal adornment which were believed to confer on them certain benefits.
Perhaps most important was the use of amulets (articles of
jewellery worn or carried) to ward off evil or hostile forces, such as
animals, dangers, natural disasters, and illness. The shapes the
amulets took – animals, parts of the body, hieroglyphs, images of
gods, special signs with a particular magical significance – were
believed to protect the wearer against specific or general dangers.
The materials used in the jewellery were also believed to contain
special properties; gold and some of the stones – carnelian, lapis
lazuli and turquoise – would bring assistance through the magical
potency of their colours, while other natural materials, such as
shells, brought protection to the wearer through their actual
shapes. The idea of protecting the wearer with jewellery was
extended to that made for the living as well as for the dead,
although funerary jewellery tended to be more traditional in
design and less well constructed.

Jewellery was also used to indicate status and wealth. Kings
gave constant employment to their jewellers, requiring sets of
jewellery to mark important events in their reigns, such as
marriage, accession to the throne, and jubilee festivals; funerary
equipment for the ruler and his relatives was also produced.
Jewellery was also presented to foreign powers, and as a mark of
royal esteem to honoured courtiers and officials, as well as to
signify the appointment of royal delegates. On special occasions,
kings would receive gifts of jewellery from their courtiers.

Throughout Egypt's long history, the materials used for jewellery varied very little. With the richest deposits of gold in the
ancient world, the Egyptians favoured this metal because it could
first be easily collected in granules in sands and gravel and then
melted into larger rings. Later, more advanced methods of mining
were introduced, when the gold was extracted from veins in
quartz rock. Also, gold did not decay or tarnish, and its colour
reflected the sun, one of Egypt's most important gods, and could
thus confer special magical benefits on the wearer. The supplies
came from Nubia, to the south, and from the Eastern Desert.
Other precious metals, such as silver, which the Egyptians called
'white gold', and electrum, were also used for setting stones.
Electrum was imported from Punt and the Eastern Desert, and
most of the silver came from Western Asia. Native 'silver' – a
low-grade gold with a high proportion of silver – was rarer than

gold in Egypt and was highly prized. By the New Kingdom, the jewellers had learnt how to experiment with various alloys and to produce different 'coloured' metals for their goldwork.

The metals were set with semi-precious stones, chosen for their colours and polish rather than their refractive properties. Most popular were carnelian, turquoise and lapis lazuli. Carnelian pebbles were picked up in the Eastern Desert; turquoise was mined in the sandstone outcrops in Sinai, where Hathor, the goddess of miners, was given a special cult; and lapis lazuli was imported from Badakhshan. Other stones – jasper, garnet, green falspar, amethyst, rock-crystal, obsidian, calcite, chalcedony – were found locally and utilised in the jewellery designs. The demand for some of these natural stones led the Egyptians to develop artificial methods of imitating them. Transparent stones such as calcite and rock-crystal, backed with coloured cements, were used as inlays, while to imitate the relatively rare imported lapis lazuli, they developed an imitative substance known today as 'Egyptian faience'. By the New Kingdom, there was also large-scale glass manufacture, and factories were established at the main centres of Thebes, Amarna and Gurob.

The craftsmen who produced these fine pieces were highly skilled and much esteemed in ancient Egypt. They were mainly employed either in the royal workshops or in temple workshops associated with the most powerful gods. Gold, levied as a tax, was collected and entered the state magazines, although some may also have entered the temple treasures, or have even been made available for the limited private work which was carried out. It was then carefully weighed, recorded and allocated to the gold-smiths in the workshops.

Goldsmiths, bead-makers, workers in precious stones and other associated craftsmen always appear, in tomb scenes, to work together under joint supervision. There was probably a chief jeweller, who had received a scribe's training, and had some freedom to design individual pieces as well as supervising the work of the others. Generally, the crafts were probably handed down in a number of families, but in the Middle Kingdom, it is possible that foreign craftsmen, perhaps from the Mediterranean area, were attracted to work in Egypt. Some of the royal jewellery at Dahshur shows a very non-Egyptian influence, although it is possible that these pieces were received as gifts from abroad. In the Old Kingdom, the first workshops were undoubtedly situated at Memphis, and the important god of Memphis – Ptah – became the patron god of jewellers. However, over the years, other centres undoubtedly became important and it is not inconceivable that craftsmen at Kahun produced some of the fine 12th Dynasty jewellery.

Wherever they were based, the jewellers only had access to simple and primitive tools. Before the New Kingdom, the furnace consisted of a pottery bowl supported on a stand filled with charcoal; the blow pipe was made of a reed tipped with a clay nozzle. By the New Kingdom, a blast furnace had been introduced, which was worked by means of a leather bellows, but before this, the craftsmen could not achieve really high temperatures to fuse metals and had only limited control over the level of the heat. Other tools included polished pebbles used to hammer the metals, and possibly limestone and bronze hammers; sandstone and quartzite stones used as files; bronze or copper tongs; and bow-drills to perforate stones. The softness of the high carat gold made the task of working the metal slightly easier, but with the limited tools available, the results are nevertheless remarkable.

A limited range of techniques were employed by the jewellers, including repoussé and chasing, engraving, granular work, possibly brought in by foreign craftsmen in the 12th Dynasty, and cloisonné-work, which reached its peak in the Middle Kingdom. Various techniques such as drilling and polishing were also used in the bead jewellery at which the Egyptians excelled. Many beads were also manufactured, from faience which was introduced in the predynastic period, and much later, from glass.

The treasure from Lahun is remarkable because of the high quality of the craftsmanship despite the availability of such a limited range of tools. Nevertheless, it is based upon the same principles of design which influenced most Egyptian jewellery. Although some items in the Lahun hoard are rare, such as the beaded belts owned by the princess which may reflect a foreign fashion, there are also examples which are entirely Egyptian but which developed in the Middle Kingdom and are representative of that period. These include the famous pectorals, trapezoidal in shape and decorated with the king's name. The representation of a shell motif was also popular and often took the form of a gold shell, inscribed with the king's name.

CHAPTER 3

The Towns of the Royal Workmen

Much of our knowledge of ancient Egypt is derived from tombs and temples – from the scenes carved and painted on the walls, and from the artefacts buried in the tombs. These sites, built of stone to last for eternity, are well preserved and in many cases have not been built over in more recent times. However, the towns – or settlement sites, as they are called – should also play a major role in any consideration of Egypt's society and civilisation. Because they were built of mud-brick, and in many cases have successive levels of occupation, they have survived less well and have therefore not received the same degree of attention as the funerary and religious monuments. Nevertheless, they are of vital importance in providing a more complete picture of life in Egypt.

Some archaeologists have suggested that true urban development never existed on a widespread scale in ancient Egypt; that because of environmental, political and religious systems, the walled city with different building levels and continuous settlement was not found throughout the country. It has been argued that, because a stable centralised monarchy had been established by King Menes at the beginning of the 1st Dynasty, subsequently there was no real political need for walled towns, and that the natural barriers provided by the deserts and mountains protected Egypt from most external threats. Thus, the need for true towns was limited to areas where products entered Egypt or along the east–west trade route involving the Red Sea and the oases in the Western Desert. In between, it is claimed, there was only a string of small 'harbours' along the Nile, in place of substantial town development. Each nome or district also had its modest centre, where the offices and houses for the administrators and officials were situated. The royal capital, or centre of government, was moved by different kings from one site to another; kings also had numbers of residences scattered around Egypt to which they paid occasional visits. In addition to housing the officials, all these urban developments also attracted craftsmen, traders and farmers to supply food for the townspeople. However, most of Egypt's resources were directed towards the construction of temples, tombs, and especially the king's mortuary complex, rather than to the towns, and this state of non-urbanisation persisted until the New Kingdom. By contrast, in Mesopotamia, urbanism was highly developed from the earliest times, and the city-state persisted as the most important element of the society.

The disappearance of the mud-brick towns in Egypt, which have been lost either because they have disappeared under the alluvial mud of the inundation or because the bricks have been removed by successive generations of locals for use as fertiliser, has not facilitated a correct assessment of the number and size of real towns in Egypt in the earlier periods. However, sufficient evidence exists to allow the concept of non-urbanism to be strongly contested by other archaeologists. It has been claimed that, as well as the major sites such as Memphis, even in the Old Kingdom, at sites in Upper Egypt such as Edfu, Abydos and Thebes, it is evident that there were walled towns of various sizes and types, and that towns existed at most or all of the places known from other sources to be administrative centres. These towns were occupied by officials with local duties, agricultural workers, and craftsmen and did not merely exist as the result of socio-economic conditions. In some cases they were specfically created to house personnel associated with temples or other monuments, at the behest of the government. This alternative concept of urbanism in Egypt presents a view of a country with an ordinary pattern of town development, rather than the sparse townships previously suggested. However, although they were obviously an important element in the society, the existence and development of settlement sites is a subject which does not find adequate coverage in the surviving inscriptional sources on which much of our understanding of the society is based.

Although the quantity, importance and spread of settlement sites in Egypt is disputed, it is apparent that two main types of urban development occurred. One was the natural, unplanned growth which evolved from the conditions of the predynastic villages. The second was a planned growth; certain towns were initiated for specific reasons in particular areas; they continued for the duration of the project, and were finally abandoned. Because their location was dependent upon the site of the project, they were not natural choices for continuing occupation and therefore were not levelled down for re-settlement. Some of these towns were built to house the royal workmen engaged on the building, decoration and maintenance of the king's funerary complex, and although they are not the oldest settlements, they are particularly important and also relatively well preserved.

In the Old Kingdom, there would certainly have existed work-forces to build the pyramids, and new excavations by the Egyptian Antiquities Organisation throw light on these. However, no details remain of how these men were controlled and managed. Most of the labourforce was made up of conscripted peasants. I theory, every Egyptian was liable to perform corvée-duty and was required to work for the state for a certain number of days each year. The wealthier evaded the duty by providing substitutes or paying their way out of the obligation, so it was the peasants who effectively supplied this labour. At first, their duties consisted of building and maintaining the network of irri-gation systems, but since the land was annually covered with water for several months because of the inundation, the peasants were later gainfully employed during this period on the construc-tion of tombs (especially the royal tomb or pyramid), and on the tem-ples. This provided them with food (they were paid in kind) and acted as a focus for the use of Egypt's manpower and resources. It has been suggested that the early use of the labourforce in this way – when they were engaged in building the king's pyramid dur-ing the Old Kingdom – provided a strong, unifying factor which enabled Egypt to develop as a powerful centralised state. Each pyramid project acted as a political, social and economic focus, and also, in the Old Kingdom, as a potent religious force, since at that time it was believed that individual eternity could only be attained through the king's own ascension to the heavens after death. Thus, the labourers and craftsmen sought to ensure their own eternity through service in constructing the royal tomb. The peasants were not slaves in the strict sense of the word, although their freedom and choice of action in terms of their place and type of work was strictly limited by social and economic factors.

Although most of the workforce were conscripted peasants, even in the Old Kingdom there would have been professional craftsmen and architects responsible for the more detailed work on the funerary complex, and these would have been housed near the pyramid sites. Petrie maintained that he had uncovered some traces near Giza of the barracks in which the workforce was housed, and the recent excavations have revealed other evidence relating to the workforce. The earliest complete example of a purpose-built royal workmen's town which has so far been revealed is Kahun. However, two other towns of a similar type have been excavated – the site known as Deir el-Medina, built to house the workmen engaged in building and decorating the royal tombs during the New Kingdom at Thebes, and that at Tell el-Amarna, the capital city with its associated rock tombs built by the heretic pharaoh, Akhenaten, at the end of the 18th Dynasty.

Although these towns were constructed at different periods, they shared a common functional purpose, and certain physical and environmental characteristics.

The three towns were conceived and built to a predetermined plan and none grew out of any previous random settlement. Each was enclosed by a thick brick wall, designed to confine the workmen and their families to a certain area. It is evident that the sites, all on the desert edge, were chosen because they were near to the worksite, but also because, isolated and surrounded by hills, they could be guarded. The inhabitants, after all, had knowledge of the position and structure of the royal tomb, and it was essential that such knowledge was retained as effectively as possible within an enclosed community. Planned within boundary walls, there is some evidence both at Amarna and at Deir el-Medina (occupied over a much longer period) that random growth of houses eventually occurred outside the walls. It is also noteworthy that even the proximity of a good water supply was not considered essential to these town sites, the requirements of isolation and security being greater. It is evident in all the towns that they were built to conform to a definite plan, with walls dividing them in a north/south orientation. Constructed for speed and efficiency, they are distinguished by regular rows of terraced houses for the workforce, and at Kahun and Deir el-Medina, some officials were also resident. At Amarna, there were 74 houses, at Kahun 100, and 140 at Deir el-Medina.

Each town also has some unique features, both in terms of its original concept, its development and occupation, and also in the quantity and type of artefacts discovered there by archaeologists. The three towns provide us with excellent examples of early town planning and give a fascinating insight into the everyday lives of special communities in Egypt.

Tell el-Amarna

Towards the end of the 18th Dynasty, King Amenophis IV patronised the cult of the Aten and introduced a period of solar monotheism which some scholars have regarded as a religious revolution; others prefer to see it as an evolution or culmination of the beliefs which had been developing throughout the earlier part of the 18th Dynasty.

The king, regarding himself as the god's agent on earth, changed his name to Akhenaten. He moved the capital from Thebes, administrative centre of his predecessors and the cult city of the pre-eminent state-god Amen-Re^c, to a virgin site midway between Thebes and Memphis. Here he built a new city, Akhetaten, which today is widely known as Amarna, or Tell el-Amarna. This city, which housed the administrative offices, the royal palaces, and temples to the Aten, stretched along the east bank of the Nile, encircled by cliffs. The North City was occupied by a palace, temple and government offices; the Central City had a palace, temple and a government office and was essentially the business quarter; and the South City housed officials and courtiers and was the industrial centre. During this brief period of heresy, the king and his courtiers planned to be buried in a series of rock-cut tombs in the cliffs surrounding the city. The situation of these tombs on the east, like so much else at this period, flouted tradition – in this case, the time-honoured custom of burying the dead on the west bank.

To build and decorate the city and the tombs, however, a traditional workforce was needed, and their purpose-built town lay in a fold between the cliffs and the South City. A shallow secluded valley in the side of a low, narrow terrace which runs out from the desert cliffs, divided it from the main city. Almost half of this village (37 houses) was cleared by the Egypt Exploration Fund in 1921 and 1922, but a preliminary survey in the 1970s indicated that there would be potential for further fieldwork, despite considerable damage at the site. Its similarity to Deir el-Medina, the compactness of the site, and the probable variety of the remains were all factors that encouraged the archaeologists to undertake further work there. Current excavations under the auspices of the Egypt Exploration Society are now revealing new facts about the site and one of the main aims of the present fieldwork has been to complete the excavation of the remaining houses within the walled area.

Like Kahun, the town was divided into two unequal sections, but this division did not reflect a class segregation as at Kahun. The houses appear to have followed a common design, except for the house of the commandant. Each house had four areas: an outer hall; a living room; a bedroom; and a kitchen leading to the roof. The building materials included wood, brick and very little stone. The recent excavations have shown that two distinct types of brick were produced: in one, standard Nile alluvial mud was used, mixed with gravel, and in the other, the material was pebbly desert marl quarried from the hills around the village. The enclosure walls of the village, and the foundations and parts of some of the houses, were of the alluvial mud. It has been suggested that perhaps at the beginning of building works at Amarna, a government agency had supplied proper mud bricks and possibly an architect to build the village enclosure walls and to lay out the foundation courses of some of the houses. Subsequently, each family perhaps had to obtain its own materials to finish off the work, and since mud-bricks were in short supply, they used the crumbly reddish-brown bricks from the nearby hillside quarries. In some cases, these were replaced with rough stones. If this theory can be proved, it would indicate the extent to which the state was actually involved in the construction of the village, and would also explain why some variations occur in the internal design of the houses. The importance of this excavation centres on providing new information such as this, and on revealing domestic architectural details of houses lived in by one section of Egyptian society.

Amarna village therefore, like Kahun, was probably built by a single architect. It shared certain principles with the other work-towns, as well as distinct differences from the randomly-developed villages. It had no wells, and the water was brought from the river a couple of miles away. However, it was enclosed and guarded, indicating some degree of official control. The houses, although not elaborate, were sturdily built, with painted walls and ceilings, and the articles found here, although not as comprehensive as those at Kahun, indicate that the same type of tools, household goods and toilette objects were used. Organic materials, including animal bones and grains, have also been preserved, as well as a mass of pottery. It also seems probable that the labour force here, as in the other workmen's towns, included some foreign elements. Although Amarna village has not revealed such a wealth of inscriptional material as Deir el-Medina, it is of unique religious interest. Here the finds indicate that, although the city of Akhetaten was built for the pursuance of the monotheistic cult of the Aten, represented by the sun's disk, the workmen themselves retained some religious independence and continued to worship traditional deities such as the cow-goddess Hathor, and the long-revered household deities Bes, the god of jollification, dancing and marriage, and Tauert, the goddess of fecundity and childbirth.

When Akhetaten was abandoned and the court returned to Thebes after Akhenaten's death and to the restoration of the traditional religious beliefs, the workmen's village at Amarna would have fallen into disuse once the centre of royal activity went elsewhere. The craftsmen and their families took up residence once again in the village of Deir el-Medina.

Deir el-Medina

The community of workmen at Deir el-Medina was involved in the construction and decoration of the kings' tombs. Together with their wives and families, they occupied the town for some 450 years, from the beginning of the 18th Dynasty to the end of the 20th Dynasty.

The princes of Thebes, who succeeded in driving out from Egypt the Hyksos rulers who had occupied the country for many years, established themselves as kings of the 18th Dynasty. This inaugurated the third great period of Egypt's history – the New Kingdom – when foreign policy changed after the Hyksos occupation from one of defence to one of aggression. The early part of the 18th Dynasty was devoted to pursuing this aim – the conquest of an empire – and areas of Asia Minor, Syria and Palestine were brought under Egyptian influence. Egypt became the wealthiest and most powerful country in the ancient world. At home, great temples were built and extended, and Amen-Re^c, the supreme state-god of Egypt whose cult centre was the Temple of Karnak at Thebes, was given a special role as father of all gods and creator of a universe which now included foreign subjects.

However, although Egypt was secure and wealthy, the kings now chose not to be buried in pyramids. They sought instead to gain protection for themselves and their possessions by choosing a burial site which was less obvious and more readily guarded against tomb-robbers. It was a futile hope, for of all the kings laid to rest in their tombs in the Valley of the Kings at Thebes, the only tomb which has so far been discovered in a more or less intact state is that of the young pharaoh, Tutankhamun. Nevertheless, the Theban cliffs on the west bank of the Nile provide a dramatic setting for these tombs. The natural cliff formation resembles a pyramid shape, and this may have lent additional support to the 18th Dynasty rulers' choice of burial site. The highest point, known as 'The Peak', was personified by the Egyptians as a goddess who was believed to protect all those resting in the rocky cliffs below. One of these barren, rugged areas in the western hills is known today as the 'Valley of the Kings', for here the rulers of the New Kingdom were buried in deep rock-cut tombs. In a nearby cleft, some of their queens and princes occupied similar tombs in the so-called 'Valley of the Queens'. In a number of places scattered across this rugged landscape, the rock is honeycombed with the tombs of courtiers and officials who were sufficiently honoured to be buried near their kings, in the same way that the nobles of the Old and Middle Kingdoms had lain in mastaba-tombs clustered at the pyramid's base.

Only the first king of the 18th Dynasty – Amosis I – was buried in a pyramid. His successor, Amenophis I, was the first to build a tomb separate from the associated Mortuary Temple which had adjoined the king's burial place in the pyramid complex. His successor, Tuthmosis I, the first ruler to be buried in the Valley of the Kings, seems to have also built the workmen's village at Deir el-Medina, as the bricks in its enclosure wall are stamped with his name. However, the devotion of the workmen to Amenophis I and his mother, Ahmes-Nefertari, may indicate that they had been instrumental in setting up the corps of workmen. In later times, they certainly held a special place and were worshipped by the community as patrons of the royal workmen. Little is known of the earliest years of the community although the men were probably drawn from a number of places and were already segregated from other workforces in the area employed on temple building projects. Their names indicate that they were of Egyptian origin, but included some who descended from Nubian or Hyksos ancestors.

The town was continuously occupied until the 21st Dynasty, although, even if it was still inhabited during the Amarna period, some of the workforce was probably moved to Akhetaten which, as we have seen, briefly became the centre of royal activity. Although the Court returned to Thebes in the reign of Tutankhamun (Akhenaten's half-brother and son-in-law), it is unclear if Deir el-Medina was again immediately in use. It had certainly resumed its role under King Horemheb at the end of the 18th Dynasty, and flourished again in the 19th Dynasty when, at the time of King Ramesses II's death, the craftsmen reached their highest numbers and greatest prosperity. It is evident that fear of the increased Libyan raids, general unrest and decline, and the aftermath of the major tomb-robberies finally forced the inhabitants to abandon the town. Ramesses XI owned the last tomb to have been built in the Valley of the Kings, and his successors were buried in the Delta at Tanis. So, by the early 21st Dynasty, the workforce had left Deir el-Medina, either forced to flee in fear, or conscripted for duties elsewhere. In its heyday, however, the town supported a thriving community, and the evidence which is preserved to us in the houses, the nearby tombs, and the papyri, ostraca, stelae and inscriptions provide an unparalleled source of detailed information. Unlike Kahun or Amarna, the excavations here have yielded large quantities of written material – official records, private letters, and literary texts – making it possible to identify the names of the workmen, their wives and their families, the houses they occupied, their legal transactions, and their working conditions. In addition, the artists' sketches on limestone flakes and potsherds which have been found in large quantities here provide a vivid insight into their everyday concerns and show us something of their humour. Thus, although in size, length of occupation, and date, Deir el-Medina differs from Kahun, it was built according to the same principles, and in addition provides literary information on the organisation and conditions of the royal workforce. To some extent, these must reflect the situation in the other two towns.

The physical arrangement of the village of Deir el-Medina closely resembled the situation at Amarna and at Kahun. Situated on the west bank near Thebes, it was hidden from the river; the only approach was along a narrow road which ran in a north to south direction through the valley, and this must have been the route taken by servants bringing supplies to the village and by members of the community who went to trade goods with those living in the cultivation. However, like Kahun and Amarna, its isolation afforded ease of surveillance, and it was also near to the worksite – considerations more important than proximity to a good water supply. The town had no well and the water had to be brought from the river which was about 1.61 km away. Special parties went to fetch the water supplies on donkeys, and it was then kept in a large tank outside the north gate, under the watchful eye of a special guard. From this, women drew their rations and kept them in large pots at the entrance to the house, to be used for domestic requirements.

The original town was enclosed inside a thick mud-brick wall. There is little information about the layout of the town within this wall during the 18th Dynasty, although it seems that not all the area was taken up with buildings at that time. This first village was destroyed by fire, perhaps during the Amarna Period, but under the restoration of King Horemheb, when the Court had already returned to Thebes and there was a return to earlier traditions, Deir el-Medina expanded. New houses were built, the damaged ones restored, and in the 19th Dynasty, the community reached its zenith. Then, the village occupied an area some 132 metres long and 50 metres wide. The area within the wall contained seventy houses, but other houses, numbering between forty and fifty, grew up outside the wall. Although there were over 400 years of occupation, there was no evidence of continuous levels of building within the enclosure walls and the floor levels of the houses were never raised. The expansion in numbers of the community was dealt with by erecting houses for them outside the walls, some of which were built amongst and over early tombs. This was perhaps the result of official policy not to extend the village itself. Certainly, the enclosure wall, originally conceived as a means of isolating and perhaps defending the community, eventually became a distinction between two social levels, with the descendants of the original inhabitants living inside the walls and considering themselves a superior category, while the less privileged remained outside.

The original village was bisected by a main north to south

street; with expansion in the number of houses, further side roads were created. The houses were arranged in blocks and the village presented a rectangular appearance, within its enclosure wall. The houses were all terraces; the earliest ones had no foundations and were built entirely of mud-brick, but the later ones, built on rubble, had basements of stone or brick and stone walls topped with mud-brick. Stone was also used for some of the thresholds. The houses had just one storey, and the roofs were always flat, constructed of wooden beams and matting, with small holes left to let in some light. Wood (from the date-palm, sycamore, acacia and carob trees) was readily available here, unlike Kahun, where the mud-brick roofs were vaulted. At Deir el-Medina, stone or wood was also used for door-frames, and the small natural light supply was doubtless augmented by leaving the wooden doors ajar. Hieroglyphic texts, painted in red, often occur on the door jambs and lintels and make it possible to identify some of the occupants. It seems that the houses were originally assigned to individual tenants by the government, but that, over the years, their families took on the tenancies on a hereditary basis.

Generally, the houses were quite cramped and dark. They all opened directly on to the street, and followed a basic pattern, although variations reflected some difference in status and wealth. The more affluent might plaster and whitewash their outside walls and paint their doors red but the floors were all made of earth. An average house had four rooms. An entrance hall led off the street, and here there was a brick structure which resembled a four-poster bed, often decorated with painted figures of women and the household god, Bes. This has been variously described as a 'birth-bed', or an altar. Here, also, there were niches in the walls to contain painted stelae, offering tables and ancestral busts, and the area probably acted as a household chapel.

A second room led off this; this was the main living room and it was higher than the first, with one or more columns to support the roof. Here, there was also a low brick platform, probably used as a sitting or sleeping divan. Small windows set high in the walls provided this room with some light. In a few houses, the archaeologists discovered child burials beneath this main room, a custom also encountered at Kahun.

One or two small rooms were entered from the main room, which were probably used as sleeping and storage quarters. At the back of the house, a kitchen was situated, consisting of a walled, open area, with storage bins, a small brick or pottery oven in which to bake bread, an open hearth and an area for grinding the grain supplied as payment to the workmen. A staircase to the roof led from the first, second or fourth rooms, and cellars under some of the houses were used to store possessions.

The walls of the rooms were either decorated with frescoes or whitewashed; the columns, window and door surrounds were coloured, and blue and yellow were favourite choices. Although Deir el-Medina has not provided the wealth of domestic artefacts which Petrie uncovered at Kahun, since most of the furniture had disappeared from the village, nevertheless, scenes on the walls of the workmen's tombs show the type of furniture which would have been used in the houses. Furniture was sparse and functional, and would have included stools, tables, and headrests for sleeping, and chests, boxes, baskets and jars to contain the family's possessions.

The accommodation of the workmen was not, however, spartan, and reflected their comparative affluence as highly skilled craftsmen in a society that valued their importance as builders of tombs and artificers of funerary equipment.

Documentary evidence provides information about the organisation of the gang of workmen employed on the royal tombs. The word used in Egyptian for 'gang' is derived from the word for a 'ship's crew'. There is no conclusive evidence about the strength of the gang; the full complement may have numbered as many as 120 men, but it was probably usually much lower, and it has been suggested that at the beginning of a reign, when the major work on a new tomb was inaugurated, the number was at its highest. However, it would have declined as the reign progressed. The figures, based on the records of grain rations supplied to the workmen, can in any case only be tentative, as the workmen may simply have been absent from work at various times for different reasons.

The gang was divided into a right and left side, with the right taking precedence. The men were usually permanently attached to a particular side, but they could be transferred, either permanently or temporarily, to balance the numbers, although the size of the two sides varied and they were not always equal.

The gang contained different categories of workmen. Most important were the chief workmen – 'Great one of the gang' or

'Chief of the gang'. There were usually two of these allocated to the tomb, each commanding one side. They were expected to direct the workmen, and they also represented the gang in dealings with the authorities. They were approached over any legal matters concerning the community and they received correspondence from the vizier. They settled disputes, received complaints, and were the leading members of the local 'court' which dealt with the community's legal problems. They were also responsible for instituting an enquiry when a workman died. They mediated between the workmen and the authorities and were supposed to regulate the workmen's behaviour. Although on some occasions, as when the gang went on strike in Ramesses III's reign, they attempted to persuade them to return to work, at other times, they encouraged the workmen to oppose the authorities. Other duties included supervising the tomb materials and receiving wood and colours for the workmen, as well as issuing new tools to them when necessary, and providing them with supplies of wood, clothes, oil and wicks.

Each gang also had two deputies, assigned to the two sides of the tomb. These men deputised for the chiefs but otherwise had the same duties as the rest of the workmen. A deputy was a member of the group to whom reports were made concerning supplies; he acted with the chief in receiving supplies for the gang and issued commodities to them which included loaves, fish, wicks, timber, charcoal, gypsum, oil and jugs of beer. He acted as a member of the court, and witnessed legal and commercial dealings; with the chiefs and the royal scribe, he participated in investigations and inspections, especially those associated with the strikes, and shared the responsibility for maintaining order in the community.

Another group were the tomb guardians who, although not members of the gang, were closely associated with it. Indeed, it has been suggested that these men may have been workmen before they became guardians; they were also connected with the tomb 'door-keepers' which may have been the appointment preliminary to becoming a guardian. There was one guardian for the tomb, and his main duty was to protect the stock of tomb materials, such as wicks, oils, pigments, jasper, leather, sacks and clothes, and issue them to the workmen. The copper tools were especially valuable, and he was in charge of these, exchanging new tools for blunt ones which he sent to the coppersmith to be repaired, and distributing the replacements to the workmen in the presence of the chiefs and scribe. As a man of responsibility, he was a member of the local court; he acted as a witness to oaths and other transactions; he was a member of the committee which inspected tombs in the area; he reported disturbances, and escorted prisoners and suspects.

The next group, the door-keepers, numbered two for a tomb, and were assigned to each side of the tomb. However, in some instances, there were more. It is clear from the lists that they did not form part of the gang, but were conscripted labour, appearing amongst the lower jobs, ranking below the gardener and wood-cutter but above the potter and water-carrier. They have left no tombs and practically no inscribed monuments. Their duties seem to have included acting as a bodyguard for the scribe, when he collected grain from the temple officials; receiving food and supplies for the workmen; acting as messengers for the workmen or bringing the vizier's messages to them; and witnessing barter transactions, oaths, and oracles. They also acted as messengers and bailiffs of the village court and seized debtors' property if they failed to pay.

The workmen were provided with their own servants, or serfs. Male serfs are known only in connection with the workmen in the reign of Merenptah, but they did not work at the tomb, nor did they live in the village. Their duties included carrying water, fish and vegetables; making gypsum for the tomb walls; cutting wood; making pots and washing clothes. They were equally divided between the right and left sides of the tomb, and were responsible to the scribes from whom they received payment in grain. There were probably usually five serfs allocated to each side, working in shifts. The water-carrier was a regular worker, but the other categories seem to have been less consistently employed; at the most prosperous times, a confectioner was also included amongst their number.

In regular employment for the workmen were the group of women slaves. Their number varied from time to time, with fifteen as the highest; they were attached to one or other side of the gang. It seems that they were provided by the king to grind the workmen's grain payments into flour, although this was done not at the tomb site but on the grindstones in the village. They were the king's property, whom he assigned to the community, but the custom probably ceased towards the end of the 20th Dynasty.

Certain categories associated with the Royal Tomb held very important responsibilities. The scribes carried out the administrative duties associated with the tomb. There were two, assigned to the two sides. They kept records of the activities and wages, and wrote most of the documents associated with the community. Every day, they noted down if all the workmen were present and if not, their reasons for absenteeism, as well as any unusual events. The preliminary notes were made on limestone flakes which were eventually thrown on to the rubbish heaps, when the final report, incorporating any additional details, was copied on to a papyrus roll. This diary was kept in the scribe's office, but extracts with detailed reports were sent at intervals to the vizier's office.

Detailed accounts were also kept of the payments received for the workmen, and of the tools and commodities which they issued to the community. The scribes also had considerable legal and administrative responsibilities. They recorded all the complaints and disputes of the village, they interrogated suspected thieves, settled divisions of property and generally dealt with cases which were too trivial to come before the local court, of which they were also members. They were responsible for the serfs and could administer punishment to them without reference to the court. Other duties involved presenting questions to the oracle of Amenophis I to obtain a decision and witnessing the replies, and delivering instructions or information from the authorities to the community.

In the village, they were much in demand to write letters and to read them for the inhabitants. They also augmented their income by using their knowledge of writing to decorate inscribed funerary equipment for the villagers. Their houses and their tombs were situated close to those of the workmen and they were an essential part of this tightly knit community.

In rank, the scribe was second only to the chief, and whereas the chief workmen were responsible for the technical progress of the tomb, the scribes were concerned with the administrative side. They were both responsible for maintaining order, and during the strikes, were expected to encourage the workmen to return to work. Both chiefs and scribes claimed the title 'Overseer of the Work', but the scribe was not responsible to the chief, but directly to the vizier. Scribes, with their expert knowledge of writing, would also have advised on the drawing and painting of hieroglyphs in the tomb.

The 'captains of the tomb', numbering three or four, provided the collective authority over the tomb, and belonged to the gang although they were not included in it. This group consisted of some of the scribes and chiefs, and combined the authority of both. The captains jointly distributed grain rations and working materials to the gang. They were responsible for the workmen's behaviour and brought them back to work from strikes. They represented them in front of the vizier and officials, and protected the community's rights. They wrote letters to the vizier, they heard disputes, and they took charge of promotions within the gang.

Finally, there were the police or 'medjay' of the tomb. Originally, in the Old and Middle Kingdoms, the 'medjay' had been Nubian nomads, but they had come to play a considerable role as mercenaries in the Egyptian army, helping to drive out the Hyksos, and by the middle of the 18th Dynasty they were established as police, protecting towns in Egypt, and especially the area west of Thebes. Responsible to the 'Mayor of Western Thebes', the main duty of those (probably numbering about eight) who were assigned to the royal tomb was to secure the safety of the tomb. They also ensured the good conduct of the workmen and at times protected them from danger, as when incursions of Libyans threatened their safety in the later New Kingdom.

Other duties included interrogation of thieves, inflicting punishments, witnessing various administrative functions, inspecting the tomb, and bringing messages and official letters. They could also be asked to augment the workforce, and to help to transport stone blocks. Although they were closely associated with the community, they never belonged to the village nor were they buried in the cemetery, but lived in the area, still on the west bank, between the Temple of Sethos I at Qurna and the Temple of Ramesses III at Medinet Habu.

Thus, the records from Deir el-Medina are most informative about the duties and responsibilities of the workforce, and other details can also be gleaned about their working conditions. We can, for example, learn something of the promotion procedures. Wages over a period varied considerably, and although some of the discrepancy was probably because some workmen were absent from work for part of the month, it has been suggested that some of the lower payments were part of a policy to pay the men at two levels. The workmen supporting wives and families may have received the higher payment, while the bachelors were given less. Part of any gang included these young men, or 'striplings', who received training in one of the specialisations – as stone-masons, carpenters, sculptors or draughtsmen. These young men were either newly recruited to the gang, or succeeded their fathers.

The families at Deir el-Medina were large, and therefore, only some of the children could hope to join the gang. Boys who were destined to do so were known as 'children of the tomb'. With few vacancies, competition was intense to get the 'boys' promoted to 'striplings' and eventually to 'men'. Fathers sought to persuade the chiefs to appoint their sons with flattery and bribery; presents, mostly of wooden furniture, were given, and one father kept 'a list (of all things) which I gave to the agents (of the Tomb to cause) them to promote the boy, they being my own and there being nobody's things among them'. In theory, the appointments were made by the vizier, but in practice the tomb officials chose the candidates who were formally approved by the vizier, and heredi- tary employment was a strongly established tradition. Those boys who were unsuccessful would have sought work outside the village and the gang.

Promotion to the higher jobs also caused conflict. The chief workmen's posts were not hereditary, but it is evident that the holder of this position made every effort to secure it for his son. Otherwise, the appointment was made from amongst the work- men of the gang. However, problems arose with regard to the deputies; each chief wished his own son to succeed him and not that of the previous chief, and to solve the conflict, the deputy was frequently chosen from the gang. In the case of the scribes, the office, appointed by the vizier, was expected to pass from father to son.

The wages also varied. The chief workmen received higher wages than the ordinary members of the gang; deputies, however, did not get a higher payment. The tomb guardians, although not members of the gang, received their payment at the same time as the workmen. The royal scribe, however, although second in rank to the chief, received only half his payment. The women slaves received wages very much smaller than those of the workmen, but it has been suggested that this was a secondary family income, since they were probably married to slaves who worked elsewhere in the administration and also received payment.

The payments were made on the 28th day of the month, for the following month. The basic payment was in grain, authorised by the vizier, and drawn by the royal scribe from the king's granary. Sometimes, however, it had to be collected from the storehouses of local temples or from nearby farmers, when the scribe was often accompanied by two doorkeepers with sticks. The grain included emmer wheat which was ground into flour, and barley which was made into beer. Other payments supplied by the government included fish, vegetables and water; and, for domestic use, wood for fuel and pottery. Less regular deliveries were also made of cakes, ready-made beer and dates, and on festival days or other special occasions, the workforce received bonuses which included salt, natron, sesame oil and meat. Some clothes were also supplied by the government. Generally, the payments were more than sufficient, and families could barter their supplies for other products. In addition, some of the royal workmen were much in demand to produce fine articles for the houses and tombs of the well-to-do, and their standard of living was comfortable.

The payments were divided out amongst the workforce, the officers, guardians and doorkeepers and female slaves, by the chiefs and scribes who themselves received a higher wage. The doorkeepers and guardians also received more than the workmen, as did the member of the gang who acted as the local physician.

While the payments were regular, the community was prosperous, but on occasions, either because of crop failures or other demands, the granaries became empty or depleted, and the workforce suffered considerable hardships. In the 20th Dynasty, there were frequent complaints about the delay in forwarding the rations, and when this was ineffectual, the workforce withdrew its labour. A major strike occurred in Year 29 of Ramesses III (c. 1158 BC) and there were shorter strikes in later reigns, the latest being recorded in Year 13 of Ramesses X. In the strike under Ramesses III the supplies were late; the scribe Amennakhte attempted to reason with the workmen when the grain was delayed for twenty days, and he went himself to the nearby Mortuary Temple of King Horemheb to obtain grain for them. Supplies were still delayed, and later in the same year, the workmen went on strike again and sat down in front of the royal funerary temples, refusing to return to work. Eventually, supplies were found, but the problems continued and strikes were a not infrequent part of labour relations. Although it was expected that the officers would encourage the men to return to work, some sided with the gang. In the major strike under Ramesses III, one chief encouraged his men to take the offered provisions, which he considered to be insufficient, but not to return to work:

> The foreman Khons said to the gang: 'Look, I am telling you: accept the ration and go down to the port to the gate, let the minions of the vizier tell him'. And when the scribe Amennakhte finished giving them the ration they started towards the port as he (Khons) had told them.

In the same strike, Mentmose, the chief of the police, who was supposed to persuade strikers to return to work, says:

> Behold, I tell you my advice. Go up, collect your tools, lock your doors and bring your wives and your children. And I will go in front of you to the Mansion of Menmaetre (the Temple of Sethos I at Qurna) and install you there in the morning.

He thus encouraged the strike to continue, and some days later, he brought some bread and beer for the workmen.

These Ramesside strikes are important, as they provide the first known fully documented evidence of collective protest by a workforce. Because the nature of their work on the royal tomb had a special significance, and its early completion was essential to ensure the king's safe passage to the next world, it was possible for them to bend Pharaoh's arm and eventually to obtain their rations. However, it is possible that such strikes were not limited to the New Kingdom, and there are indications that the workforce at Kahun may have used similar methods. Nor were the strikes the only delays to completing the royal tomb, for at Deir el-Medina, the records also indicate that absenteeism was not uncommon, for a number of reasons, and sometimes the whole gang seems to have been away from the tomb to carry out unofficial duties for the chiefs and scribes. The attendance register kept by the scribe also lists other reasons for absenteeism, such as illness, nursing other workmen, attending family funerals or actually preparing the body of the deceased for burial, offering to the gods and attending festivals. Even personal activities were included such as quarrelling with one's wife, brewing beer or getting drunk, and attending to household repairs!

However, in addition to providing information about difficulties experienced in their labour relations, evidence from Deir el-Medina also throws light on the gang's working conditions. Although the workmen were resident with their wives and families at the village, it was necessary for them to spend their working days in the Valley of the Kings and to stay overnight in huts nearby. They worked continuously for eight days, only returning to the village for rest on the ninth and tenth days. Each day, they worked two shifts, each of four hours, with a lunch break at noon. In addition to their six rest days every month, there were sometimes other free periods in the week, and official holidays and religious festivals were also quite frequent. In addition, long weekend breaks were sometimes taken, and 'unofficial' time was spent preparing their own tombs. While the men were away at the rest station near the Valley of the Kings, the women organised the life of the village; retired men, the sick, men on special duties, and servants were also permanently resident. However, in addition to household duties and supervising the slaves who ground the grain, the women had almost total responsibility for bringing up their families in the father's partial absence. Some of the remains of the buildings in which the workforce camped have been discovered on a pass leading to the Valley of the Kings, and indications of a similar stone camp have been discovered at Amarna, suggesting that here, too, the workmen engaged on major building projects were accommodated at night close to the work site, so that they could be closely supervised.

The selection of the site of the royal tomb was the responsibility of a royal commission, headed by the vizier. The various phases of constructing and decorating the tomb were carried out in close concert, but there was clear specialisation of the various crafts, with one phase following another in each area of the tomb. The men were supplied with tools by the state, and we have seen that certain posts carried the responsibility of handing these out as required, and attending to those that needed repair. In addition to the copper tools, wicks and oil or fat were supplied to provide artificial lighting. Salt, it has been suggested, was added to prevent the wicks from smoking.

The construction of the royal tomb was obviously a major undertaking, commenced as soon as a ruler ascended the throne. If the king's tomb was finished in good time, then the workforce was employed on tombs in the Valley of the Queens, and in some cases, on those of favoured courtiers. However, in most cases, the nobles had to obtain craftsmen from elsewhere and doubtless employed some of those artisans from Deir el-Medina who were unable to find a place on the royal gang.

The workmen were also much concerned with their own burial places. Finds at Deir el-Medina indicate that many of the inhabitants were prosperous and had aspiring social ambitions. This is evident in the titles which they presumed to give themselves. They chose to be known as 'Servants in the Place of Truth'; tomb guardians sometimes called themselves by the title of 'Chief Guardian in the Place of Truth'; and in their own private inscriptions, scribes would often affect the personal description 'King's Scribe in the Place of Truth'. There is never any indication that they were slaves, or even serfs, and although their total freedom of habitation and movement was evidently restricted, there is no indication that there was any strict regulation of their domestic lives or religious practices.

Indeed, they had considerable opportunities to augment their income and attain a comfortable standard of living. They accepted commissions for private work, and such was the demand for tomb equipment and funerary inscriptions that they could regularly increase their income. They held privileged positions, and some were able to acquire their own expensive metal tools, to own land and livestock, and slaves.

Their relative affluence is nowhere better illustrated than in their tombs which they built in the nearby cliffs. They devoted much of their spare time to these, which provide a valuable source of information, for, although the tombs were usually plundered, the walls, beautifully decorated with scenes of the deceased in the underworld in the company of the gods, provide information and frequently give the name and position held by the workman.

The tombs were built on a basic plan, with a small open courtyard and a vaulted chapel surmounted by a brick pyramid topped with a pyramidion. At a time when the kings had abandoned pyramids in favour of rock-cut tombs, the wealthier necropolis workmen were incorporating miniature pyramids in their funerary monuments. A shaft in the courtyard led to an underground passage and a vaulted burial chamber. Stelae were set on the side of the mud-brick walls, and in the courtyard there was a large stela which commemorated the deceased and depicted his funeral.

The tomb equipment included coffins, canopic jars, ushabtis, statuettes, furniture, clothing, jewellery, tools, pottery and stone vessels. The villagers made their own tomb equipment as well as that for sale to private buyers. Amongst themselves, they paid each other for required items. They also acted as embalmers and priests at each other's funerals. The tombs that have survived well date mostly to the early Ramesside period, when conditions were stable, but tombs were used at different periods for family burials and passed on in Wills.

Indeed, sufficient documentary evidence exists to enable us to consider briefly some of the legal aspects of the community.

In the New Kingdom, the two main centres of legal administration in Egypt were the High Court, situated at the capital city and presided over by the vizier; and the local court (Kenbet) which was composed of certain categories of people and which dealt with many of the less major crimes that did not require the death penalty. At Deir el-Medina, the village had its own Kenbet. It settled all civil matters and the less important crimes, and could deal with even more serious crimes, although the vizier had to give a final judgment and apply capital punishment if necessary.

The Kenbet at Deir el-Medina consisted of special categories of workmen who were considered to be responsible and of some significance – the scribes, foremen and deputies, the tomb guardians and some selected ordinary workmen. The Kenbet was mainly concerned with cases which centred around non-payment for goods or services. An individual would conduct his own case; the court's decision was not final, however, and a dissatisfied petitioner could appeal to the gods, by means of an oracle, for another decision. Difficulties were encountered in enforcing the payment of debts, and the court appointed the tomb door-keepers to attempt to exact these payments as one of their various duties. The police were not members of the court, but helped to uphold the law in the community. They also made arrests and ensured that the accused appeared in court. Another duty of the court was to register deeds of gift or divisions of property. The Kenbet would have sat at times when the workmen were not required at the tomb. Its existence shows the degree of autonomy given to the royal workmen who were allowed to conduct their own judgments and punishments for all except the most serious crimes.

The literary evidence from Deir el-Medina also illustrates the situation regarding domestic law – marriage, divorce, inheritance and ownership of property. It is clear that the wife was equal to her husband under the law and retained full control of her own property, whether she acquired it by inheritance before or after her marriage. Her rights to a share of the marital property were also assured.

Perhaps the most famous legal conflict which affected the inhabitants of the west bank and the village centred on the major tomb robberies of the 20th Dynasty. At this period, the economic conditions in Egypt had begun to deteriorate. Delays in the payments of the workers' rations increased, and in addition, Libyan raiders were constantly causing problems for the people settled on the west bank. For example, under the rule of King Ramesses IV, it was recorded that there was, in 'Year 1, 1st month of the winter season, Day 3, no work out of fear of the enemy'.

Troubled times led to an unprecedented spate of tomb robberies, and the Tomb Robbery Papyri preserve the account of the associated legal proceedings and also, the social background of intrigue and unrest. One major robbery took place before Year 9 of Ramesses IX (c. 1117 BC) and involved the violation of the tomb of Ramesses VI, but none of the thieves who were caught and punished included any of the residents of Deir el-Medina.

However, also in the reign of Ramesses IX, tomb-robbers, organised into a gang, plundered the tombs of some of the nobles, of some of the kings of the 17th Dynasty, and some situated in the Valley of the Queens. The conflict of interests, and accusation and counter-accusation which passed between the Mayor of Thebes-west and the Mayor of Thebes-east over this case makes fascinating reading even thousands of years later. However, culprits were finally brought to justice; they were in fact employees of various temples in the area, and not the royal workmen, but further evidence finally implicated members of the community. Eight royal necropolis workmen, including senior members of the gang, were arrested, and held at the Temple of Ma'at at Thebes. A house-to-house search at Deir el-Medina finally enabled the authorities to recover the stolen goods. The lists of the men from whose houses the goods were removed provide useful information not only concerning the robberies, but also because they give an idea of the range of occupations held by the villagers. The trials which ensued were followed up by a change in the administration of the community, and the senior workmen – the chiefs and their deputies – were replaced by men drawn from the ordinary workmen.

Although the workmen were probably not the instigators of the royal tomb robberies, they were undoubtedly implicated. Once the tombs were opened and plundered, they took a share of the treasure, and in some cases advised the robbers of the exact whereabouts of particular tombs.

The area was restored to order by Year 19 of Ramesses XI, and the royal mummies with their remaining treasures were collected and reburied together in two caches, but the position of the community subsequently declined. Ramesses XI built the last royal tomb at Thebes, and thereafter, the reason for the village's existence and importance disappeared.

We must now turn briefly to another important aspect of the community's life. The necropolis workmen at Deir el-Medina set much store by their religious beliefs and practices. In this, they exhibited the same general attitudes as all other inhabitants of ancient Egypt, for it was a society in which religion played a major role. Indeed, religion permeated most aspects of the civilisation. However, in the workmen's communities, it is possible to consider the more personal devotions which were followed by the workmen and their families. It is also important that these were the practices carried out by the men and women of the community during their lifetime, and not the customs which were primarily associated with death and the funerary cult. Evidence of such beliefs provides a valuable insight into a special aspect of Egyptian religion.

The Egyptians worshipped a pantheon of gods. In the earliest, prehistoric times, every village possessed its own local deity, worshipped by the chieftain and the community. As the country became unified politically, the deities of the various towns and villages were also gradually amalgamated, so that, although an individual might still offer his prayers to one god or a small number of gods, the 'official' pantheon came to include many deities. Some of these gods, who survived because their worshippers were more powerful than their opponents, adopted the characteristics and attributes of the conquered deities who were ultimately suppressed.

By the Old Kingdom, powerful groups of gods had evolved, supported by their own priesthoods. There was considerable rivalry between the various priesthoods, especially concerning the role of their own particular supreme god in the creation of the universe. Each priesthood tried to emphasise the importance of its own god as the prime creator from whom all else had been derived.

To simplify a complicated subject, it is possible to classify the gods of ancient Egypt into three main categories. Some gods, of whom the solar god, Re^c, is the first example, became so powerful that they came to be regarded as 'state gods'. These deities often enjoyed royal patronage, and indeed, their priesthoods were not infrequently involved in selecting and supporting a particular line of kings. Other similar gods, including Osiris and Isis, had wide-spread popular support as well as royal acceptance. All these deities received cults in the great state temples of Egypt, where the king or his deputy, the high-priest, approached the god, embodied in a statue, with ritual offerings of food, drink, clothing and other goods, in order to obtain certain benefits, such as longevity and prosperity, for himself and his people. A number of state gods existed at any one time, but usually, one was singled out for royal preference. The kings often elevated to this position the deity who had been the important local god of their own region. Thus, we have seen how Amun became the state-god of the kings of the 12th Dynasty. As a Theban god, he now achieved even greater power under the kings of the 18th Dynasty, who had formerly been princes of Thebes.

The second category were 'local gods'. Many of these were obviously derived from the old tribal deities who had been all-powerful in predynastic times. In later times, these gods received worship in local temples dedicated to them and were served by their own priests. The temples and the rituals were basically the same as those enjoyed by the state-gods, although the temples were smaller, owned less land, and did not have national import-ance.

Both the state-gods and the local gods were regarded as divine beings, with almost human needs, who lived in their 'houses' (temples) and were attended to by their 'servants' (priests). On certain occasions throughout the year, each god had a festival to mark some important event in his mythology. Then, the god's statue would be paraded outside the temple sanctuary and the people of the town and area would become onlookers, enjoying the spectacle of the festival, when the shaven-headed priests with their white robes and incense burners accompanied the god's procession. However, for most of the year, these gods played no direct part in the people's lives and their personal prayers and worship were addressed to another group of deities.

This third group, which undoubtedly received widespread attention, are called 'household gods', because, unlike the state and local gods, they possessed no temples or priests but were worshipped in people's homes. Some of them are known to us from the amulets – magical charms or tokens which were carried around in life and placed amongst the funerary goods in death. Some amulets take the form of household gods, to protect the wearer in those crises of life which almost everyone encountered. Thus, the goddess of childbirth and fecundity – Tauert – is frequently seen, and also the god of marriage and jollification, Bes, whose goodwill was essential for a happy life.

The stone temples dedicated to the state and local gods have frequently survived, and their wall reliefs, illustrating rituals and events in the gods' lives, provide an insight into the role of these deities. However, the household gods, widely revered and the undoubted objects of intense personal piety, have no such memorials in stone. They also feature less frequently in the traditional funerary equipment and official mythology, and evidence concerning these gods and the nature of their worship must usually be sought in the towns and villages once occupied by the living.

Discovery and excavation of such sites is rare, and of those yet explored, the workmen's communities figure largely amongst those to be considered. One major problem, therefore, in studying the religious artefacts from these sites is how to decide whether the material from Amarna, Deir el-Medina and Kahun is peculiar to them, as special workmen's villages, or whether it is a fair reflection of personal religious belief and practice in most living communities of ancient Egypt. Since one assumption holds that numbers of foreigners lived in the workmen's towns, we must consider whether the statues and other religious artefacts found at these sites give any indication of this. This problem will be considered more closely in relation to the Kahun evidence.

At Deir el-Medina, there were various religious buildings of some importance. There were several large temples to the north and north-east of the village, and chapels to various gods were carved into the cliffs near the village. In the temples and the chapels, there were stelae, statues and offering tables dedicated to various deities. Dedications were also made to deceased relatives on offering tables and on stelae, placed in the chapels or in the houses. Ancestral busts, placed in the houses, were the subject of family devotion, but it is unclear whether this was a custom

unique to Deir el-Medina, or whether it was also common elsewhere. From these domestic cults, it is also evident that, here,
Osiris and Isis, the deities who had enjoyed widespread worship
since the Middle Kingdom, were largely replaced by Amun and
Hathor.

The personal role which Amun or Amen-Re^c played at Deir
el-Medina is especially interesting. In the New Kingdom, he was
of course the great state god of Egypt, who had gained the empire
for the king, and who took on a supreme role both as the creator
not just of the Egyptians but also of their subjects, and as king of
the gods. His splendid temple at Karnak on the east bank at
Thebes was unparalleled in size and magnificence. Yet, at Deir
el-Medina, he received the personal prayers and devotion of the
workmen and their families, and was regarded as protector of the
weak and poor, and the arbiter of divine justice. A temple was
dedicated to him here, as were most of the stelae.

Another important cult at Deir el-Medina was that dedicated to
the deified king, Amenophis I, and his mother, Ahmes-Nefertari.
Although the village was actually founded by Tuthmosis I, the
workmen regarded Amenophis I as their patron, perhaps because
he established the royal workforce. A temple was dedicated to him
and he is shown being worshipped on many tomb walls and stelae.
Although some other kings received cults in the New Kingdom,
that of Amenophis I was of special significance here.

Three popular deities were Hathor, Bes and Tauert. Here,
Hathor became a goddess associated especially with domestic
ritual, although, in general, she enjoyed great popularity on the
west bank at Thebes, being represented as a cow-goddess and
associated with Isis, Egypt's great mother-goddess. She had a
shrine at the Temple of Hatshepsut at nearby Deir el-Bahari, and
Sethos I erected a large chapel to her near the village. Other
goddesses who were also sometimes identified with her occur at
Deir el-Bahari. Mertetseger, the necropolis, serpent goddess often
shown as a cobra, was identified both with Hathor and with the
'Peak of the West', the personification of the tip of the cliffs which
tower above the Theban necropolis. Rennout, another goddess,
was also identified with Hathor, and received a cult here.

Bes, the ugly dwarf-god who received widespread although
humble worship, was originally mentioned in the Pyramid Texts
of the Old Kingdom. Although he may have originated in Ethiopia
or Asia, his existence in Egypt was long-established and by the

New Kingdom he had gained a considerable following. He was regarded as the devoted guardian of Horus, son of Isis and Osiris, and he was believed to assist at childbirth, as well as protecting the young and the weak. He was also present at the circumcision ceremony, and fought evil forces, using music, singing and dancing as his weapons. He is sometimes shown playing a drum or other instrument, and always wears a hideous mask, often painted blue. Many figures of Bes were found at Deir el-Medina, and it is obvious that he played an important role there.

The third deity, Tauert, was also widely worshipped. She symbolised the waters of chaos out of which the world was believed to have been created. She was the goddess of childbirth, and was associated with Meshkent, the personification of the birth bricks on which women were delivered. Tauert appears as a figure with the body of a hippopotamus, and the head of a woman, a lion, or a crocodile; sometimes she has the tail of a crocodile.

Other deities at Deir el-Medina included Anubis, the jackal-headed god of embalming who roamed the necropolis; Thoth, the god of writers, builders and architects, represented as an ibis or a baboon; the crocodile god, Sobek; Re-Harakhte, a form of the sun-god; Ptah, the patron god of craftsmen; and the Aten, the solar deity who was the object of King Akhenaten's exclusive monotheism towards the end of the 18th Dynasty, but who was probably just one of many gods worshipped at this village. Osiris and Isis are also featured, as well as gods from the Cataract region of Elephantine – the ram-headed god Khnum, and the goddesses, Anukit and Satit. Foreign Asiatic gods were popular in Egypt during the New Kingdom, reflecting the generally cosmopolitan attitudes, and are represented at Deir el-Medina by Reshep, a war god, and the fertility goddesses, Qudshu, Anat and Astarte.

This wide range of gods therefore perhaps indicates the cosmopolitan nature of the community; the gods of any foreign residents were simply, in the usual Egyptian fashion, included in the pantheon. Thus, loyalty to one's own god, albeit of foreign origin, in no way affected an individual's acceptance of the Egyptian state gods. Another important feature was loyalty to the founders of the community, and despite a remarkable diversity of gods, the inhabitants of the village were obviously sincere and pious in their devotions.

The forms this worship took can be reconstructed, to some degree, from the physical and literary evidence. Of particular interest was the existence of an oracle at Deir el-Medina. The use of the oracle is well attested in the great temples, but at Deir el-Medina, it was the deified king, Amenophis I, who was consulted regarding the community's problems. His decisions were sought on such diverse matters as personal quarrels and family concerns, as well as definitive judgments on cases associated with the local law court. A petitioner could seek his answer in place of or subsequent to a ruling by the Kenbet.

The physical arrangements for working the oracle centred around the priests. The workmen acted as their own priests in the cults of the community, and performed the rituals for all the gods. For the oracle, certain workmen acted as priests and were responsible for the official maintenance of the cult – manipulating the oracle, keeping the god's sanctuary in order, and attending the god's festivals. To 'work' the oracle, the god's statue was held by the priests, in front of the petitioner. They manipulated it to move, from one side to another or up or down, so that the god's statue could indicate its reply to the question posed by the petitioner.

In the household shrines, filled with stelae and offering tables, lamps, water jars, braziers and vases, the family worshipped their selected gods with sacred rites. These, like the rituals in the great temples, doubtless included offering food, pouring out libations, and burning incense before the god's image. The village also enjoyed festivals, when the statues would be carried by the priests in procession through the village, and these occasions seem to have been times for meditation as well as rejoicing. The community also probably took part in some of the great state festivals of Thebes, when Amun's statue came from Karnak to visit the temples on the west bank.

Further insight into the personal feelings and devotion of the workmen has been revealed by the study of the memorial stelae erected by the workmen in the chapels. These appeal to various gods, and in some instances indicate humility and gratitude for recovery from an illness which was believed to have been brought about by the workmen's own misdemeanours.

The idea that an individual should be humble before his god because of his sins is not one that is widely found in Egyptian religion. However, in a study of this aspect of the religion, based on the material from Deir el-Medina (B. Gunn, 'Religion of the Poor in Ancient Egypt', in *Journal of Egyptian Archeology* 3

(1916), 81–94), it was shown that the people approached their gods, confessed their sins and appealed for mercy.

Some of these prayers occur on documents; others are on the memorial stones from the necropolis. A most interesting stela, now in the British Museum, was discovered in one of the small brick temples dedicated to Amun, which was used by the necropolis workmen. The stela was dedicated to Amun by one of the draughtsmen, Nebre, and his son, Khaᶜy; it gives thanks for the return to health of Nekhtamun, another of Nebre's sons. Another stela, dedicated to the god Haroeris by Nebre, the son of Pay, asks the god to 'let mine eyes behold my way to go'. It has been suggested that this may be a plea for a cure of blindness, or perhaps to receive spiritual enlightenment. Another stela addressed to the goddess of the Peak by Nekhtamun, scribe of the necropolis, states 'Thou causest me to see darkness by day.' Blindness was probably a fairly common condition and Gunn indicates that phrases suggesting blindness occur frequently in these prayers. He questions whether this frequency was because blindness was an almost occupational hazard for men engaged in decorating the badly lit tombs, or whether blindness in particular was regarded as a punishment for impiety, for which prayers had to be offered to the gods.

It is not clear how the petitioners had transgressed. Some examples, however, suggest that swearing falsely by the deity's name was regarded as an offence. One record states: 'I am a man who swore falsely by Ptah, Lord of Truth. And he caused me to behold darkness by day.' In another instance, a certain Neferᶜabu was punished with sickness, which was later withdrawn, for his 'transgression against the Peak' (the Goddess of the Peak).

Whatever the nature of the supposed sins, it is clear that the community regarded these transgressions as serious offences which incurred the god's wrath, and which were punished directly by illness. However, prayers and contrition could persuade the deity to withdraw the sickness.

The workmen of Deir el-Medina were literate because of their occupations, and could make inscribed stelae, which have preserved their religious sentiments. These men were, therefore, in a special category. However, some other prayers and hymns of the same period indicate that these ideas were not held exclusively by the inhabitants of Deir el-Medina. It perhaps formed part of a popular religious development during the later New Kingdom, and Gunn has suggested that the ideas of divine mercy and man's dependence on it may have been introduced into Egypt by Syrian immigrants. Alternatively, these ideas may always have been part of popular faith, but did not find expression in the written form before this period. This aspect of the religion nevertheless provides an insight, unparalleled elsewhere, into the beliefs of the community.

The literacy of the members of this community is in fact attested by the wealth of literary ostraca and papyri which have been discovered at Deir el-Medina. The Greek word *ostracon* (plural *ostraca*) means 'potsherd', but in Egyptology it usually refers to the sherds of pottery or limestone flakes which, as cheap substitutes for papyrus, were used for writing and drawing. Broken clay pots from the houses and limestone flakes from the nearby cliffs provided the people of Deir el-Medina with a ready supply of writing material, and many thousands of ostraca were discovered in the rubbish heaps of the village by the archaeologists Schiaparelli, Moeller and Bruyère. Most of these date to the 18th–20th Dynasties, and many are now in the Turin and Berlin museums.

They are generally inscribed in the cursive form of the Egyptian language known as 'Hieratic', and probably a large proportion of the male population of the village, and not just the scribes, were literate in Hieratic, if not in the sacred picture writing, known as 'Hieroglyphic'. Some of these ostraca were inscribed with official or semi-official records or accounts – bills, work diaries, reasons for absenteeism, inventories and so forth. Others, however, were obviously for private or teaching use, and included wisdom literature, to instruct youngsters in the required attitudes for advancement in the society; popular stories, of which one of the best known was the famous Middle Kingdom tale, the 'Story of Sinuhe'; hymns to deities; poems to the kings; love songs; and magical spells to protect the individual against various dangers.

However, another class of ostraca is also of considerable interest. The so-called figured ostraca or pictorial sherds provide a unique record of the personal artistic expression of the workmen. These sketches are important because, unlike the official art in the tombs and the temples, they provide a rare insight into the artist's own imagination and wealth of ideas. At home in his village, the same man who was engaged in producing the traditional wall scenes in the royal tomb picked up a limestone flake,

made his sketch, and later discarded the flake in the rubbish heap.
For such drawings, the themes and motifs were of his own
choice, and they often do not occur in the official art. He was also
free to express his own artistic style, without the restrictions
imposed by the rigid religious traditions on his official work.
Again, in some cases, these pieces provide information about the
training and techniques of the artist. Many of the ostraca are now
held in museums in Cairo, Turin, Berlin, Stockholm, Brussels,
New York, London, Paris and Cambridge.

There were undoubtedly schools in the village for training the
sons not only of the scribes but also probably of the ordinary
workmen to write in Hieratic. There were also art lessons in which
students, apprenticed as assistants to a master or taught in a
group, learnt their basic skills; some of these figured ostraca are
the students' trial pieces. The teacher would supply models which
the pupils were required to copy. Most of the ostraca have designs
in paint with only a very few examples in relief. These preliminary
sketches would sometimes be corrected by the teacher.

In addition to the novice pieces, there are also ostraca which
show fully fledged artists' drafts; some of these are copies of the
large tomb paintings, and as such, are examples of official art.
These men used the same tools and materials for their sketches
that they employed in their work in the tombs – primary colours
derived from mineral paints and brushes made of reeds chewed at
the tip.

Some ostraca scenes, however, were personal doodles. Inspired
by folklore and by the events of daily life, they introduced themes
which are not found in the official art. Here we can see something
of their vivid world – figures of gods, kings, musicians, dancers,
their household decoration and furniture, sport, games, enter-
tainment and even erotic scenes are all represented.

A number of ostraca acted as substitutes for the large stelae
which the wealthier inhabitants possessed. On these pieces, coloured religious scenes occur as well as invocations to various
deities; the snake-goddess Mertetseger, Ptah, Thoth, Amun and
Re^c were especially popular.

However, one group of figured ostraca has particularly captured the imagination of the modern student of Deir el-Medina.
These show sketches in which animals are represented, posing,
dressed and acting out roles as human beings. Various explanations have been offered for these. They can be regarded as

illustrations of ancient animal folktales and perhaps particularly represent the story of the war between the Cats and the Mice, since quite a number show cats in service under the authority of lordly mice. However, it has also been suggested that these are in fact satirical sketches, with a much wider political significance, and that they reflect the workmen's own criticism of the social order, and their awareness, despite their relatively low status, of their own importance.

The range of animals in these sketches is wide, including most common types except sheep or pigs. They appear dressed as humans and they walk upright; they also act out human situations – offering flowers, food and drink; dressing their hair; playing musical instruments; taking part in religious processions; nursing their young in shawls; doing accounts; playing games; working in the kitchen; drinking beer; and sitting in judgment. They also use human language but no texts of stories have actually survived to accompany these scenes. The ostraca may have been used in conjunction with oral versions of well-known stories, to illustrate more vividly the characters and events in the tale.

The animal scenes occur mainly on ostraca, although three 'satirical papyri' with similar themes (now in Cairo, London and Turin) have also been found. These animal ostraca have been found in larger numbers at Deir el-Medina than elsewhere, and although this may simply be due to the inhabitants' particular artistic ability or an accident of preservation, it is also perhaps possible to see something of the community's remarkable autonomy and independence of spirit in these scenes. Human foibles and social aspirations are expressed in the animal forms, and these are surely the forerunners of modern cartoons in which the 'underdog' ultimately triumphs. Whatever their real significance, the ostraca undoubtedly illuminate another aspect of the community.

In general, the evidence from Deir el-Medina indicates that the workmen enjoyed a relatively good standard of living, with an income from their official work and also ample opportunity to augment this with private commissions. They had considerable legal and religious autonomy, with freedom to appoint the members of their own law court and the priests to serve their gods. When the occasion arose, they could bring work on the Pharaoh's tomb to a standstill, and, by a collective protest and withdrawal of their labour, they could force the authorities to obtain the overdue rations.

However, they were also pious and devoted to their particular gods; and despite family feuds and legal wrangles, they were a close-knit community. To some extent, these characteristics were fostered by their physical, environmental and social conditions, and although some of these elements were different at Kahun, and the documentation from there is comparatively limited, we should expect to see a community which shared at least some features with Deir el-Medina.

Gurob

The site of Gurob, or Medinet Gurob, was worked for over thirty-three years, but the first legitimate excavations were carried out there by William Flinders Petrie in two seasons, from 1888 to 1890. This was one of the excavations which was substantially financed by the Manchester textile merchant, Jesse Haworth.

Like Kahun, Gurob lies in the Fayoum oasis, some 25 miles west of the Nile on the edge of the desert, and a short distance west of Bahr Yusef. This site consists of the remains of the town of Mi-wer and of an earlier foundation, Southern She, as well as the associated cemeteries.

Petrie assumed that the occupation of the site lasted from the 18th to the 19th Dynasty, and although there may have been limited settlement here in the 1st Intermediate Period, it was the foundation of a temple at Gurob by Tuthmosis III that established it as a major town. Doubtless, houses were built here at this time for the workmen engaged on the temple, although little evidence was found of these. The temple was subsequently dismantled, except for the foundation stones, either before the end of the 18th Dynasty, when this may have been carried out on the orders of King Akhenaten as part of his religious revolution, or, more probably, by Ramesses II for his own buildings at Ahnas. Houses were then built, with apparently no preconceived system or arrangement, over the remaining blocks of the temple. These, Petrie suggested, were occupied by the masons who had dismantled the temple.

From the time of Akhenaten until the reign of Merenptah (some 146 years), the town was occupied continuously. Petrie believed that the fall of the town began in the early part of the

Merenptah's reign, when, in Year 5, he led a great campaign against the Libyans, and drove them from Egypt, where they had already penetrated to the south of the Fayoum. As a result, Petrie suggested, the foreign inhabitants of Gurob were expelled during this war. However, other evidence seems to indicate that Gurob was still flourishing in the reigns of Ramesses IV and V, and it is more likely that famine and a decline in the cultivation in the area finally drove the inhabitants to new homes.

Various interpretations have been offered regarding the purpose of the site. One archaeologist, Bruyère, regarded it as a workmen's town inhabited by artisans, but the physical evidence – the random arrangement of the houses – indicates that, unlike Kahun, Amarna or Deir el-Medina, it was not built at one time for a specific reason nor to a pre-arranged plan. The houses were casually built amongst the ruins of the temple, and there is no evidence of an architect's scheme in their layout.

The reason for the development of the town can be seen in the environment of the Fayoum. The pleasures of fishing and fowling here had been appreciated by the kings of the Middle Kingdom, and they had established a harem at Re-hone (Lahun). A royal harem was a pleasure palace built to accommodate the king during his visits around the country and each had its own staff and administration which, during the king's absence, continued to function.

By the New Kingdom, the harem had been moved from Lahun to Gurob, which literary evidence has identified as the ancient town site of Mi-wer. The harem required its own permanent network of officials and administrators; artisans, servants and workmen were also needed, to look after the building and to cultivate the land belonging to the harem and to the temple. These men and their families were brought into the area, and accommodation was provided for them at Gurob.

Thus, although Gurob, as a recreational centre for the king and court was state-controlled and developed because of a royal need, it differed from the other workmen's towns, built primarily to house royal necropolis workers. There was less rigid organisation and control, and security was not so important here as in a town associated with the royal tombs. However, the people of Gurob had to be housed and fed, and the archaeological evidence suggests that their everyday existence was probably not very different from that of the inhabitants of the necropolis workers' towns.

The town buildings at Gurob were never completely planned or accurately reported, although excavation notebooks provide some additional information to the publications. Petrie's time at Gurob was fraught with difficulties. His relationship with the volunteer worker, Mr W.O. Hughes-Hughes, who carried on the excavation at Gurob while Petrie devoted himself to Kahun, was unsatisfactory, and illness prevented Petrie from returning to complete the site. Subsequently, the site was ransacked and although studies were made by various other archaeologists, the nature of the buildings – not conforming to a clear plan – and the somewhat chequered history of its investigation have posed considerable problems in reconstructing the layout of the town and the specific provenance of the articles found there.

Petrie's work at Gurob, never completed and never published in full detail, appears to have centred on the town-site near the temple, and most of his finds came from the houses and surface rubbish of this area. The houses, some built before the dismantling of the temple, had begun to encroach on the temple enclosure, and with its destruction and the removal of the stone blocks, more houses were built over the temple site.

His excavations also extended to some tombs of the 19th Dynasty situated to the north of the walled area of the town, and to the cemeteries of the New Kingdom and Ptolemaic periods west of the town. In addition to those found in the town, some of his finds were also from these tombs, but in many instances, the exact place of discovery of an object is not recorded.

Despite these limitations, certain facts about the layout and type of architecture in the town have been established. It seems that the town site was surrounded by a large wall which formed a square enclosure. The second season at Gurob was supervised by Hughes-Hughes, because of Petrie's occupation with Kahun. Although his work was incomplete, it was evident that the temple, in its own enclosing wall, was surrounded by a great square enclosure. Nearly all the town dwellings, including the harem and palace, were restricted to these enclosures and few buildings were erected outside. The high quality of objects discovered in the dwellings over the temple ruins suggest that the harem remained here until the late 19th or even 20th Dynasty. After the harem, the temple was the most important feature of the town, supplying work for many people. Of the main temple, built by Tuthmosis III, very little survived, although it seems that Tuthmosis III himself and the crocodile god, Sobek, were probably both worshipped here. There was also probably a cult at Gurob to the Nile perch, since a large fish cemetery was discovered in the vicinity. In the Ramesside period, there was again almost certainly one temple, and possibly two, at Gurob, reflecting its significance as an important town.

There is no evidence to confirm the arrangement of any street plan at Gurob; indeed, the houses seem to have been built randomly and expanded laterally, since there is no indication that rebuilding took place on the same foundations. The town was apparently divided into three areas, with a southern, main and northern section. Unlike the necropolis workmen's towns, no guardhouses or barracks were found at Gurob, again suggesting that surveillance of the population and visitors to the town was not considered necessary here.

The intimate details of the houses – the overall number at the site, and the internal arrangement of the rooms – remain unrecorded. Originally, Petrie was of the opinion that the houses were relatively poor, with no coloured dados, no granaries, nor stairs leading to the roof. Again, because he discovered no intact examples, he concluded that the furniture was sparse. Only a type of pottery container, which Petrie discribed as a 'sort of fire-box or stove made of very rude pottery', was found. Similar examples were discovered at Kahun, Amarna and Deir el-Medina, and their use will be considered later.

However, despite the paucity of furniture found in the houses, fragmentary pieces from Gurob indicate that they were originally furnished with chairs, stools, boxes and baskets to contain their smaller possessions, and headrests. There were also probably pottery storage vessels for food and water, beds, tables and floor-coverings, and the quality of these would have reflected the family's status. Petrie also later discovered granaries, although he does not indicate their exact location, and these were used as rubbish pits once their function as grain stores was finished.

Altogether, the apparently low standard of housing at Gurob is more likely to be a modern misconception, based on the less-well-preserved structures found there. The houses and their furnishing were probably not unlike those at Kahun and other towns, although the random building pattern at Gurob may indicate that the inhabitants were expected to build their own dwellings. Consequently, the building materials and methods of construction may have been of a lower standard at Gurob than at those places where the planning and building of the town were supervised by the royal architect and the materials were at least in part supplied by the state. However, the poor preservation of the site and its history of excavation prevents further conclusions being drawn.

Despite these drawbacks, sufficient evidence exists to give some idea of the lifestyle of the people of Gurob. Here, as elsewhere in Egypt, the majority of the population were engaged in agriculture, cultivating the land owned by the temple and the harem, and producing food for the officials and artisans of the town. Although relatively few agricultural implements have been discovered at Gurob, they suggest that life here was little different from Kahun, where a wealth of agricultural tools were uncovered. At Gurob, animals – sheep, goats, and oxen – were also kept, as well as domestic animals such as dogs and cats. Fishing, a major activity in the Fayoum, was also important at Gurob, both to supply food and also as a source of employment, for there is evidence that fishing nets and netting needles were manufactured here on some scale. Other crafts were also important to the community. Although no complete items of furniture were discovered, fragments of stools, chairs, boxes and headrests were found, and indicate that a woodworking industry existed at Gurob. Tools had to be made for this, and there was obviously a considerable production of metal implements in the town. A complete change is seen in the tools manufactured at Gurob from those found at Kahun. In the 12th Dynasty, flint-chipping was still a highly skilled art, which had lasted since predynastic times, and although the Middle Kingdom stone tools were influenced by the shape of the metal tools, they still greatly outnumbered the metal items. However, by the 18th Dynasty, this pattern was reversed, and the few flints which do occur are badly worked. On the other hand, the metalworking industry had developed considerably, and was now highly skilled and organised. The main metal was bronze, but copper was used for some items; there were also lead netsinkers, used for fishing, and gold and silver were employed for delicate pieces.

The range of metal goods was now wide. Carpentry tools – adzes, axes, chisels, awls, borers, knives, rasps and nails – were found; hunting and fishing equipment included barbs, netsinkers, arrowheads and lance heads; metal jugs and pans for domestic use were also made. Some ornamental and decorative metal products also occurred, including rings, amulets, scarabs, kohl-sticks and tweezers. Tools were also manufactured for the stone-working industry, which utilised not only the readily available supplies of limestone and alabaster to produce domestic and cosmetic dishes and vases and funerary stelae, but also the stone for royal building projects.

A major industry at Gurob was weaving. This was directly associated with the harem, and was under its jurisdiction. The archaeological and literary evidence suggests that this industry was very important at Gurob, and was highly organised.

Papyrus fragments from Gurob, which date to the reign of Sethos II, make reference to the training of textile workers. The workers, some based at home while others were employed in workshops, were apparently given instruction and training by the state, which was also their employer. At Gurob they were directly responsible to the harem, and other papyri from here refer to garments and cloth which were kept in the stores at the harem, and sent to the king or to various houses.

From the evidence, it seems that the ladies resident in the harem, far from leading lives of idle luxury, were, in many if not most cases, given the task of supervising and training the textile workers. It is unclear whether or not the royal women themselves engaged in the actual manufacture of the textiles, but their supervisory duties were undoubtedly undertaken seriously. The male Overseer of the Harem would have been responsible for the overall administration of this industry, and for the harem's special involvement.

The weaving industry was obviously long-established at Gurob, for another piece of evidence – an ebony statuette found at Gurob, inscribed with the name of the Lady Teye, who bore the title 'Chief of Weavers' – dates to the reign of Amenophis III (c. 1430 BC).

The development of weaving technology and evidence for this obtained from the sites of both Gurob and Kahun will be considered in more detail later, but the quality of the cloth produced by the weavers can still be seen in a pair of sleeves from a child's jacket which were discovered by Petrie, new and unused, in the clean sand filling of a 19th Dynasty tomb at Gurob. The cloth was in near-perfect condition and showed no signs of wear, and Petrie suggested that the sleeves may have been lost, while still new, by a labourer's wife as she sat down to rest on the sand-heap thrown up while the tomb was being dug. The sleeves are how housed separately at University College London and at the Manchester Museum.

The textile industry employed people engaged in the various branches of sewing, spinning, weaving and net-making. Gurob, as a centre for fishing and fowling, produced large nets for bird-catching as well as smaller ones for fishing, and also netting needles of bone and wood to make the nets. Other discoveries indicated that rope-making and basketry were carried out there; flax, rush and palm fibre were used to make ropes, while palm leaves and fibres were turned into a variety of basketwork items.

Pottery was produced at Gurob, as at all Egyptian sites. Some of it bears a marked resemblance to the pottery uncovered at Tell el-Amarna. In general, the coarser pottery was found in the town area, while the finer ware comes from the cemeteries. Glass manufacture was also important at Gurob and remains of factories and kilns were discovered. Decorative, multicoloured glass was produced, and turned into vases, perhaps used for perfumes and cosmetics, vessels for other purposes, and a range of beads, amulets, and earrings. Faience objects were also made, and included kohl-jars, beads, jewellery, scarabs, amulets and ushabtis.

Generally, the objects found at Gurob indicate that the style and quality of life of at least some of the inhabitants were above average. This is not surprising, since Gurob was not only the town which was honoured with periodic visits by the king and his royal entourage, but also boasted many of its own officials and functionaries. Some of these held posts in the palace and harem, while others were town dignitaries, or held temple priesthoods. The names and titles of the more important officials are preserved on funerary stelae and equipment.

These men and their families would have enjoyed the pastimes of wealthy Egyptians throughout the ages – hunting wild game in the desert, fishing and fowling in the marshes and entertaining their friends at banquets, where food and drink were lavish. Their wives, and indeed even the lower orders, adorned themselves with a wide range of cosmetics and jewellery, and there is ample evidence at Gurob that the women at the palace and elsewhere paid considerable attention to their appearance.

The personal and toilet articles are more frequently encountered at Gurob than at Kahun, perhaps because the lifestyle was more sophisticated there, or because the tombs as well as the town at Gurob have delivered up a multitude of these items.

Bronze mirrors have been found, some of which Petrie believed showed an Asiatic influence. He suggested that these could have been produced by a foreign artisan, trained in Egypt and resident at Gurob. Wooden combs, bone and wood hairpins, and a bronze hair-curler suggested that hairdressing was commonly practised here as elsewhere in ancient Egypt. Facial make-up was also popular; kohl was used to outline and enlarge the eyes, and was stored in vases which were tubular in form. These were usually made of wood, although examples in stone, reed and ivory are known, and the kohl was applied to the eyes with a kohl-stick. At Gurob, examples made of wood, haematite and even bronze have been found. Boxes, vessels and spoons were also made, to contain and handle the creams and ointments with which the Egyptians perfumed their bodies.

The jewellery consisted of beads, bracelets, earrings and rings, in a variety of materials. The beads were found both in the excavations and on the surface of the site, left by the denudation of the soil. They were very varied in materials and style, but differed markedly from those found at Kahun. At Gurob, Petrie also noticed significant differences between those beads which he attributed to the 18th Dynasty and to the 19th Dynasty. The 18th Dynasty beads were rarely made of glass, but contained a preponderance of glazed coloured pendants in the form of fruit and leaves, a style which had been introduced as part of Akhenaten's religious and art revolution, but which died out in the 19th Dynasty. Also, there were numbers of thin flat blue disc beads and pendants depicting gods – again styles introduced under Akhenaten. In the 19th Dynasty, however, all the beads were coarser and poorer, but there were new developments in glass beads which were now produced in clear as well as opaque glass, and in very different designs. Beads in multiple colours were common, and glass earrings were also manufactured as part of an important glass-making industry which had begun to develop in Egypt in the 18th Dynasty.

Scarabs and rings were discovered in considerable numbers, many bearing the names of different kings. The large number of blue glazed faience rings were mass-produced, it has been suggested, to distribute to the people, as the king's gifts to mark special state occasions or royal visits.

Evidence for life at Gurob is mainly material. Although there must have been a substantial collection of papyri – written records and administrative documents pertaining to the palace and the temple – very little indication of major scribal activity has survived. Only two writing palettes were uncovered, and the few papyri that have survived were not in such a good condition as those found at Kahun. The only royal name mentioned in the Gurob literature is that of Ramesses II; none of the papyrus rolls were sealed, and many had been crushed up for use as waste paper.

It is, therefore, the artefacts from Gurob which most clearly illuminate the lifestyle of the inhabitants. The architectural remains do not permit us to draw many firm conclusions regarding the accommodation of the various levels of the society, or the disposition of the 'wealthy' and 'poor' areas within the town. However, it is evident from the finds that there were several quite distinct social categories, made up of the officials and administrators, the artisans and craftsmen, and the agricultural workers. This is borne out by the cemeteries at Gurob, which were excavated by Petrie and other archaeologists. They were extensive, because of the long occupation of the site, and were arranged around the town, stretching out for some distance into the desert. The cemeteries were organised into areas, according to the type of burial and the status of the occupant. There were differences not only in the type of construction of the tombs, but also in the amount and quality of the tomb goods; the cemeteries therefore illustrate not only the different periods of the town's occupation, but also its social divisions.

It is evident that the town came to support several quite major industries, apart from the original reason for its foundation as a place of royal recreation. For many of these, the raw materials were at hand, but in some cases, they were perhaps brought in from outside. The resident population provided the market for some goods and services, whereas for others, most notably the textile production, some of the goods were produced for other parts of Egypt.

It is therefore possible, from the finds, to reconstruct a fairly accurate picture of life in the town – the people's clothing and adornment, their food and drink, and the furnishing and equipping of their homes.

The quality of everyday existence in all these ancient towns would have differed only in degree from one place to another, and, to some extent, according to an individual's social status. However, a common factor which has been claimed for some of these work-towns and which would distinguish them in a number of ways from other Egyptian settlement sites, is a substantial presence of resident foreign labour. Petrie claimed that this situation existed at both Kahun and Gurob, and the evidence for such a presence at both sites will be considered later.

PART II

THE TOWN OF KAHUN

CHAPTER 4

The Site and its Excavation

The site of Kahun was excavated in two seasons by William Flinders Petrie, 1888–89 and 1889–90. Limited work was also carried out there by Petrie and Brunton in 1914.

The town was built originally to house the officials and work-force engaged in the construction of the pyramid of King Sesostris II at Lahun in c. 1895 BC. Sesostris ordered a town to be built which adjoined the temple in which he was to be worshipped; both the town and the temple were given the name of 'Hetep-Sesostris', meaning 'Sesostris is satisfied'. The pyramid has already been described; it was built on a natural rock mass which was cut into the required shape, and the upper part was constructed of mud-brick. It was situated in the desert, about 805 km from the cultivation, and on its east side there was a small temple which was decorated with offering scenes to supply the king's spirit with sustenance after death. About half a mile away, opposite the east side of the pyramid and situated on the edge of the desert, a larger temple, also dedicated to Sesostris II, was built. These buildings formed the mortuary and valley temples usually seen in the typical pyramid complex.

The king's more distant valley temple was surrounded on three sides by a massive brick wall, some 12.19 m in thickness, and lined with fine limestone blocks. It stood on a prominent rocky slope, just on the edge of the cultivation. Petrie's excavations here led him to the conclusion that the greater part of the temple area had been open, and that there was probably a colonnade around it, while at the back of the enclosure (west end) stood a chamber which had been decorated with fine wall reliefs. He also found the remains of some sandstone objects, and pieces of two statues of the

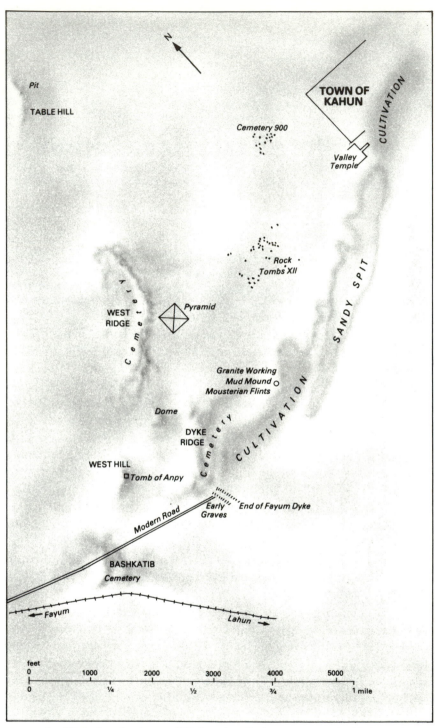

FIGURE 3   Plan showing town of Kahun in relation to pyramid of Lahun (Petrie, *Lahun II*, pl. II).

king, one of which probably stood in the decorated chamber.

However, the most exciting find made here was the discovery of foundation deposits which remained intact, buried under two blocks of stone in a hole about four feet deep which had been excavated in the rock. Four sets of these objects were found here, placed in the hole without any order or arrangement. In Egypt, foundation deposits were put underneath temples when work began on the building. A possible explanation for such deposits (which, in Petrie's day, had only previously been found in association with later Egyptian buildings) was that the spirit of the temple would require maintenance and repair and the tools were provided for the workmen's spirits to use in this respect. In each of the Kahun sets, there were seven model tools of bronze – chisels, knives and a hatchet; a pair of corn rubbers; strings of beads; a couple of pieces of green carbonate of copper ore; a piece of galena; a quantity of pottery vessels and some baskets.

The temple doubtless fell into disrepair some time after Kahun ceased to be occupied, but it was apparently still standing in the 18th Dynasty. However, its final destruction came in the 19th Dynasty, and debris of this date, presumably belonging to the masons who carried out these orders, was found at the site. The stonework was removed from the temple, at the instigation of Ramesses II, to be re-used in his own temple at Ahnas (Heracleopolis). The same fate befell the smaller temple which adjoined the east face of Sesostris II's Lahun pyramid. That these blocks had been re-employed at Ahnas was confirmed for Petrie when he saw a granite column drum there, reused for Ramesses II, but bearing the Ka-name of Sesostris II. The temple area was subsequently deserted for thousands of years, but finally had a new use, this time as a Christian burial ground, in the 7th Century AD.

At the north end of the larger of Sesostris II's funerary temples, Petrie discovered another building, which he believed was a porter's lodge. It had a large room, in which a stone trough was let into the ground, with sloping stone slabs around it so that water could run down. Other similar troughs were found in the town of Kahun, and Petrie believed that they were provided for daily ablutions. To the north of this temple lay the pyramid workmen's town known as Kahun. A bay about 402 m across, formed by the sweep of the high ground, occupied the area north of the temple, and here the town was built. The buildings all lay in a slight hollow, and were enclosed on three sides by a thick wall.

This ran northwards from the end of the north side of the temple for about 402 m; it followed the edge of the bay and then fell down into the desert behind it. Then, it turned eastwards at right angles to enclose the town and then turned southwards for a short way. Thus, the town wall extended along the north, west and partly along the east sides, but on the south side, the site lay open to the Nile Valley. However, at the east wall, Petrie discovered the remains of a gateway, and this led him to the conclusion that, although the site now lay open to the south and along part of the eastern end the wall was also missing, originally Kahun had been completely walled on four sides. However, the south wall and over half of the east wall had since been entirely lost. Within the town, an area of high ground was cut back to form an elevated platform. This area, called 'The Acropolis' by Petrie, was used to accommodate an important building.

In his two seasons, Petrie cleared over two thousand chambers which he believed comprised over three-quarters of the total extent of the town. In his first season, he probably cleared away only part of the western sector of the town, and an area in the middle of the eastern part. The remainder of the eastern section and the whole of the southern section were never excavated or planned, because Petrie considered them to be hardly worth any further efforts, since they had been so disturbed in Roman times. He was able to plan the whole of the extent of the town which was cleared; it was of particular interest, not only because this was the first of the royal workmen's towns ever to be uncovered, but also because it was the first occasion on which it had been possible to produce an almost complete plan of an Egyptian town.

Kahun had been laid out on a regular plan, evidently by a single architect who was almost certainly the man also responsible for the king's pyramid at Lahun. It was rectangular in shape, surrounded by a thick brick enclosure wall and inside it was arranged in two sections. The eastern part was nearly as long as it was wide, and the western part, divided from the other by a thick wall, contained the smaller houses of the workmen. There was little difference in the date of these two sections. In fact, the wall separating the eastern and western sections probably marked a change in the ground level, with the western sector being somewhat higher. However, the division was also utilised to separate the wealthier quarters from the most concentrated area of workmen's houses.

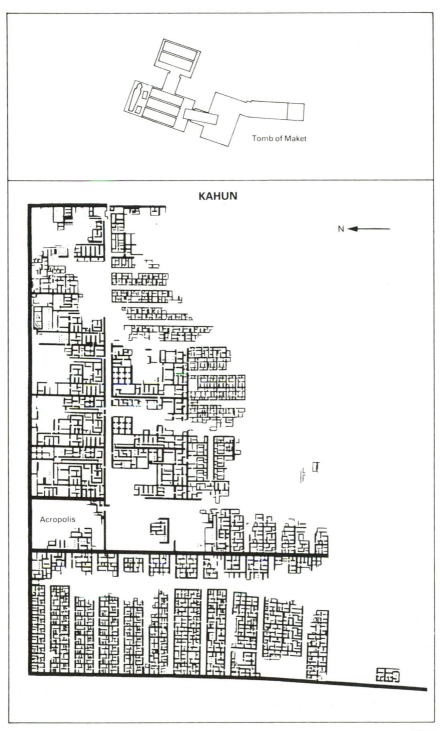

FIGURE 4   Plan of Kahun town. (Petrie, *Illahun, Kahun and Gwob*, p.l. XIV).

The streets and houses were laid out in regular lines, and in an arrangement so that access to the western blocks of houses could be easily guarded by a single watchman. The town divides readily into several main areas and can be considered in these sections. The most important part was the 'Acropolis'; because it was higher, it had been destroyed by denudation more than any other section. The buildings stood on a banked platform which was shored up with a massive retaining wall; from here, the occupants could gain an excellent view of the roofs of all the other houses in the town. The whole of the acropolis was occupied with one very large house; access was provided by a front entrance which led to those rooms which overlooked the town in an eastwards direction, while two smaller stairways provided entrance to the back rooms. These stairways showed very little evidence of wear, and had subsequently been filled up with the debris from the fallen walls. In some areas, Petrie had to remove as much as 3.04 m of rubbish in order to clear them. At the foot of the retaining brick wall of the acropolis, to the south, there was an open area with just one building which Petrie identified as a guardhouse. The Acropolis house was obviously important; Petrie discovered stone bases of columns and pieces of brightly painted dado in the rooms, but, at the same time, the place had obviously been deserted early in the town's history. The building was filled up with broken pottery and debris of the 12th Dynasty date, left there by the people of the town. The building's size, obvious significance, and physical eleva- tion, which ensured that it could be easily guarded, led Petrie to infer that this was an official residence built for the king to rest when he visited the town to inspect the progress of the work on his pyramid at nearby Lahun. The pyramid was finished long before the town was finally deserted, and the acropolis residence, no longer used for the royal visits, fell into disuse.

In general terms, the houses at Kahun included a number of elements; there were rooms used as a reception hall or living room, and harem or women's quarters, a room with washing or bathing facilities, and a kitchen, and there were also cellars and circular granaries. However, Kahun was a considerably more important centre than merely a place to house the pyramid workforce, and the wealth and status of some of its inhabitants – officials associated with the pyramid administration or temple – are evidenced by a number of large houses. Along the north wall, there were five great houses which were all built according to one plan, with four of them joining in a row. The house entrance was from the street to the south; here there was a moderate-sized doorway with a stone lintel and facing it was a doorkeeper's room. The entrance provided three separate means of access to the rooms which lay beyond. By passing along a passage at the left-hand side of the entrance, the visitor reached the offices and other rooms where the master carried out his business, as well as the rooms of the men-servants and guests.

In the centre of the house, behind these rooms, there lay a group of private chambers which opened on to a four-pillared hall. Behind this was a large area which, in the northernmost part, was open to the sky, while along the south ran a colonnade. This was the reception hall where the master entertained his visitors. The colonnade provided shade for him and his guests, who could reach this reception area directly from the street entrance by means of a large passage. Other rooms which could only be reached from the reception hall were used as the private chambers of the master and his family. These included the master's own court, which had a stone tank sunk in the middle of a paved floor. Although the roof area immediately above the tank was probably open to the sky, around it ran a roof supported by twelve columns. The tank provided a washing area for the master and his family, a place of refreshment in the centre of the house. The importance of these tanks, which may have been used for personal ablutions per-formed in connection with the religious family observations, is indicated by the fact that Petrie found similar tanks, but con-structed as separate boxes of stone, let into mud floors in poorer dwellings.

On passing through the main house entrance, another passage led off to the right and gave access to several small rooms and a columned hall. This area, with its own private entrance passage and direct access to the main reception hall, almost certainly comprised the harem, or women's quarters.

Anyone visiting these houses would therefore be expected to take one of the three routes of entrance into the house according to his personal business. The total area of each house was 42.06 m × 60.35 m, and each contained many rooms and passages. These were substantial dwellings, designed to fulfil the business and domestic requirements of the senior officials who lived there. They provided large, cool rooms, with their roofs supported by columns made of wood, with flat, wide stone bases. Some of these columns were made of stone and were fluted or ribbed, with capitals decorated either with plain abaci or with the palm leaf form. The houses, similar to some found today in the Middle East, were conceived as oases of cool and shade protected from the glaring sun. They were centred inwards, away from the heat and dust of the streets, to the halls and colonnaded courts, where the master could entertain his guests. In the women's quarters, the family's privacy was maintained and the women occupied themselves with household matters and the rearing and education of the smaller children.

On the south side of the town, there were three more great houses, which were exactly the same size as those on the northern row, but had somewhat different internal arrangements. The plan of these was difficult to determine, because they had been much altered in antiquity, by division into tenements and by the insertion of new doorways. However, the general arrangement seemed to be that the entrance opened into a vestibule with a column and, from here, a short passage led to the main rooms, while a longer one gave access to the back area of the house. Another passage led along the opposite side, from the middle of the house to storerooms at either end. Nine storerooms which formed a square block (three each way) were arranged as a complete unit against the street wall.

To the south of the Acropolis, backing on to the thick wall which divided the town into east and west sections, were blocks of dwellings or stores which were built on one repeated plan. Some items were found here, including a set of copper chisels and hatchets in a basket, and a copper dish. Here, there were also rock-cut cellars, their entrances barred by stout wooden flap-doors, one of which was still found in position. The largest cellar which had two chambers was used as a family tomb in the 19th–20th Dynasties and was given the name of 'Maket's tomb'. The tomb, a rare example of an undisturbed burial, was carefully cleared, and Petrie describes in some detail his discovery and recording of the objects which he found. It was also in the middle block of this building that some of the papyri of the 12th and 13th Dynasties were uncovered.

Behind the southern mansions, on the east, there lay five streets of workmen's houses. In each house there were about seven rooms. To the east of the southern mansions there were more workmen's dwellings. These were smaller, with only four rooms apiece. Petrie had difficulty planning these streets, because the southern end had been completely erased by denudation and even in the part that he managed to plan, the remains of half the area were only a few centimetres deep. In several of the small streets he found evidence of a stone channel running down the middle of the street, which had originally sloped towards the centre. This was an early example of street drainage; the waste water from the houses and also the occasional rainfalls would have been removed by it, thus ensuring that the streets did not become muddy. Petrie believed that this system was probably in general use in all the streets of Kahun, and that, considering that this was not a capital city, the concept of street drainage must already have been a feature of other more important towns in Egypt.

In the western division of the town, separated by its own thick wall, there were eleven streets containing workmen's houses, each of which had four or five rooms. It was five streets of this area that Petrie managed to plan and publish at the end of his first season. In these houses the rooms were grouped together, with one outer door to the street. The walls of the houses at Kahun were mainly built of mud-brick, and were of one storey, but the flat roofs were probably used as sitting areas and places to store fuel and straw. Each house had a series of steps leading to the roof-top, built in two parts, with a turn in the middle.

Although Petrie found many of the walls standing, the upper parts, including the roofs, were usually destroyed. However, fragments of roof have been found and it is evident that most of the roofs would have been constructed of beams of wood on which poles were placed. Bundles or reeds or straw were then bound firmly on to these, and mud plaster was applied to the inner and outer surfaces. In some houses rooms were entirely roofed with a barrel vault of brickwork, and indeed, architecture at Kahun provides sufficient evidence that the arch was in common use in the Middle Kingdom. The method of constructing these arches may have been to fill the chamber with sand while work on the brick vault was in hand, and then to clear the sand away once the roof was finished.

The doorways had semicircular arches of brick spaced with chips of limestone, while there were wooden door-cases, thresholds, doors and door bolts. The door pivots were arranged quite differently from those used in later times. Stone sockets were placed against wooden door sills; the door pivot passed down inside the socket and rested on a block of wood beneath it.

The physical arrangement of the rooms was obviously pre-planned, the architect making use of round numbers of cubits. The design of the houses followed a repetitive plan in each block and it is evident that the houses and the sections of the town were carefully constructed to meet specific official requirements.

Inside the houses, columns were used to support the roofs over the larger rooms. The marks left by these on their stone bases indicate that they were octagonal in shape and were probably of wood. An entry in Petrie's *Journal* for 24–31 October 1889, records his discovery of one of these columns:

> At last I have a piece of one of the octagonal wooden columns of which I have so often seen the marks on stone bases in the chambers. It is of a hard dark brown wood . . . about a foot high remains of it, the upper part having been burnt away.

Many granaries were also found; these were conical in shape and built of brick, plastered on both the inner and outer surfaces. They were frequently found in pairs, in the room of the house which was used as the kitchen. There was no one place built to take the fire and it was generally situated at one side of the room, in a slight depression in the floor.

The inside walls of the best rooms of the houses were frequently mud-plastered and painted with a dado. On to the smoothly plastered surface a series of coloured borders were painted – a dark colour or black in the lowest area, and then, between three and five feet above, black and red lines on a white ground. Above this, the wall was covered with a yellow wash. However, some wall decorations were more elaborate. In two of the workmen's houses behind the southern mansions, paintings were found with the subjects coloured in red, yellow, white and black paint. One illustrates a large house showing, at the bottom level, the outside of the building, while the upper level is cut away to reveal the interior. The house is represented as having a series of arched chambers, and may depict one of the brick-vaulted buildings in the town. The interior scene shows the master being attended to by his servant. The painting in the other house depicts a strange building with columns of a form which Petrie claimed was un-known anywhere else in Egypt.

Petrie's work at Kahun required his continuing and dedicated attention. He was allowed to use the inspection house at Illahun as his base, and his devotion to the task at Kahun meant that much of the work at Gurob (the other site which engaged his attention at this time) was carried out under the supervision of Mr W.O. Hughes-Hughes who took on the excavations there in November 1889. In January 1890, Petrie's second season and his work at Kahun drew to a close; with the exception of the eastern side of the town, he had finished clearing the site by the end of December 1889. About this time also, Hughes-Hughes had completed his task at Gurob, and in March 1890 Petrie left Egypt. He published the results of these excavations in two volumes, *Kahun, Gurob and Hawara* (1890), and *Illahun, Kahun and Gurob* (1891).

The cost of these excavations was largely borne by Jesse Haworth and Martyn Kennard, and, towards the end of his second season at Kahun, in his *Journal* entry for 30–31 December 1889, Petrie states:

> I do not expect that my friends (i.e. Haworth and Kennard) will hear of anything more now from Kahun and Gurob; the places are done for, and well have they repaid us, by the insight we have gained in the life and manufactures of the 18th and 12th Dynasties. I have now really outlined the greater part of the long blank of hitherto undefined history of domestic and personal objects, which had been such an attractive unknown region to me. If I can now do the 6th, 4th and possibly earlier times, in as complete a way in future, I shall accomplish what has been my particular aim in Egypt.

Petrie's ambitions were later to be realised, but at Kahun he had an early opportunity to develop his own special, painstaking methods of excavation. Altogether he cleared more than 2000 chambers in his two seasons, and each had to be measured and entered in a working plan which he kept. His method of working was to clear all the rooms in one block of houses along a street front. The earth was removed from them on to the street. He next cleared the line of rooms further in, and into the first set of rooms (which had by now been planned and recorded) he then emptied the debris from the second set. In this way, he not only devised a system of ensuring that every object was uncovered, but also that the buildings were filled in and covered over again, so that the brick walls were preserved. He refers to this method of working in his *Journal* for 8–15 April 1889, where he says: 'I am planning all the chambers as we go on; and shall have a complete survey of the place.'

In addition to his systematic method of clearing the chambers, he also took the precaution of sounding the floors of the rooms with a rod to see if they concealed any hollows or pits which had been filled in. This precaution was rewarded by the discovery not only of objects, but also of baby burials, which he records thus in his *Journal* (8–15 April 1889):

> Many new-born infants were found buried in the floors of the rooms, and, strange to say, usually in boxes made for other purposes evidently, by their form. In short, unlucky babes seem to have been conveniently put out of the way by stuffing them into a toilet case or clothes box and digging a hole in the floor for them. . . I fear these discoveries do not reflect much credit on the manners and customs of the small officials of the 12 Dynasty.

Possible explanations for this custom at Kahun will be considered later.

At Kahun, Petrie also devised a method of paying his workmen who assisted in the excavations. Every chamber, when cleared, was carefully measured and marked in on the general plan which Petrie kept in his notebook; these plans, together with triangulation, eventually enabled him to draw up the general scheme of the corner of the town and temple. The men were each paid $\frac{1}{2}$ piastre for one cubic metre of a cleared chamber, which, in the late 1880s, worked out at the English equivalent of a little under one penny a yard. They were paid additional sums for everything which they uncovered and brought to Petrie, and top prices were given for finds of papyri or bronze tools.

According to Petrie, the archaeological evidence indicated that, at the site of Kahun there were two periods of occupation. The first, which perhaps lasted about a century, started with the foundation of the town in the reign of King Sesostris II in the 12th Dynasty (c. 1895 BC) and finished towards the end of the 13th Dynasty, long after Sesostris II had been buried in his pyramid at Lahun and the area had ceased to be used for royal burials. We shall consider the possible reasons for the desertion of Kahun later. However, the foundation and construction of most of the buildings, and the date of the majority of objects of daily use found at Kahun, can be assigned to this first period. Petrie was able to identify the town as a 12th Dynasty foundation because of a number of factors. First, its position adjoining and built square with the temple of Sesostris II and the fact that it was laid out at one time by a single architect, convinced him of its date. Also, various distinctive artefacts were found there; these included the papyri; the alabaster objects which showed the quality of the 12th Dynasty; the stelae and offering tables of that period; pottery unlike that of any other period of which he was aware; the ivory castanets which resembled those of a similar date which had been found at Thebes. These all persuaded him that this was a town built and occupied in the Middle Kingdom.

However, he also believed that Kahun was briefly inhabited during the New Kingdom in the reign of Amenophis III; numbers of objects of this later date were found at the site, but he considered that only some of the rooms in the western quarter (the original 'workmen's area') were now re-occupied.

Until recent years, virtually nothing remained to be seen of the town site, which has been completely covered over by drifting sand. Even in Petrie's time, the site had already suffered considerable denudation. The height of the walls which Petrie excavated would have varied in different places, probably from one to ten courses of bricks. In the south part, because of severe denudation and the encroaching cultivation, there would have been few remaining traces to assist Petrie in his planning of the site. Nevertheless, the results of the excavations, despite the difficulties imposed by the working conditions, were remarkable; they revealed, both in the written records and in the property left behind in the houses, many aspects of the religious, civil, and domestic life of the town. Nearly all the excavated possessions of the town's inhabitants were objects of daily use, and these provided a unique illustration of the domestic conditions and current technologies of the period.

Today, a new archaeological survey of the site has been in progress for several years, initiated by the Royal Ontario Museum, and this will add more information to earlier discoveries.

CHAPTER 5

Legal and Medical Practices, Education and Religion

> . . . so intimate may you now feel walking their streets, and sitting down in their dwellings, that I shall rather describe them as a living community than as historical abstractions.

Thus Petrie described the inhabitants of Kahun to his readers in the 1890s, when he was excavating the town. Subsequent research on the artefacts found there, and the translation of the papyri from the town, have further enabled a picture to be drawn of 12th Dynasty Kahun.

Kahun's prosperity and importance was not entirely dependent upon the pryamid and temple of Sesostris II. The significant Middle Kingdom irrigation works in the Fayoum, the subsequent construction of the pyramid for Amenemmes III at nearby Hawara, and Kahun's position as a centre for business in an area which the kings had developed, all ensured that the town continued to be of some importance. Indeed, it was far larger than the other workmen's towns that have been uncovered, and long after the pyramid of Sesostris II had been completed, it continued to house religious and civil officials as well as the lower classes. As a town which continued to maintain the mortuary cult of the king at his pyramid temple, Kahun would have accommodated the priests and their families, and all the employees engaged to supply food and perform other services for the temple. All the services which were needed to support a significant town of this size grew up and were to be found at Kahun in the Middle Kingdom; there was an important legal office there to deal with local problems, and there is firm evidence of the provision of community medical care.

One of the most important sources of our knowledge of certain aspects of the town is the collection of papyri (over a thousand fragments) which Petrie brought back from Kahun, as well as from Gurob. Some were complete enough to be intelligible without too much study, but the vast majority were fragments no larger than one inch square. They were inscribed in Hieratic and the decipherment was laborious. The major work on this was carried out by the scholar Francis Llewellyn Griffith, who painstakingly pieced the fragments together and translated the texts. The results of his labours were published in three volumes in the late 1890s.

Those from Kahun were most ancient and more numerous than those found at Gurob; it is doubtful that any of the Kahun papyri fragments date to the reign of Sesostris II himself, but they span the reigns of several other kings. A hymn and perhaps one of the legal documents may be attributed to Sesostris III's time, but most of the Kahun papyri date to the reign of Amenemmes III and indicate that he ruled for some forty-five years. One papyrus dates to the time of Amenemmes IV, and others may belong to the later reigns of the 13th Dynasty. The papyri which can be attributed to the brief occupation of Kahun in the 18th Dynasty under Amenophis III are not connected with the organisation of the town.

The Middle Kingdom papyri can be divided into two main classes. There were those which were original compositions put together by the scribes, and included letters, accounts, legal documents and memoranda, although some of these were copies. However, there were also copies of early texts, which included literary, scientific and religious works, and school exercises. Together, although they lack the breadth of the documentation found at Deir el-Medina, a site occupied for considerably longer than Kahun, they nevertheless provide invaluable insight into major areas of the town's organisation. The medical, veterinary and mathematical papyri are particularly important sources of information.

Legal administration

The legal documents were well preserved; some were the first known examples of their types. The *amt-pr* was a deed which recorded the transfer of property from one individual to another, and some types of Will and marriage settlement seemed to have been thus classified. One Will, made by a certain Mery, transferred to his son his priestly office and the title of his property, house and contents. The son was to be taken on as a partner in this office, and although the older man would retire from active work, it seemed that he also retained some control. It would also appear that, although in this case the successor to the post was the old man's son, the transaction was purely a business arrangement. The son was to be 'as an old man's staff; even as I grow old let him be promoted (thereto) at this instant'.

The other two settlements or Wills refer to members of one family. The Will of Sahu, an architect, probably dates to the reign of Amenemmes III. He leaves all his property and his Asiatic slaves to his brother Uah, who was also an architect and a minor priest of Sopdu. In his deed, Uah in his turn transfers this property to his wife, Sheftu, giving her the freedom to pass it on to any of their children; he also gives her the foreign slaves whom she can transfer to any of the couple's children. He grants her the undisturbed possession of the house in which she lives, which was built for him by his brother, and makes provision for the selection of a certain Gebu as their son's tutor. The deed is witnessed by a list of named witnesses, and this almost certainly constituted a Will or arrangement of affairs before death.

The next group, known as *aput*, were official lists of a man's household. These gave the names of the family members, and their serfs and slaves in the groups in which they were acquired. The lists are drawn up in double columns, one written in black and the other in red, to accommodate the two personal names which Egyptians usually had. They include the names of the father, mother, young children and female relatives; in richer households, female slaves and their children are included, but not adult male slaves. It has been suggested that the total absence of male serfs from these lists is because they were listed elsewhere, in connection with their employment as labourers, soldiers or clerks, or indeed as heads of independent households. One *aput* list from Kahun belonged to a man who had migrated to the town from an area of the eastern Delta; the list includes the man, his wife, a grandmother, and three of his father's sisters.

Another list gives the households of a soldier's son, Hera, and his relatives, showing how the guardianship and accommodation of unmarried female relatives was undertaken, by combining households when the male head of one household died.

There are various wider social aspects about Kahun which also become evident from these lists. The soldiers and the priests, who made up the two leading groups at Kahun, could be called upon to take part in the actual construction work on the pyramids at Lahun and Hawara. The soldiers, with their military engineering skills, could be required to direct operations at the pyramid site; the priests, with their knowledge of the religious layout of the buildings and of the rituals which were necessary to protect them, would act as advisers and perform the required rites. The soldiers and priests who are known from the Kahun documents were therefore probably actively engaged at the pyramid site, as well as performing their other traditional duties.

It seems that the town probably suffered a reduction in import- ance and manpower after the 12th Dynasty, when work on the pyramids in the area ceased. Griffith suggested that in the 1st Year of the 13th Dynasty, the official recording of the household of a priest associated with the Lahun pyramid of Sesostris II may have indicated that his property was to be confiscated, or his household resettled.

The third group of legal documents are the *am rem.f* lists. These were accounts kept at Kahun which referred to the superinten- dents and workmen. Some were lists which the scribes kept for their own reports, whereas others were kept as part of an official journal which recorded the rations of the workmen, their attend- ance at the site, and some division of land and property.

The lists of workmen provide some information about their organisation, although they are less detailed than the documenta- tion discovered at Deir el-Medina. One list gives the muster of men for shifting stones at Kahun from the '4th month of Khoiak and 1st month of Tybi'. From the combined information of the lists, it seems that these were professional 'stone-shifters' who worked for a two-month period. At the head of the list there is a man of some importance – a 'director' – and also a scribe; the gang follows and is composed of ten or five men, the first one of whom is the foreman. The men's two personal names are often given, and in some cases the name of a man's mother.

In one list, after the gang's details are given, the officials appear on a second page; they include soldiers, priests, chief cook, royal scribes, 'dwellers in the domain of the lady of the house', and temple doorkeepers. All were doubtless residents of Kahun. According to these papyri, many people at Kahun seem to have been given the name of 'Sesostris', after the town's founder.

The official journal also illuminates several interesting points. On one fragment some details are given of figures and dates which obviously record the times and quantities of materials which were either produced or received by the workmen. It has been suggested that these may have been mud-bricks supplied for royal buildings. Large bricks (those used for the pyramid of Lahun measured $42.24 \times 21.32 \times 13$ cm) seem to have been reserved for pyramid construction, whereas the bricks used for the houses at Kahun were much smaller. The wooden mud-brick mould which Petrie discovered in the town was obviously used for making domestic bricks.

The journal also apparently recorded the days of the workmen's attendance at the site, although only part of this record is preserved. It seems that at Kahun, four months of the year were particularly busy; each gang worked continuously for just two months, so that in this period, it could have only worked for a maximum of sixty days. This list, although it is inadequately preserved, mentions twenty-nine gangs which, at maximum strength, would have supplied a total workforce of 290 men. However, this undoubtedly represented only a fraction of the number of men working at the site. The gang probably enjoyed four days of holiday in each month, which coincided with the lunar quarters.

The journal is also important for another reason. It contains abstracts of a communication and reply, which seem to centre around the vexed question of withdrawal of manpower. The communication infers that some people were remaining at home instead of attending their work, and the writer asks for advice on how he should deal with the situation.

The reply, perhaps written by the vizier's secretary, tells the enquirer to ascertain what orders have been given and to stop the people coming to the palace to state their grievance. If the situation is resolved, the vizier will send at once to fetch these people.

It would therefore appear that some grievance had upset the men, and that they had taken a collective action to show their annoyance, by staying away from their workplace. The officials wished to keep them away from the palace but decided that the situation was sufficiently severe to warrant the vizier's personal intervention. Although the details are unclear, it seems that perhaps this disturbance at Kahun foreshadowed the much more clearly stated conflict in the 'strike papyri' discovered at Deir el-Medina. It is quite possible that royal workmen engaged on the king's tomb had recognised their potential power in much earlier times, and that their strikes had always been part of the labour relations in ancient Egypt. Where a situation existed involving royal tombs, a workforce and food rations, there would almost inevitably have been conflict.

Another type of legal papyrus, the *sunu*, was an official document either appointing a government officer or engaging a servant. Finally, there were memoranda, written on small squares of papyrus and usually bearing the name of the writer and the recipient on one side and the message on the other. One memorandum gives the price of services and was made by Ameny, 'Sealkeeper of the office of providing labourers'. The payment seems to have been made, probably as an honorarium by the government, to two brothers on their appointment to particular offices. However, the point of interest is that the payment consisted of four Asiatics, two women and two children.

The Egyptian legal system is known to us only through the kind of documents that have come down to us from settlement and temple sites. At Kahun, accounts and correspondence were found at the temple, whereas papyri dealing with various other matters were discovered in the houses. Nowhere, however, has a law code, similar to those possessed by some other early civilisations, come to light.

The Kahun documents show that the town was both busy and important. It also was governed by strict administrative measures. Individual documents reflect the same legal practices which are evident in material from other sites. They are dated, the parties concerned in the transactions make statements, and the documents are witnessed by named individuals. The papyri which refer to the family of the priests of Sopdu provide evidence of family law, and the existing group was apparently only part of a much larger collection of documents which probably dealt with the family's whole legal history. It is clear that the inhabitants of Kahun entered into legal transactions over a period of many years.

However, there are perhaps two most important contributions which these documents make to our overall understanding of the society. Firstly, they show that a significant number of 'Asiatics' were present in the town, engaged in a variety of occupations. Secondly, they illuminate some aspects of the employment and working conditions of the royal workmen, although there are few details of the type of work and techniques involved. They also indicate that the vizier's authority here, as elsewhere, was only required for more important cases. This underlines the severity of the problem which lay behind the apparent refusal to return to work, when it became necessary for the vizier to be involved.

Education and literature

The second major group of papyri from Kahun are those which, at different levels, attempt to deal with literary skills. It was the custom in Egypt for children to be educated in groups. There were different kinds of schools for different classes of people, but essentially, the children were taught a range of subjects. Their most essential skill, however, was the ability to read and write. They were frequently trained by means of sets of model letters which they would copy on to sherds, limestone flakes, or, less frequently, papyrus. These were intended to be formal exercises which would not only improve the children's writing and spelling ability and accuracy, but in some cases, by their very content, instruct and inspire the youngsters with wisdom and desired attitudes. At Kahun, a book of these model letters was found. Unfortunately, although its existence indicates that formal education existed at Kahun, and that this took the same form as in other towns and at different periods, the book adds very little to existing knowledge of the Egyptian educational system. Here at Kahun, as elsewhere in Egypt, the sons of the priests and officials would have received quite a lengthy education, designed to create a socially acceptable as well as an intellectually competent young person. It is not known whether more than a rudimentary education was extended to the workmen's sons at Kahun.

Amongst the objects excavated in the town, a few other items of educational interest were discovered. A wooden counting stick, made from an old piece of furniture, was used for teaching children. It was designed to enable them to count many of the numbers up to 100. Some fragments of writing tablets were also uncovered. These were made of wood and the surface was faced with a polished layer of stucco. This was so fine that the ink would not soak into it, but could be washed off.

One model letter thus used to instruct the children will suffice to show their general level –

> The servant of the *wakf*, Ser, saith to . . . life, prosperity,
> health! By the favour of Sobek, Lord of Kheny, as the servant
> there desireth. It is a communication to the Master, life,
> prosperity, health! about causing to be brought to me a little
> peppermint (?) for the servant there. It is good that thou
> hearken.
> (F.LL. Griffith, *Hieratic Papyri from Kahun & Gurob*, [1898]
> p. 69 (letter 7).)

Numbers of original letters were also discovered. Letters were sent to Kahun from other cities – Thebes, Heliopolis, Heracleopolis, Crocodilopolis, and other places associated with the cult of Sesostris II – as well as being written by the town's residents. Many letters were folded up in vertical folds; they were folded two or three times from the sides, and then the folded roll was bent double or treble. The two ends were tied up with a strip of papyrus or string. This was sealed with a clay seal, and the impression, produced by a scarab, often gave the name of the town so that, from this evidence, it was possible to determine that Kahun's original and ancient name was 'Hetep-Sesostris'. In all but one example, the letters were begun on the recto and addressed on the verso, usually in the form 'The Master X, from Y'.

One letter and its reply are especially interesting. They follow the usual pattern, but the contents give the impression of an angry exchange between the writers. The reply implies that the writer wishes numerous evils on his correspondent, ending with the words –

> 'Ill may be thine hearing, and a plague! (or, 'May you be
> plague-stricken!')'

However, he follows with a postscript –

> 'Come that I may see thee. Behold, we are passing an evil
> hour.'

Although the Middle Kingdom was the great period of literature in Egypt, there is little evidence of such a golden age in the papyri found at Kahun. Part of a hymn addressed to King Sesostris III was discovered, which will be considered later as an aspect of religion at Kahun. The only other literary piece is a portion of an episode from the myth of the conflict between the gods Horus and Seth, which was written in a popular form.

However, the Kahun mathematical and scientific fragments are of more interest. It would appear that the Middle Kingdom was the time when scientific literature flourished; all known mathematical documents are either believed to have originated then or to be copies of documents of the 12th Dynasty. At Kahun, various mathematical works were discovered; two small papyri were found together, one giving an arithmetical table and the other a calculation regarding the contents of a circular granary. Another was an account of fowl. This was a 'balance sheet' of an account, which lists the values of the birds named in relation to a common factor – the *Set*-duck. Those people who were in charge of animals and birds were apparently required to provide a tax return which was either a fixed annual amount or fixed proportion of their produce. If the produce fell in one year, it could be made up in another, and paid at intervals throughout the year. Such lists were drawn up by scribes to provide updated accounts of the tax situation.

Veterinary and medical practice

Animals were an important concern to the inhabitants of Kahun. One of the papyri – a narrow strip inscribed with veterinary prescriptions – is unique. It relates to the treatment of diseases in animals and probably details eye complaints suffered by a bull and perhaps by a fish, a bird and a dog. The symptoms suffered by each animal are listed. This is the treatment for a bull suffering from wind (a cold?):

> Let him be laid on his side, let him be sprinkled with cold water, let his eyes and his hoofs and all his body be rubbed with gourds or melons, let him be fumigated with gourds. . . .

However, one of the most important discoveries at Kahun was part of a medical papyrus which contained instructions and prescriptions for physicians or midwives. It consisted of three pages, closely written in Hieratic, in a distinctive hand which enabled the fragments to be picked out from the heap and reassembled: the third page was pieced together by Griffith from 46 separate fragments. The papyrus was apparently found damaged in ancient times, and had been repaired with new papyrus pasted along the back.

A major source for our knowledge of the concepts and practice of medicine in ancient Egypt is the group of nine principal medical papyri; these are either named after their original owners – Edwin Smith, Chester Beatty, Carlsberg – or after the site where they were found – Kahun, the Ramesseum – or after the city where the papyrus is now kept – London, Leyden, and Berlin. One is named after its modern editor – Ebers. Others of less importance also exist, but the Kahun papyrus is the oldest of the medical papyri. It was also obviously a copy of a yet older text, as were most of these papyri. All these medical papyri can be regarded almost as 'recipe books', with details of individual 'cases', and their treatment. Papyrus Kahun is not only the most ancient document on gynaecology known from anywhere in the world, but it also illustrates the relative sophistication of medical practices at Kahun in c. 1880 BC.

The first two pages contain seventeen gynaecological prescriptions without titles or introduction. These all take one form:

> Treatment of a woman (suffering and symptoms are
> described); say thou with regard to it ('it is,' etc. and the
> diagnosis); make thou for it (prescription).

No surgical treatments are indicated, but various drugs, fumigations and vaginal applications are given; the substances recommended include beer, cow's milk, oil, dates, and other fruits, herbs, incense and various offensive substances. The quantities of the substances are not usually specified, but would be decided by the physician. However, where the quantity is stated, it is given in terms of measure and not of weight; $4\frac{1}{2}$ cubic inches or $6/7$ pint for liquid are favourite amounts.

The third page contains a further seventeen prescriptions, which are concerned with various tests designed to ascertain sterility, pregnancy and the sex of unborn children.

All Egyptian medicine was imbued with a combination of rational medical practice and magic; disease was classified in two categories – where the cause of the illness was evident, rational methods could be used to alleviate it, whereas if the cause were not apparent, magic was brought in to attempt a cure. Papyrus Kahun has much in common with certain other medical papyri. Many of the same formulae are found in the Ebers Papyrus, which is the largest and most important of the known papyri and dates to the reign of Amenophis I (c. 1550 BC). It is particularly significant because, whereas the others simply list prescriptions and include magic along with rational methods, the Ebers Papyrus attempts for the first time to consider objectively the problems of disease, without recourse to magic. It was discovered with another papyrus in 1862, and in 108 pages, it deals with many gynaecological diseases which are frequently mentioned in the earlier Papyrus Kahun. Some of the subjects covered include the disease known as 'eating in the womb' which may refer to cancer, as well as eroding ulcers, contraceptive measures, methods to assist with childbirth and treatments for gonorrhoea.

The Berlin Papyrus and the Ramesseum Papyri IV and V also contain much that is similar to Papyrus Kahun. The Berlin Papyrus, which dates to the 19th Dynasty (c. 1300 BC), contains a series of fertility tests, whereas Ramesseum Papyrus IV in particular has many prescriptions which are identical to those in Papyrus Kahun, so that sometimes it is possible to complete a missing text in Papyrus Kahun by reference to the Berlin Papyrus. The main subjects of the Berlin Papyrus are childbirth, protection of the newborn, and contraceptive formulae.

Other papyri also deal with women's ailments and childbirth. There are sections such as that in the Hearst Papyrus (c. 1550 BC) which are concerned with gynaecological diagnosis. The Brooklyn Museum Papyrus contains a magical protection for the pregnant woman against evil spirits and all dangers. However, most examples in other papyri merely duplicate the Ebers Papyrus.

Gynaecology therefore occupies a major section in a number of papyri, and the various versions are so similar that it suggests that they were probably derived from the same original source. The papyri indicate that the Egyptians' gynaecological knowledge, based on detailed examination of the patient, was considerable. Other physical and psychological symptoms which patients evidenced were also frequently attributed to gynaecological causes.

The Egyptians developed the earliest medical profession in the world. From the Old Kingdom onwards, they were aware of the internal arrangement of the organs in the human body, largely because of the postmortem knowledge which they gained through the incision and opening of the abdomen and the removal of the viscera, as one of the preliminary stages in the process of mummification. Their range of medical diagnoses and surgical and pharmaceutical treatments was considerable, and it is not surprising that the diseases associated with pregnancy and childbirth, as well as methods to ascertain sterility and fertility and to prevent conception, were regarded as important concerns.

The Egyptians married early in life and therefore could be expected to produce many children. On the one hand, barrenness was considered a great personal tragedy for the couple concerned, and every attempt was made to determine if a woman would be fertile. On the other hand, however, pregnancy and childbirth were surrounded by considerable physical dangers. Many infants died in the first few months of life, and the level of antenatal care and the conditions surrounding birth must have meant that many women died or sustained injuries associated with childbirth which continued to trouble them. It was therefore not surprising that contraceptive methods were devised which limited their families and lessened the dangers presented by continuous pregnancies.

The papyri provide a fascinating insight into the gynaecology practised in ancient Egypt as well as the extent and level of medical knowledge. From the Ebers Papyrus, we learn that there was a school of midwifery in the Temple of Neith at Sais in the Delta, where midwives learnt their skills from the goddess's attendants. Probably a number of Egyptian temples taught these skills as part of the wider medical training of students. It is also evident from Papyrus Kahun that through the physicians or midwives, the people of the town had access not only to pregnancy and fertility tests, and the diagnosis and treatment of their diseases, but were also provided with knowledge of contraceptive methods.

In Papyrus Kahun, on the first and second pages of the original manuscript, occupying 59 lines, there are seventeen prescriptions which list the patient's signs and symptoms and then indicate a treatment. In every instance, some symptoms or disturbances are noted which on first sight seem to bear little relation to gynaecology. They include pains in the limbs, the eyes and the abdomen, deafness, shaking attacks of terror, and apathy. However, these are accredited to causes which the Egyptian physicians sought in a few primary disorders of the womb. Thus, in Prescription No. 8, there are:

> Instructions for a woman suffering in her neck, pubic area and ears that she hears not what is said to her. You should declare about her: 'This is disquietings of the womb'. You should prescribe for it: the likes of that prescription for driving out 'morbid discharges' of the womb.

Prescription No. 11 deals with a case of apathy, believed to be the result of hysteria:

> Instructions for a woman who wishes to lie down, she makes no effort to rise, and will not shake it off. You should declare about her: 'This is spasms of the womb'. You should act towards her thus: making her drink 970 ml. of $h^c wy$-fluid and having her vomit it forthwith.

One case is particularly interesting. In Prescription 9, the woman's symptoms are described as 'pains in her vagina and also in every limb – like one beaten', which Griffith tentatively identified as rheumatism. However, a more recent translation has been provided by Stevens – 'pains in her vagina and likewise in every limb; one who has been maltreated'. He offers a different explanation of this passage and suggests that the treatment indicated in this prescription – that the woman should eat oil until she is well – recalls the story of a woman in the D'Orbiney Papyrus. Wishing to make her husband believe that his brother had indecently assaulted her, she took oil and grease to make herself resemble one who 'had been maltreated'. This remedy seems therefore to have been the classic prescription for such cases, and Stevens suggests that the example in Papyrus Kahun may refer to a victim who had suffered this type of assault. Other 'social evils' at Kahun may also be reflected in this papyrus. In Prescriptions 1, 6 and 16, descriptions are given of a woman 'whose eyes are diseased that she cannot see, and suffering is in her neck', and another who is 'diseased in every limb, and suffering in the sockets of her eyes', while a third also suffers 'in every limb and in the sockets of her eyes'. It has been suggested that the combination of symptoms – generalised aches, pains in the eyes and a uterine disease – may suggest evidence of venereal disease. However, the existence of gonorrhoea in ancient Egypt cannot be confirmed, and if it did occur, it is impossible to determine how widespread it was.

Prescription No. 2 illustrates a number of points. The patient has become ill because her womb is 'diseased through journeying'. The physician, required to ask her 'What do you smell?' is instructed that, if the woman answers 'I smell fries', he should declare 'This is a disorder of the womb', and prescribe for her 'fumigation over everything she smells as fries'. The smell of 'fries' or burning flesh may indicate a case of cancer of the genitalia here; if so, the method of treatment was to combat it with another 'burnt odour' – the fumigation. It is difficult to determine how common this type of cancer was in Egypt, although other sources indicate that their physicians could identify those tumours for which no medical or surgical treatment would be effective, but which had to be left to the god's intervention. This passage shows that the physician considered his patient's history and her perception of her own symptoms as very important indications, which helped him to reach a diagnosis. It also makes it evident, as do other examples, that the Egyptians believed that the pelvic organs, including the womb, were freely mobile within the abdomen. If they wandered, they could cause disease, and it was necessary to 'put them again in their place' by attracting them into position with fumigations placed under the standing woman. These fumigations were often made of frankincense and oil; pessaries made of vegetable extracts and wine or beer, on which the woman sat, were also used to correct prolapse and other disorders of the womb.

Various bodily symptoms were said to be caused by 'defluxions of the womb'; these included pains in the 'hindquarters, pubic region and the bases of her thighs', and also urinary problems. In another case (No. 4) the woman's symptoms were deemed to be due to giving birth, while in No. 6 the symptoms were said to result from 'want in her womb'; it has been suggested that this may have meant that the woman strongly desired to bear a child. Prescription 5, for a woman 'suffering in her teeth and her gums that she cannot open her mouth', recommends fumigation but also warns that further painful symptoms in this case indicate 'an incurable disease'.

Apart from the fumigations, various dietary prescriptions were given: a woman should eat the raw liver of an ass; or prepared concoctions of nuts, grain and milk; or cereal blended with water or mixtures of grass, beans, seeds and beer. In most cases, a specific number of days were stated during which the patient was required to take the medicine. One patient, suffering from pains in her feet and legs, was to be instructed to smear her feet and legs with mud until she was well, and another, for similar symptoms, was to be given 'strips of fine linen soaked in myrrh'.

Various cases dealt with problems associated with menstruation. In Prescription No. 12, a remedy is given which may have been intended to promote menstruation; aromatic concoctions to be employed as vaginal douches so that 'the blood may be made to come away' are found in the Ebers and Edwin Smith Papyri as well as Papyrus Kahun. The Egyptians also considered some other conditions to be associated with menstruation. In Prescription No. 1, inflammation of the eyes was regarded as a symptom of uterine disease, and indeed it is accepted today that some cases of iritis are manifested during menstruation.

Case 17, 'Instructions for a woman bleeding. . .', may be a prescription to deal with a threatened miscarriage; once again, the woman was required to sit over a prepared concoction, and as a further measure, to drink a mixture which had been boiled and cooled.

From this first section of Papyrus Kahun, it is clear that the physicians adopted a systematic approach. They questioned their patients, assessed their symptoms, and then prescribed the treatments. The observations were noted and documented with care and it is obvious that local examinations and the consideration of patients' own histories played an important part in the final diagnosis.

A second section begins on page 3 of the Kahun Papyrus and includes Prescriptions 18 to 25. These passages deal with conception and contraception and indicate that many aspects of the procreative process were already recognised and understood by the Egyptians.

Prescriptions 18 and 20 are both concerned with fertility; it has been suggested that No. 18 was a recommended aphrodisiac (half a dipper of milk poured into the woman's vagina), while in No. 20, a recipe is given for a fumigation, which should be used 'by suppertime', to cause conception. A number of contraceptive preparations are then given, which were designed to act as either

barrier or spermicial methods. These include 'excrement of crocodile dispersed finely in sour milk', which is similar to a prescription given in the Ramesseum Papyrus IV; a concoction of honey
and natron which is to be injected into the woman's vagina; and an
insertion of sour milk.

The third and final section of the papyrus (page 3, lines 12 to 24)
describes a number of tests which were used to prognosticate a
woman's fertility and ability to conceive, to diagnose pregnancy,
and to determine a child's sex. Many similar tests are included in
other medical papyri, and show the importance which the Egyptians attached to such predictions.

Some of the tests were designed to distinguish between fertile
and infertile women. These were based on the erroneous idea that,
in fertile women, there existed a free passage for certain substances to pass from the vagina to the rest of the body. Thus, in
Prescription No. 27, the physician is instructed to ask a woman to
sit over a mess of dates mixed with beer. If she vomits, she will
conceive, and the number of vomits indicate the number of
children she will bear. If she does not vomit, she will remain
barren. A prescription in the Berlin Papyrus has similar implica-
tions. Papyrus Kahun has another prescription (No. 28) in which
an onion is inserted in the woman's vagina; if the odour of the
onion appears on her breath the next day, she will conceive, but if
not, then 'She will not give birth ever'. A parallel to this is to be
found elsewhere in the Egyptian texts (Papyrus Carlsberg IV)
and also, some 1500 years later, in the writings of the Greek
physician Hippocrates (Aphorism, V, 59).

Papyrus Kahun also indicates (No. 26) that the physician
should examine the woman's breasts to distinguish 'who will
conceive from who will not conceive'. If the vessels of the breast
are distended, she will conceive. This again finds a parallel in the
Berlin Papyrus. Other methods to assess fertility included the
examination of the woman's abdomen (No. 29) and her counte-
nance (No. 31), by which it could be decided if the woman would
bear a son, although, if 'you have noticed something upon her
eyes, she will not give birth ever'. Various parallels exist in the
Berlin and Carlsberg Papyri, as well as in a text from Hippocrates,
in which the sex of the unborn child is prognosticated by observing
the mother's facial features, and the consistency of the breasts.
This idea was based on the theory that the fluids in the body of a
woman who was carrying a boy must be different from those of a

woman who would give birth to a girl. Although no reference is made to it in Papyrus Kahun, another most significant test is mentioned in the papyri, which sought to determine the unborn child's sex through examination of the mother's urine. The properties of the urine would vary according to the child's sex, and the woman was asked to urinate daily on two cloth bags, one containing wheat and the other barley. If both germinated, it was claimed that the woman would give birth – if the barley grew first, it would be a boy, but if the wheat germinated first, she would bear a girl. If neither cereal grew, then she would not give birth.

Modern pregnancy tests are based on the principle that, in pregnant women, a particular hormone is present; this was only demonstrated in 1927. However, the ancient Egyptians probably held the belief that, as the pregnant woman's body carries life, her urine would also contain a life-force and would thus cause growth in cereals. Indeed, tests by Professor Ghalioungui and others have shown that these ancient pregnancy tests, if not the reasoning behind them, have some scientific foundation, for in a series of modern tests, in about 40 per cent of the cases, the urine of pregnant women caused barley and wheat to germinate, whereas that of men and women who were not pregnant prevented growth in the cereals.

In Papyrus Kahun, there was one final method by which fertility could be determined (No. 30). This is the only example in the papyrus of a magical incantation, as opposed to a rational diagnosis and suggested treatment. The incomplete text seems to provide a spell to induce a nosebleed – '. . . if there is a coming away from her nostril, she will give birth. If however, there is no coming away, then she will not give birth ever'. Perhaps, by contrast, this last magical prescription illustrates how the rest of Papyrus Kahun reveals a sophisticated attitude both to the diagnosis and treatment of gynaecological problems, and to methods of community medicine. The papyrus remains one of the most important sources for the study of the history of world medicine and the development of medical practice in Egypt. It also provides a major contribution to our understanding of medical care and social organisation at Kahun itself. However, the existence of such a document should not obscure the significance of other physical facts from the site. Petrie discovered that almost every house at Kahun had been invaded by rats; nearly every room was tunnelled through in the corners, and the holes had been stuffed with stones and rubbish to hold the animals back. Despite some advanced socio-medical ideas and practices, the standards of hygiene and probably the general incidence of disease at Kahun would have endangered lives.

Religion at Kahun

At Kahun, as elsewhere throughout Egypt, there were different levels of religious practice. The official cults, performed on behalf of the king and the gods in the elaborate setting of temples, certainly existed there. So, also, did the worship of humble deities in the inhabitant's own dwellings. The official religion at Kahun shows no specific evidence of non-Egyptian beliefs or practices, but some aspects of the popular religion at Kahun are perhaps unusual. It will be necessary to consider later whether these peculiarities can be accounted for by the fact that our knowledge of domestic religion at settlement sites is limited, or whether the Kahun situation reflects 'foreign' practices, brought in by those residents whom Petrie claimed had migrated to Egypt.

The official religion at Kahun was centred on the pyramid temple of Sesostris II. This, we have seen, was one of the main reasons for the town's continuing existence and prosperity once the king's pyramid was completed. The pyramid temple played an important part in the king's burial service, and thereafter, it became the place where the priesthood performed daily rituals, offering food and drink to the dead king's spirit so that he might enjoy an eternal food supply. In this, the funerary temple had the same purpose as the offering chapels attached to humble tombs of the non-royal deceased, where their families and special funerary priests presented food offerings. In the funerary temple rituals, it was also the intention to ensure the dead king's acceptance by the gods and to constantly reaffirm his role as a god and king in the next world.

The two temples attached to the Lahun pyramid – one immediately joining it, and the other, where the rituals continued to be performed after the king's death, about 805 m away at Kahun – were both excavated by Petrie. Originally they would have been linked by some kind of causeway although at this site, this link was more 'spiritual' than actual. In both, he discovered foundation deposits placed there when the construction was started, and in the Kahun temple, a mass of papyri were discovered which provided information about the personnel and administration of the temple.

Amongst the papyri there was a list of royal statues which were kept in the temple at Kahun. The four members of the royal family who were represented in this group were Sesostris II as a deceased king, Sesostris III (still alive), the 'King's Wife and Mother', who was already dead, and the 'King's Wife' who was still alive. It was doubtless these royal persons who received worship and divine honours at the temple during the reign of Sesostris III. Another papyrus recorded the attendance of dancers and singers at festivals in the same temple. It makes reference to the 35th Year of the reign of a king, whose name is lost. It also contains a number of tables; the most complete preserves the names of sixteen persons, grouped together under various mutilated headings, but it is clear that they were all dancers or acrobats and singers. In the remainder of the table, the festivals are grouped according to the months in which they occurred.

Generally, the papyrus makes it clear that each epagomenal day was a festival. Also, each group of individuals had their own set of festivals which they were required to attend; this seems to be an account of the number of individual attendances and it may also be a record of the absences or days on which sickness prevented the performer being present. The total individual attendance for a year seems to have been thirty-two days, an average of three days in every month.

In one list, a number of festivals are mentioned and include those of Sokar, of Khoiak, and of the reigning king. There is also a festival of 'Receiving the Nile' which was probably connected with the cutting of the dam at the inundation. Table 3 is concerned with the 'Festival of Rowing Hathor, Lady of Heracleopolis', which may have celebrated the visit by the goddess to the Kahun temple.

Further interest is provided by the names of the performers; their two personal names are given, in addition to that of the person's father or mother. Many of them are named after Sesostris, the town's founder and patron. As well as in other Kahun lists, this custom can also be noted on a large stela which records the offerings for a high-priest at Kahun, named Sesostris-ankh-tef-pen. In Table 2 of the papyrus, four groups are recorded; the first three are headed either 'acrobats' or 'dancers' and then divided into '?' and 'singers'. There appear to be two singers in each group and these are all Egyptians. However, in the subdivision where the title is lost – '?' – the individuals are nearly all distinguished by the term which implies that they are foreigners.

Other documents referring to temple administration include a table giving thirty days of a month (which is not identified), divided into lucky and unlucky days; these are classified as 'good', 'bad', or as 'good/bad' meaning 'mixed'. Such lists are known from other Egyptian sources and were doubtless derived from observations of certain magical signs which indicated the advisability of carrying out particular functions on various days. Another papyrus lists a number of jars, probably including a honey-measure, which were perhaps used in the offering rites. There is also a record of the daily payments to various temple staff who are specified as being 'upon the free list (?), eating bread of this day'. These include the superintendent, who received eight jugs of beer and sixteen loaves of bread of different sizes, the chief cook, porters and others. It appears that about a sixth of the daily revenue of the temple was paid out in this way; a much larger amount would have been paid to the priests who offered food to the deceased king and to his favoured deceased relatives and officials.

The temple records tell us little about the major cults at Kahun. Undoubtedly, Hathor was favoured here, as at Deir el-Medina. Sobek, the crocodile god who was held in special esteem in the Fayoum, would have received official worship here also, although it is surprising that no mention is made of his festivals in the Kahun temple documents. However, a beautiful inscribed black basalt statue, found standing in the corner of a room in one of the large northern mansions, belonged to a royal relative whose name, Se-Sobek, underlines the importance of the god's cult at Kahun.

The family of Uah mentioned in the Kahun legal papyri held priesthoods of the god Sopdu or Soped. He was a falcon deity, 'Lord of the Eastern Desert', who, together with Hathor, the 'Lady of Turquoise', protected the crossing to Sinai. It is perhaps surprising to find such a god worshipped at Kahun, and Petrie suggested that some of the Kahun settlers may have come originally from east of the Delta, and introduced his cult at Kahun.

The only other major religious document which was discovered at Kahun in 1889 is a hymn addressed to King Sesostris III during his lifetime. It was composed as a form of greeting by the inhabitants of a city, to celebrate the king's entry into 'his city'. Whether reference to Kahun or another city is intended is unclear. The king's virtues and attributes and prowess against his enemies are extolled, and the hymn commences with the words:

> Praise to thee, Khakaure! Our Horus, divine of forms!
> That protects the land and widens its boundaries, restraining the foreign lands with his crown . . .

Turning to evidence of popular religion at Kahun, we find that offerings of food were made in the houses, as at Deir el-Medina. A number of roughly carved stone dish-stands were discovered in the houses. Each of these generally consisted of a simple column, which supported a dish, into which the dough or bread would have been placed. However, some took forms which are not known elsewhere in Egypt. Curious primitive stone figures act as supports for the offering dish, and in some examples two men stand back to back and support a cup with raised arms. In another instance, an arm supports a cup and this was obviously intended to project from a wall into which it would have been built. Most columns had a plain capital, but Petrie also discovered 'a small stone stand in the form of a lotus column, which supported a saucer which had obviously been used for burning incense'. It was cut from one block of limestone, and again, although its form was traditionally Egyptian, this use of the lotus column for such a purpose has not been seen elsewhere. The evidence seems to indicate that these stands formed part of some daily ritual which occurred in the houses, when bread and perhaps other offerings were made to deities. It is impossible to determine if these household gods and rituals at Kahun differed to any considerable degree from those which existed in towns and villages elsewhere in Egypt. The strange design of the stands suggests a purely local artistic development; this may indeed indicate that the worshippers were foreign and had different religious customs but it could simply represent a variation on the design of the stands introduced here by native Egyptian householders.

Other physical evidence for the popular deities at Kahun is unremarkable. Two figures were discovered which represented the goddess of childbirth, Tauert; one large rough figure shows that all the characteristics of the goddess which are seen in later representations are already present in the Kahun forms.

Perhaps one of the most interesting groups of objects was found in a house on the south side of the second street from the top, in the western sector of the town. Petrie discovered this between 6 and

13 November 1889. He described it as his 'most complete find of
the week', and referred to it in his publications as 'Group 9'. The
whole group is now in the Manchester Museum, and, according to
Petrie, could be dated by the flint and copper implements and
the forms of the alabaster vases to the Middle Kingdom. The
group consisted of a wooden spoon with the remains of a little
figurine at one end; three fine alabaster vases all of one type and a
green paste vase of the same shape; a selection of flint knives, one
with binding on the handle; seven flint flakes in a leather bag,
with some nuts and roots, metal items, and a whetstone; a
selection of copper tools including a large knife, two small chisels
set in wooden handles, a piercer set in a nut handle, and some
other pieces without handles. There was also a wooden box, and
most importantly, a fine metal mirror, with a wooden handle
carved on either side with the cow-eared, human face of the
goddess Hathor, together with a torque. With the exception of the
metal part of the mirror and the large knife, all the items were
discovered in one room of the house. They have been mentioned in
some detail because the overall impression they give is of a group
of ordinary possessions belonging to a workman and his wife – his
tools, some woody rhizomes, perhaps for chewing, and her cosmetic jars, mirror and precious necklace.

However, the mirror and the torque are of special interest.
Petrie could not recall another instance of a torque found in
Egypt. However, a few other examples have been discovered
there: a silver torque was found in a woman's grave at Abydos;
another belonging to a group was discovered at Ballas; two more
were excavated in a Pan-grave, Tomb 1008, at Mostagedda; and a
grave in the Fayoum was found to contain part of a torque.
However, although this type of jewellery is apparently so rare in
Egypt, the torque is a distinctive ornament which was worn for
over five centuries in western Asiatic areas. The earliest well-
dated example comes from a pre-Sargonid grave at Ur in Mesopotamia, and it has been suggested that the 'torque-wearers' may
have been an ethnic group who came from elsewhere and settled
in Byblos and Ras Shamra, on the coast of Palestine, at the
beginning of the Middle Bronze Age. It seems that torques were
thereafter produced locally at Byblos. The few analyses of specimens which have been carried out have shown that they were
made of almost pure copper, or of bronze, containing a high
proportion of tin.

The Kahun example is therefore of unique importance; it is the only torque found in Egypt which was obviously a piece of jewellery worn in the owner's lifetime. A likely explanation is that she or perhaps her husband were foreigners residing at Kahun, and that she had brought the treasured torque from her original homeland.

However, even in this house, the representation of Hathor, an Egyptian goddess, is found on the mirror handle. Does it imply that the residents, even if they were foreign, had adopted the worship of an Egyptian goddess who was particularly favoured at Kahun? Or did they already worship her in their original homeland? Hathor, as one aspect of Egypt's mother-goddess, had a wide appeal. Her popularity in cosmopolitan communities is evidenced elsewhere, in the copper-mining community in Sinai and in the workmen's village at Deir el-Medina. She was also worshipped in Palestine in the 12th Dynasty, which, as we shall see, is a possible place of origin for Kahun's 'foreign residents'. It is interesting to note also that the Hathor mirror handle resembles, in a much poorer version, the splendid example which Petrie discovered in the royal princesses' treasure at Lahun. Perhaps the royal fashions established a style that was followed by the humbler inhabitants of the pyramid workmen's town, but this is the only example which Petrie discovered at Kahun. It is not inconceivable that a relative of this woman had been involved in the design or production of the royal mirror, and had copied its shape and decoration, in a simpler form and with cheaper materials.

Another group with magical and perhaps religious significance was found in a hole in the floor of a room in one of the houses. This group included a wooden figurine, representing a dancer wearing a mask and a costume with a tail, as well as a pair of ivory wands or clappers. In the next room in the same house, a full-sized cartonnage mask was found. This was made of three layers of canvas covered with stucco and painted black with arches above and below the eyes, spots on the cheeks, a band across the head, and red lips. The nostrils and the eyes were pierced, to enable the wearer to breathe and to see. It had obviously been worn quite frequently, since some of the stucco had fallen off; to repair it, black paint had been applied directly to the canvas base.

The features of the mask resemble the face of the god Bes, who was the popular household deity of jollification, music and dancing. A mask of Bes in moulded clay was also discovered at Deir el-Medina, and a comparison has been drawn between these masks and a figure shown in a wall-painting in Tomb 99 at Thebes, which dates to the 18th Dynasty.

The Kahun wooden figurine was stolen in 1892. However, although it was a unique piece, a similar statuette was discovered at the Ramesseum at Thebes, where a wooden figurine of a masked woman, holding a bronze snake in either hand, was uncovered.

The Kahun group probably belonged to a dancer who often wore the mask and used the ivory clappers, perhaps in some kind of magico-religious ceremony. It would appear that such activities, perhaps intended to imitate the god Bes and to utilise his magic powers, were part of popular religious custom in these communities. Further discoveries of figures of Bes and of pottery moulds to produce amulets suggest that the popular beliefs regarding religion and magical protection were much the same at Kahun as elsewhere.

One feature of funerary customs at Kahun, however, is unusual. It has already been stated that numbers of baby burials were discovered here by Petrie, underneath the floors of many of the houses. Many of the babies, who were sometimes buried two or three to a box, were several months old, and their bodies were sometimes decorated with protective beads and amulets. The boxes in which they were buried had been used originally for other purposes, such as holding clothes, tools and other possessions.

As far as can be determined, the practice of interring bodies at domestic sites was not an Egyptian one. From early times, most communities had taken their dead and buried them on the edges of the desert, to leave the cultivation free for agricultural and domestic purposes. However, such customs were practised elsewhere in the ancient Near East. Particularly at Mesopotamian sites, in certain periods, the burial of children in wooden boxes underneath the floors of houses was an accepted custom. The burials at Kahun may again indicate the introduction of foreign funerary practices there. The bodies of these children were frequently returned to the earth by Petrie, although some were brought out and given to museums. Unfortunately, despite an intensive search, it has been impossible to trace any of these babies in museum collections around the world. One baby was received in the Manchester collection, but the rapid deterioration of the body led to its later disposal. Possibly the other bodies met a similar fate, but a detailed study of the anatomy of these remains, if they could be located, could provide valuable information not only about the possible cause of death but also about the ethnic origin of the children.

The adult cemeteries at Kahun are situated in a number of areas in the vicinity of the town and the pyramid. Work on them is published in *Lahun II*.

Early dynastic tombs were discovered about three quarters of a mile south west of the side of the Lahun pyramid, on the edge of the cultivation, and these consisted of open graves, shallow and deep shaft tombs, and stairway tombs. However, it is from the 12th Dynasty tombs situated in the vicinity of Sesostris II's Lahun pyramid that some idea can be gained of the original significance of the Kahun cemeteries.

It is evident that the court officials from the reign of Sesostris II were buried here, near their king's pyramid in the time-honoured fashion. It also seems that, when the king died after a reign of some nineteen years, Lahun ceased to be the burial area for members of the royal court. Sesostris III built his pyramid at Dahshur, and it is likely that his courtiers and officials were buried there. A number of tombs at Lahun were unfinished or unoccupied, suggesting that these had been planned during Sesostris II's reign, but that their owners had then decided to be buried elsewhere.

The 12th Dynasty tombs at Lahun are scattered over several areas. As already stated, the Kahun temple was the Valley Temple of Sesostris II's pyramid. It lay some distance (1.21 km) to the east of the pyramid, and in a typical pyramid complex would have been joined to the pyramid and its mortuary temple by a covered causeway. At Lahun, however, the archaeologists suggested that this 'causeway' or line joining the two buildings was a purely spiritual concept, and that there was no actual physical processional route. No clear route had been left for a roadway here, and indeed the 'causeway' line of approach ran through a group of deep rock-cut tombs which were apparently of the 12th Dynasty. These had all been severely plundered, and had frequently been re-used in the Roman period. To the north-west, on the higher ground, there was another group of 12th Dynasty tombs; again, these had all been plundered. Many others, built in the high ridge on the west of the pyramid, were re-used in the 18th and 19th Dynasties, while, close to the pyramid on the north-east, there were ten tombs of the 12th Dynasty, but none of these had ever been occupied. Another ridge, close to the end of the dyke which runs out from the modern village of Lahun, contained many other tombs of different periods, but these have never been excavated.

Finally, an isolated hill lying further west, known as 'West Hill', was found to contain a number of 12th Dynasty tombs, the most important of which was the mastaba of Anpy, architect of Sesostris II, who was responsible for building the Lahun pyramid and presumably also the town of Kahun.

His tomb, which crowns the hill, is typical of those found in the pyramid cemetery; they are larger and are covered by better-constructed mastabas than the tombs in the surrounding areas. Anpy's tomb (No. 620) was the most elaborate of its type; the owner was 'overseer of all the works of the king in the land to its boundary', and his names and titles also occur on a stela found at Kahun town. The tomb consisted of four underground chambers, entered from two shafts, one of which was vertical, the other sloping. To the east, partly situated in the hill, was the funerary chapel. The mastaba or superstructure of the tomb had almost entirely disappeared, but the archaeologists discovered fragments of sculpture from the walls of the funerary chapel. These pieces indicated that the inside walls of the chapel had been covered with offering lists. On one scene, an inscription occurs in front of Anpy's children or relatives, one of whom, named Anpy-Senb, held an official appointment connected with Kahun. The tomb, mostly plundered, contained two pottery cylinders; these objects were not uncommon at Kahun town, but only rarely occurred in tombs, and their possible purpose will be considered later.

Anpy's tomb was situated on one of the highest sites, a position favoured by the wealthiest nobles buried at Lahun. At least one other mastaba (Tomb No. 608) was as large as Anpy's, but it was too damaged to plan.

In fact, only one complete Middle Kingdom tomb was found at Lahun, situated on an isolated knoll of rock between the dyke and the western ridges. Here, a coffin was found, as well as two skeletons, one of a man named Ankh-mesa and the other of a woman, but these showed no signs of mummification. From the later periods, only a few 18th Dynasty tombs were discovered; these included two undisturbed burials in the western quarry near the pyramid and the tomb of Maket situated in Kahun town.

Later cemeteries in the area probably dated to the 22nd to 25th Dynasties and to the Roman period. From the second century AD, situated about a mile to the north of the pyramid, the excavators discovered a crocodile cemetery. Mature crocodiles were buried here in pits some 1.06 m deep, and young crocodiles were also found in graves, together with a quantity of eggs either placed on the mummified animals or stored in amphorae. The crocodile was the cult animal associated with the god Sobek, whose worship was particularly significant in this area.

The excavations of the cemeteries at Lahun, carried out on behalf of the British School of Archaeology in Egypt in three seasons (1914, 1920 and 1921), produced some information regarding the burials of the inhabitants of the Middle Kingdom town of Kahun. The tomb plans of the mastabas belonging to the wealthiest nobles indicated that, in each tomb, the architects tried to include as many chambers (usually up to four) as time would permit. An entrance passage (the length varied in the different tombs) led south into one or two rooms, while, in the western portion, a pit or trench would be sunk to take the burial; this gave access to the burial chamber itself. Because the tombs had been so heavily plundered, virtually no human remains were found which could have supplied information on the incidence of mummification or provided evidence of disease and possibly ethnic types. Only examples of 12th Dynasty pottery remained, since the rest of the tomb goods had been stolen in antiquity. The archaeologists queried whether any distinction could be drawn between the types of pottery found in the town and in the tombs. They concluded that the tomb pottery did not seem to include special funerary styles, but that some of the pottery found in Kahun town was not found in the tombs and seemed to have had definite domestic uses. In particular, the distinctive incised pottery dishes appear to have been found and used only in 'household' contexts.

However, not all the funerary items were discovered in the cemeteries around Kahun. Offering lists, stelae, statuettes and parts of tomb wall scenes appear to have been removed from tombs and brought to the town. Petrie suggested that the inhabitants of Kahun ransacked the tombs for materials towards the end of the 12th Dynasty or beginning of the 13th Dynasty.

Although the much plundered cemeteries are not particularly informative about the religious and funerary practices, there is nothing to indicate that the tomb-owners had burial customs that differed from those at other Egyptian sites.

In general terms, therefore, it is not possible to draw firm conclusions about the religious beliefs and practices of the inhabitants of Kahun. Some customs suggest that perhaps they were introduced by people who were not of Egyptian origin. However, because so few of the towns of ancient Egypt have been fully excavated, it is unwise to draw conclusions about the apparent peculiarities at Kahun. It is not appropriate to assign these customs to 'foreign' origins, when they could in fact be representative of aspects of Egyptian popular religion for which we have relatively little evidence from other excavated sites.

Nevertheless, it would be equally wrong to conclude that there were no foreigners involved in the religious life of the town. Quite apart from any private devotions in their own houses, it is evident from the papyri that foreigners played a significant if minor role in the official temple cult. The deities who were chosen to receive official worship at Kahun included Hathor who, although Egyptian in origin, had associations beyond Egypt's boundaries and was widely accepted in communities elsewhere. Another god who apparently received worship at Kahun was Sopdu, who again had connections with the region beyond Egypt's eastern Delta. Both religious and other evidence indicates that Kahun's inhabitants included some people of non-Egyptian origin. The Egyptians, in their customary way, probably took the official line that the immigrants could continue to worship their own gods, who would be absorbed into the Egyptian pantheon, and the official cults in the town may have been centred on deities who would appeal both to the Egyptians and to the 'foreigners'. It is impossible to tell whether the immigrants brought these deities with them to Kahun from their original homelands, or whether Egyptian officialdom consciously introduced cults at Kahun which they knew would be familiar and acceptable to both native and foreign residents.

CHAPTER 6

Everyday life at Kahun

Apart from the papyri and literary sources, the objects of daily use which were discovered at Kahun provided us with an unequalled opportunity to study many aspects of life in a Middle Kingdom community. Most of these objects were found in a 12th Dynasty context, and unlike so many examples of excavated material from Egypt, these were articles of everyday use rather than tomb goods intended for the owner's benefit in the next world.

Tomb goods frequently included such items as clothing, jewellery and furniture, but some of the most mundane objects of common use were never placed in the tombs. For example, the implement which the ancient Egyptians designed to produce fire was not known to archaeologists before Petrie discovered a number of these firesticks at Kahun. Again, other objects, especially some of the workmen's tools, were previously known only from the tomb wall-paintings.

Many of the finds from Kahun are therefore particularly significant because they enable us to understand how an Egyptian town functioned some 4,000 years ago. Some of the discoveries were unique, and others provided sufficient information so that Egyptologists could begin to assess the developments in various branches of ancient technology.

Hunting, fowling and fishing

From earliest times, the inhabitants of the Nile valley had hunted the game which surrounded them. In c. 5000 BC, the people were still living in primitive hunting communities, and the chase,

rather than being a form of amusement, was a necessary occupation to feed and clothe the community. By c. 4000 BC, however,
agricultural and pastoral methods had arrived in Egypt, and
hunting became increasingly a secondary pursuit. Gradually,
people hunted only to supply additional delicacies for the table or
to amuse themselves, and by the Old Kingdom (c. 2500 BC),
hunting in the desert and catching fowl in the lush Delta marshes
had simply become favourite pastimes of the nobility. During this
period, scenes occur which show the wealthy tomb-owner with his
family and retainers in the act of hunting, fowling and fishing.
These were intended to provide the deceased tomb-owner with the
ability to enjoy for eternity the pleasures of some of his best-loved
occupations.

Parts of the open desert were used for the hunt, and also areas
of the Nile Valley; however, the northern Delta and the Fayoum
oasis were perhaps the richest preserves. The chase was highly
organised. Attendants in the service of the wealthy noblemen had
specific duties; they looked after the hounds, directed the hunt,
carried darts and hunting poles, and arranged the nets which
enclosed the ground area into which the animals were to be
beaten. They used long nets which were supported on forked poles
and which varied in length to accommodate the different contours
of the ground. Smaller nets were also employed to stop the gaps.
In addition to the nets, the Egyptians also pursued the game with
hounds and the bow and arrow. The hunting bow was very similar
to that which was used for warfare. The animals most frequently
hunted included gazelle, the ibex, oryx, wild ox, wild sheep, fox,
hyena, jackal, wolf, desert hare and leopard. Some animals, such
as the leopard, were valued for their skins, and ostriches were also
pursued for their magnificent feathers which were made into
ornate fans. In addition to their duties at the hunt, the retainers
also superintended the game preserves and obtained more animals to stock them when they became depleted. As well as the
animals already mentioned, the hippopotamus was hunted in
Upper Egypt, although it was probably something of a rarity in
Lower Egypt even in antiquity. As a danger to fields, crops and
life, the hippopotamus was a favourite target for the hunters;
additionally, the hide was eagerly sought for making whips,
shields, javelins and helmets. Another dangerous creature, the
crocodile, received ambivalent treatment in Egypt. In some areas,
especially in the Fayoum and around Thebes, the crocodile was

regarded as sacred, and was kept at considerable expense on a diet of geese, fish and meat. According to the Greek writer Herodotus (*The Histories*, Bk II, 69), they were also provided with earrings, bracelets and necklaces of gold or semi-precious stones. After death, as the cult animal of the god Sobek, crocodiles were embalmed. Elsewhere, however, they were disliked and destroyed and indeed, both the hippopotamus and the crocodile seem to have been both revered and regarded as the embodiment of evil at different times and in various places in Egypt.

Kahun would certainly have been a centre for game hunting, for it was situated in the fertile Fayoum oasis. In addition to the royalty and nobility who enjoyed these pastimes there, the ordinary inhabitants of the town would have augmented their basic diet with some of these delicacies. Finely polished wooden arrows were found there, as well as another hunting weapon, the throwstick. Both symmetric and asymmetric examples of this weapon were discovered, and one had been broken and bound together with string in antiquity. Tomb scenes again show this activity, with throwsticks being used to kill birds. They were flat and made of heavy wood, and could travel considerable distances. Fowling was in fact a favourite pastime, and the nobility and others made expeditions into the thickets of marshland, where birds were in plentiful supply, especially in the region around Lake Moeris. At the time of the annual inundation, the wild fowl were most abundant in the area around the lakes formed by the rising waters. The fowling expeditions would sail amongst the reeds in papyrus skiffs and the nobleman, accompanied by his family and his retainers, is often depicted with a skilful cat who may have been trained to retrieve the birds.

Although the birds were sometimes brought down by throwsticks or arrows, the most common practice was to catch large numbers of them in clap-nets which were set up in fields or on the surface of a lake. When a sufficiently large number of birds had gathered, a signal was given for the trap-net to be closed tight. Several kinds of net were developed and used, and the discovery of nets of different sizes, netting needles, and clay or stone net sinkers at Kahun suggests that quite a number of people were engaged in producing the necessary equipment for this sport.

Another weapon, but with limited use, was the sling. This would be employed by gardeners to frighten birds from the crops and vineyards. A fine sling was found at Kahun, which may be the earliest known example of this type in the world. It is beautifully woven, with long cords; one of these has a loop at one end to retain it on the finger, while the other end is plain. It was found with three small sling stones which were probably flung from the sling at the same time, to produce a scatter effect.

The Egyptians greatly prized fowl as part of their diet, and enjoyed partridge, bustard, quail, geese, pigeon and curlew. Some birds were preserved in salt, and to meet a demand, in addition to the fowling expeditions, the people also introduced methods of rearing poultry. Artificial methods of hatching the eggs of fowl and geese were developed and the young were reared and sold to poultry-yards. The eggs of some birds especially prized as food were supplied by the poulterers for the tables of the wealthy.

Further variety was also given to the diet by the provision of different kinds of fish. The Nile supplied a rich harvest for the fishermen, and this made a major contribution to the food of a country which had only limited pastures and herds of cattle.

The waters of the river brought the fish harvest to most villages in the Nile valley at the time of the inundation. There were also small lakes or ponds in the gardens of large houses, where fish were fed for the table. There were a number of ways in which fish were caught: the favourite method, especially amongst the wealthy, was to use a bident spear with two barbed points, which was thrust into the fish as it glided past. The poorer people fished with a short rod which usually had a single line, although some-times a double line was used; each line had its own hook, and a copper example was found at Kahun. Sometimes, also, the fish were caught with a drag-net, either trawled between two boats, or with two men working on either side of a pool. As a centre of weaving, Kahun produced nets for fishing as well as for catching birds.

The fish were either eaten immediately they were caught, or they were preserved; the fish were slit open, and then salted and placed in the sun to dry. Some fish were especially good to eat because they had more flavour, and some of the best were found in the Fayoum. As well as being cured or sold at market, a quantity of fish was also put aside to feed sacred temple animals.

Although, by the historic period, the nobility and the wealthy hunted and fished only for sport, others pursued these activities to feed their families and to take the surplus to market. However, these activities supplied only part of the people's food requirements, and from early times, cultivation of crops and animal husbandry provided the basic diet of the Egyptians.

Agriculture, animal husbandry and horticulture

From the Neolithic Period in Egypt (c. 4000 BC), crop production and the rearing of livestock for milk, meat and leather had been the main occupations of most of the people. Although, by the Archaic Period, Egypt was developing a highly organised and centralised bureaucracy which employed many officials and scribes as well as artisans, the majority of people remained peasant farmers, who produced the food for the rest of society.

Every town and village possessed an agricultural support system, and Kahun was no exception. It is evident from the objects found in the houses that at least some of the inhabitants were involved in this, to provide food not only to meet their own requirements, but also to feed the officials and craftsmen of the town.

The Egyptians kept various domestic animals. Cattle, sheep and goats provided meat, milk and clothing. Although woollen garments were not usually depicted in sacred wall scenes in temples or tombs nor included amongst tomb goods, because they were not considered to be ritually 'pure', the Egyptians undoubtedly possessed and wore them. For much the same reasons, because they were considered unclean, pigs were not represented in tomb scenes, but they were kept as domestic animals. However, cattle, sheep and goats appear in tomb scenes, and indeed, several kinds of cattle were quite clearly differentiated. Donkeys also occur, and were widely employed as beasts of burden, while other animals were put to additional use, pulling ploughs and treading the grain.

Evidence from Kahun indicates that cereal crops (wheat and barley) were grown in the fields nearby, while vegetables, fruit and flowers were cultivated in the gardens.

The agricultural implements found in the houses were similar to those depicted in the tomb scenes. It seems that, around 3000 BC, there had been great advances in early technology in Egypt, although our view of this may be influenced to some extent by the fact that, from this time onwards, there is more information about various aspects of life in Egypt because of the development of tombs and tomb scenes, as well as increased funerary goods.

However, until the end of the 4th millennium BC, it was undoubtedly the invention of the plough which, as a technological development, had the greatest effect on society. This invention resulted in vast improvements in crop yield because it allowed the farmer to sow his seed consistently and evenly in rows; it also facilitated weeding. A wooden plough coulter and a bronze ploughshare were both found at Kahun, as well as the wooden hoes and rakes which were used to clear the ground before ploughing commenced. The rakes were roughly cut from a single piece of wood and were much worn; they were cut along one side into large teeth which, in different examples, numbered between seven and ten. The wooden hoe was developed in Egypt c. 4000 BC. The Kahun examples were of the simplest kind, with the wooden blades (broad and flat in some cases and thick and narrow in others) and the handle inserted into each other and bound together in the middle with a twisted rope. This same method of attachment is shown in the tomb scenes. The blade and handle were pierced with holes or grooved to take the rope, and some of the hoes have curved handles.

In addition to rakes and hoes, the Egyptians used wooden mallets to break up the heavy clods of earth. Examples of these were found, cut from single pieces of wood. The earliest illustrations of ploughing in Egypt showed oxen harnessed to a plough by a yoke attached to the front of the animal's horns. This was later replaced by the more efficient shoulder yoke which was put over the animal's shoulders and required no further harnessing.

Ancient ploughing methods produced only narrow, shallow furrows; once this part of the work was complete, the farmer then sowed his seed. The grains found at Kahun included wheat and barley; however, early reports indicated that large quantities of weed-seed were also recovered and included clover, flax, oats, spiny medick, dock and poppy. This indicated that the fields were infested with many of the same weeds that occur today. Unfortunately these plant remains are no longer available for modern identification.

Implements were also discovered that had been used in antiquity to reap the crop. The sickles were based on the form of an animal's jawbone. In some cases, an animal jawbone was turned into a sickle by setting flints in the teeth sockets, but in other instances, the body of the sickle was made of wood, usually constructed of two or three pieces joined together, because of the difficulty of obtaining a single piece from which the required shape could be carved. A groove was made along the inside of the handle, and a line of short flint blades was set into this and held in place with cement made of mud and glue. Such flint blades were frequently discovered, and had distinctively worn, serrated edges, but the Kahun sickles showed these flint saws in position and confirmed their use. One example was made either as a back-handed sickle or for use by a left-handed person.

Once the reaping was completed, the grain was then packed into baskets, to be taken by donkey to the threshing floor where it was trodden by animals. Various baskets, made of plaited palm-leaves and fibre, were discovered at Kahun, and some may have been used for harvesting. Next, the grain was winnowed, using wooden scoops, in order to separate the chaff from the wheat – an activity depicted in some tomb scenes. Finally, the grain was collected off the threshing floor using wooden grain scoops.

The grain was next weighed and then taken to a storage area, before it was reduced to flour. First, it was ground in a stone mortar with a heavy pestle; in the Kahun example the limestone mortar has a deep bowl shape, while the limestone pestle is of a cylindrical shape and rounded at one end. The flour was then ground even more finely between two stones, with the addition of sand to aid the process. The flat lower millstone was used in conjunction with a rounded rubber or pebble, and again, these have been discovered in the town. It was this method of preparing the flour, in addition to sand in the environment and atmosphere, which was largely responsible for the condition of the ancient Egyptians' teeth. They ate large quantities of bread, and although they did not suffer greatly from caries before the Graeco-Roman Period, there is ample evidence that by adolescence, the diet of gritty bread had affected most people's teeth. In most of the skulls and mummies which have been examined, it has been found that the outer surface of the teeth had been worn away and in some cases this led to severe dental problems.

At Kahun, Petrie found examples of most of the implements which would have been used for the various stages of crop production, harvesting and grinding the corn into flour.

Here, also, considerable attention was given to cultivating trees, shrubs and vegetables. Doubtless, the *shaduf* (a water-lifting device) was used to bring an increased volume of water to the area under cultivation. The *shaduf*, which can still be seen in parts of Egypt today, consists of a beam pivoted on top of an upright post. At one end of the beam, there is a rope with a water-container at its end and at the other end is a counterweight. The water container is lowered into the river or canal by hand; it is raised and emptied into an irrigation channel, and then lowered back into the river. This, although slow and tedious, increases the volume of water that one man can raise, and in Egypt, this method was not improved upon until the water-wheel (where an animal provided the power) was introduced many centuries later.

The garden produce from Kahun indicates that the towns-people grew peas and beans as well as cucumbers. Two radishes were also identified, and these are of particular interest since the Classical writer Herodotus claimed that radishes were one element of the payment provided by the state for the workmen engaged on the Great Pyramid at Giza. Radishes were perhaps cultivated at Kahun for the same purpose, to provide sustenance for the workmen who built the Lahun pyramid.

Houses and furniture

The layout and general construction of the houses at Kahun has already been described. The major industry connected with house building was the production of mud-bricks and the Egyptians used unfired mud-bricks for all domestic buildings, including their royal palaces. Sun-dried mud-brick was the earliest domestic building material used throughout the ancient Near East and a scene in the 18th Dynasty tomb of Rekhmire at Thebes shows the process of mud-brick manufacture. Alluvial mud was mixed with water, and then packed into wooden moulds; these moulds were then removed, leaving the bricks to dry in the sun arranged in long rows. At Kahun, not only did the walls of the houses survive, but Petrie even discovered a mould – the first tangible evidence of the industry to be found at any site.

This wooden mould was oblong, and the four sides were carefully fitted and pegged together; one side projected beyond the corner to form a handle with which the mould could be lifted to allow the moulded brick to fall to the ground.

It is evident that this 12th Dynasty example is the forerunner of those depicted in the tomb of the Rekhmire and in the scene of King Taharka (25th Dynasty) making bricks, which occurs in the

Temple of Medinet Habu. Ancient peoples soon discovered that objects as well as bricks could be modelled from clay and that the material could be hardened by firing. However, in Egypt, although kiln-baked pottery is in evidence from early times, there was no urgency to introduce baked bricks, since the dry climate ensured that sun-dried bricks lasted for many years. Thus, kiln-baked bricks were only widely introduced in the Roman period, and even today, houses in country villages are often built of sun-dried bricks, which are produced in moulds almost identical to the ancient ones.

Once the building was erected, it had to be plastered with a layer of mud. Again, the plasterers' floats found at Kahun are almost the same as those in use today. One float was larger, intended for applying the rough coat of plaster. It was made of one piece of wood, and the bevelled end which projects out from the handle was to allow the plasterer to get into the corners of the room without touching the plaster on the adjoining wall. Some plaster still remains on this float, where the ancient workmen forgot to completely clean it some 4,000 years ago.

The smaller, lighter float, carved from one block of wood, was used for putting on the facing coat. This also retains a smearing of mud-plaster as it was left by its last owner.

The houses were fitted with wooden doors, and an almost complete example is in the Manchester collection. Door-bolts were also discovered; some were single and others were double. The wooden blocks into which the door-bolts slid were set into the door near the edge by means of a tenon and were fixed with a pin in the edge of the door. If it was a single door, the bolt slid through one door block and into the wall; if it was a double door, the double bolt passed through the two blocks on the edges of the double door. One double door-bolt which was found was cut from one piece of hard wood, and was flat on one side and carefully rounded on the other. It corresponds closely to the hieroglyphic sign which represents a double bolt.

A wooden key was also discovered. This was a cylindrical piece of wood, which at one end was pierced to a depth of 1.9 cm. This key was thrust through a hole in the door, and the two strings knotted through the pierced holes pushed back the bolt (of which no ancient example has yet been discovered), which fastened the door inside. The purpose of this object and the method of using it were first identified in 1907, when a certain Herr Krencher observed an almost identical key in Abyssinia.

Inside the houses, the floors were made of a layer of clay. There was little furniture; seats were provided, and also containers for personal possessions. Seats were used which were cut from one stone block; a section of stone was cut away underneath to create two legs, and the seat was slightly hollowed out to provide more comfort. Parts of wooden chairs were also found. These had apparently had carved legs, and all the angles were strengthened by L-shaped angle pieces (cut out of selected curve-grained wood) which were attached with a large number of wooden pins.

One chair was obviously finely constructed, using a dark wood and ivory pegs, but some other pieces of furniture were very coarse, such as an oblong stool with four legs which was cut from one block of wood and roughly finished.

Possessions were kept in wooden boxes. Some were small and contained personal items; one was obviously a make-up box and included powdered haematite, a kohl-stick and juniper berries for colouring the face, whereas another contained two strings of glazed pottery, garnet, quartz, carnelian and amethyst beads. The boxes were constructed so that the lid fitted into the box in such a way that the lid could not be raised at one end. On the other end there was a knob which could be fastened down with thread to another knob on the end of the box. Larger boxes, probably originally used to contain clothing and other possessions, were found to hold baby burials and also, sometimes, beads which were inscribed with the names of the 12th Dynasty rulers, thus fixing the date of the burials.

For sleeping purposes the Egyptians used headrests which supported the head and lifted it off the ground. Although these would appear to be most uncomfortable, they were widely used and were regarded as a more hygienic option than pillows or cushions. Fine examples of these occur in some tombs, carved in stone or alabaster, and these were obviously used in some houses in the owner's lifetime. However, at Kahun, the only examples are crudely carved from stone and curved slightly at the top to receive the head.

One remarkable discovery was the firestick. Previously no fire-making tools from ancient Egypt had been found, and indeed, it was not known by what means the Egyptians produced fire. The firestick is essentially a bow drill, and the complete example discovered at Kahun revealed the method of use. It consisted of four parts: a drill cap, a matrix, a firestick and a bow. The drill cap was made of a conical stone, flattened on the base and drilled with a circular hole into which was inserted the upper end of the wooden firestick. This was carefully smoothed and carved to swell out slightly at the rounded ends. The lower end of the firestick would have been inserted into the wooden matrix, which was a rough strip of wood, drilled with a number of holes which were blackened by the action of the firestick. Finally, there was the bow, made of a narrow piece of wood curved widely at one end; it was bored with rectangular holes near each end which were intended to receive a length of string to complete the bow. Heavy pressure exerted by the user on the drill cap would press the firestick into the matrix hole, and the simultaneous movement of the drill bow caused sparks to ignite at the matrix. A quantity of very dry leaves and twigs would be kept close at hand to kindle the fire once the sparks appeared. One matrix did not appear to be burnt in the holes but was very deeply drilled, and Petrie suggested that it may have been a trial piece for a learner. The discovery of the firestick was very important; because of the scarcity of wood in Egypt, most would have been used as fuel as soon as their purpose had been served, and therefore, very few complete examples of this fire-making implement are likely to be found.

Culinary equipment at Kahun was also recovered. Grains of wheat and barley were found in the houses, as well as the equipment to grind them into flour. Wooden scoops and bowls also occurred; these were common at Kahun, but are rare later. Some were plain, but others were carved to incorporate a handle. One shell implement was pierced on one side and the hole was closely bound with a rush to form a handle; the cutting edge was serrated. Its use remains uncertain but Petrie suggested that it might have been used as a scoop for soft fruit. Limestone and sandstone whetstones were also found, for sharpening tools.

The pottery from Kahun falls into several categories. Some vessels, found in special circumstances, can definitely be attributed to the 12th Dynasty; these include the temple foundation deposit pottery, the material found in a box together with cylinder seals of the 12th Dynasty, and pottery from the masons' rubbish heap. Other pottery which Petrie assigned to the same period was dated thus because he found it in the town, usually in rooms which had been deserted and then filled up with the rubbish from neighbouring houses.

This differed markedly from the pottery of later periods. The common-place 12th Dynasty pottery was either coarse, rough and brownish-grey in colour; or a softer brown ware; or of a thin, fine, reddish-brown clay which was often washed over with red, and, from the clay marks inside the pot, there was evidence that the potter had used upwards streaking with the fingers instead of turning the pot. This pottery was all in marked contrast to the rough red tile of later periods, or the fine drab ware of the 26th Dynasty, or the polished light drab and light brown of the 18th Dynasty.

The styles of the 18th Dynasty domestic pottery had changed almost entirely from those of the 12th Dynasty, and Petrie could only identify any evidence of continuation in a few examples, such as the pilgrim vases. Therefore the 12th Dynasty pottery can almost certainly be characterised by distinctive styles.

Some groups are of particular interest. There are numbers of pottery stands, which were used both to hold dry food on a raised dish, and also to support porous jars containing liquid. If such a jar was placed directly on the ground, it would accumulate dirt and grit, whereas on a ring stand, the pot always remained clean. An alternative means of support was provided by stone stands, usually made of soft limestone; these were generally rectangular with four feet, although some were circular and had three feet. They supported one or two jars which were placed in conical holes, and often there was a groove which caught and led off the water which seeped through the porous jar.

Many incised pottery dishes were also discovered. Petrie suggested that these were used to serve food, since one example had a raised centre. They have a rough surface and therefore were probably not used for cooking or serving wet or juicy food. They were generally oval in shape, and incised on the inside with patterns; some of these were derived from basketwork designs, whereas others incorporated lotus flowers, fish and lions.

Some items were unusual and interesting; one pot which was closed below but perhaps originally had skin stretched tightly across the top may have been a drum, rather like the modern *darabuka*. There were plain pottery cones, which were perhaps used as strainers; dishes with two loops inside at the bottom which were probably used in spinning; and pottery offering trays which had a space for pouring out libations and also pottery representations which included a bull's head, bird, haunch of meat, wine jars, flat and conical cakes, and radishes. One fragment of pottery was discovered which had a fine smooth surface applied to it which was then marked with black pigment to imitate marble and serpentine.

An unusual pottery object was found at Kahun which is similar to examples discovered at Deir el-Medina and Gurob. These are pottery 'coops' which are pierced with air-holes and fitted with a sliding door. The Kahun example was found in a 12th Dynasty rubbish heap in the northern part of the town. It had been partly broken while in use, because the handle was missing from the top, and one of the holes had been filled up with plaster, presumably when repairs were being carried out on it in antiquity. Various purposes have been suggested for these objects. It has been claimed that they may have been used to kindle a fire or to carry fire to a hearth, but there is no evidence of burning on them. Again, they may have been used as portable ovens. When Winifred Blackman lived at the modern Lahun village in the 1920s, she noted that the houses had both 'fixture' ovens and portable ovens for bread-baking.

However, Petrie believed that the holes were present because these containers were used for keeping live animals. He suggested that they may have held hatching eggs, and that the chicks would not stray when they emerged but could be carried away in the warm pottery cage without chilling. He noted that artificial hatching methods of this type existed in Roman times, and that they may have been used earlier for duck and goose eggs. Finally, another suggestion is that they were used to catch rats. Kahun certainly suffered from vermin, but the idea of the 'coops' as artificial hatcheries is perhaps most convincing.

Pottery from Kahun was found in several areas; some came from the tombs, some was from the temple foundation deposits, and some was discovered in the stonemasons' pottery heap just north of the temple, outside the town wall. Here, little dishes were found which were similar to those uncovered at the pyramid site of Dahshur as well as near the Lahun pyramid.

As already noted, some differences distinguished the domestic or secular pottery from Kahun from the funerary and religious wares. However, examples of one type – long, pipe-like objects – were found in the town and also in the temple foundation deposit. One of these objects, now in the Manchester Museum collection, was examined in the 1970s by a research chemist and beekeeper, Mr H. Inglesent, and his investigation has revealed the true significance of these pottery 'tubes', which had not previously been identified.

It is known that beekeeping was one of the important minor industries in ancient Egypt. From as early a time as the Old Kingdom, references to honey occur, and it also appears in lists of tribute and of offerings to gods in the temple rituals. Honey was also an important medicinal aid and appears in various medical papyri.

However, only four representations of beekeeping are known from ancient Egypt. The earliest occurred on a wall section from the solar temple of Niuserre, now in the Berlin Museum; it shows various stages in the process. Another scene in the Tomb of Rekhmire at Thebes shows jars of honey and honeycombs, while the taking of honey is depicted in the 25th Dynasty tomb of Pa-bes at Thebes. In this, cylindrical hives are shown, which were probably typical of Egypt. Finally, another scene occurs in a Theban tomb (18th Dynasty) but this is now barely visible.

Lucas, the chemist who carried out many experiments on ancient Egyptian materials, described his examination of two small pottery jars from the tomb of Tutankhamun (18th Dynasty) at Thebes. These jars were identified by Hieratic inscriptions as containers of 'honey of good quality', but chemical tests carried out on the very small quantity of remaining contents gave negative results. Another examination of a New Kingdom specimen by a different scientist also produced similar results.

Apart from the analyses of jar contents and the information from the tomb scenes, there were literary indications that beekeeping was practised in ancient Egypt, but no actual apiaries had ever been discovered. Nevertheless, sufficient evidence existed to indicate that there was a beekeeping industry, and that the hives were cylindrical and, piled on top of each other, were built up in the form of a wall. Despite the absence of written records about the process, it is fair to assume that ancient Egyptian beekeeping techniques were similar to those of the present day.

Inglesent's aim was to examine the large collection of Egyptian pottery at the Manchester Museum, to ascertain whether any of the pots had been used to store honey. In examining the unidentified pottery 'tube' from Kahun, he brushed out the contents and established that these were mainly fragments of ceramic material from the pot, mixed with some black flakes which were identified as chitin. However, he also discovered two lumps of material adhering firmly to the inside of the tube. These were removed and analysed, and were found to contain a substantial amount of material derived from beeswax. The extracted residue was examined microscopically and pollen was found as well as the metatarsus of a bee, examined and identified microscopically as being from *apis mellifera*. Inglesent has concluded that these two pieces were part of the hive 'debris' and that the pottery tubes were in fact ancient Egyptian hives. It would not be surprising to find such hives in both secular and religious contexts, since honey was part of the divine food. Again, the Kahun material has supplied an example of an object which was previously known only from tomb scenes or literary sources.

There is a wide range of pottery at Kahun used for many domestic and other purposes. Some of this pottery, Petrie claimed, was foreign, and had been introduced by Kahun's immigrant residents. The evidence for the 'foreigners' at Kahun and the associated pottery will be considered later. However, there is ample evidence to indicate that, in addition to any imported ware, the town had its own flourishing pottery industry.

Apart from the vast numbers of pots which have been recovered from Egyptian sites, scenes in tombs at Beni Hasan and Thebes illustrate the sequences involved in making pots – mixing the clay and turning, baking and polishing the vases. The clay was usually trodden by men to make it homogeneous. It was then worked and formed into a lump of a convenient size, before it was placed on the wheel. The 'wheel' was probably introduced early in Egypt, to meet an increased demand for pottery. It was more accurately a low turntable of simple construction, probably made of wood or clay and pivoted into a socketed stone at the base.

The prepared clay was taken by the potter, who squatted at the wheel, and placed in the centre of the turntable. He turned this with one hand, while he used his other hand to shape the clay into the desired form. The vessel was then cut off, any ornamentation was added with a wooden or metal instrument, and the object was removed to the kiln. This simple turntable was introduced as an improvement on earlier methods of making pottery – building up the vessel with a succession of clay rings, or hand-modelling. With some minor developments, it remained the most advanced method of pottery production for many years until, c. 700 BC or later, another innovation – the true 'potter's wheel' – was introduced which, with its continuous rotation, further increased the methods of production.

Once they had been dried on planks of wood, the vessels were carried on trays to the kiln. The Egyptian kilns, known from tomb scenes, were tall structures which resembled chimneys. They were open at the top and some had a platform at one side so that the potter could place his vessels inside the kiln through the top opening, which was partially closed with a capping of stone or mud. It is unclear whether there were platforms inside the kiln to receive the wares, or whether they were simply piled inside. The introduction of the kiln and the turntable as production methods required the potter to produce a finer, smoother and more uniform body of clay, so that the particles would not catch in his hands as the clay rotated on the wheel, and would not shrink unevenly in the kiln. Therefore, even in early times, pottery-making was highly skilled and organised in Egypt, although in later periods, it never achieved the standard of excellence which is found in some other areas. The clay was not of a sufficiently fine quality to enable the Egyptians to manufacture very fine pottery, and the industry remained one of the few in Egypt which did not aspire to an art-form of excellence. Pottery making remained to a large extent a means of producing domestic and utilitarian wares.

Clothing, personal possessions and adornment

The houses at Kahun supplied evidence not only of their owners' household goods but also of their personal possessions. One man had left behind his walking stick, which was made of wood and was well shaped and smooth; its lower end was well worn and gave every indication of much use. However, the production of clothing was obviously a major industry in the town and ample evidence exists of spinning and weaving, which will be considered later. In addition to linen and woollen clothing, the residents also required footwear, and sandals of neatly bound rushes were discovered, as well as leather shoes and sandals. These will be discussed in more detail in Chapter 11.

The women of Kahun used a range of cosmetics and beauty aids which reflect the elegance of their lifestyle even in this remote town. These personal possessions, left in the houses, are important. Most of our knowledge of such groups of antiquities is based on discoveries made in the tombs, and it could be argued that such luxurious tomb goods were collected and prepared for a specific purpose, rather than reflecting the average standard of everyday existence. However, there is no doubt that the Kahun finds illustrate the quality of goods used every day.

From earliest times the ancient Egyptian women paid considerable attention to the enhancement and preservation of their beauty. The creams and oils with which they adorned themselves were kept in containers which illustrate their love of elegant and beautiful possessions. By 2500 BC oils were pressed from various fruits in Egypt, using a simple bag press. This method was used to extract olive oil and the aromatic oils for flavourings and scents. A major industry developed in cosmetics, and some plants and herbs were specially cultivated in Egypt for this, while others were sought elsewhere in Africa.

The early cosmetics were made of animal fats or plant oils and were heavily scented with aromatic substances. These precious unguents were stored in jars or bottles which were made of stone, pottery and, later, glass.

Various small containers were discovered at Kahun, and some of these were of stone. Alabaster, porphyry, basalt and serpentine were used which the Egyptians had known since earliest times, selecting them for their fine colouring or translucent qualities. However, at Kahun some cosmetic vases occurred which were made of a fine-grained, bluish-grey marble; this, Petrie stated, was used in Egypt only in the 12th Dynasty and had perhaps been introduced from an area to the north of the Mediterranean. By the Old Kingdom, the Egyptians had perfected their skills in producing stone vases of all sizes, and this had long been a major

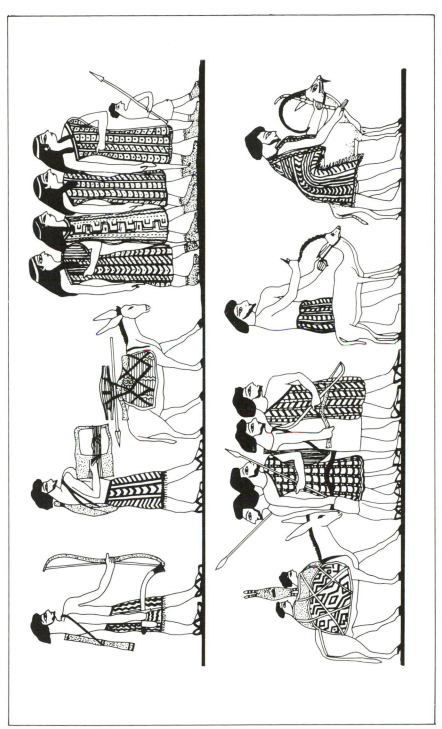

FIGURE 5   a) and b) Foreigners shown in Tomb of Khnumhotep III at Beni Hasan (P.E. Newberry, *Beni Hasan,* and Posener, op. cit., p. 82).

industry. The method was to rough-cut a solid block of stone to the required shape; a drill was then used to hollow out the centre of the vase. The bow-drill had been devised for this purpose and the drill, fitted with a crescent-shaped flint bit, was turned by hand. Heavy stones were attached to the drill handle to provide weight, and for large vessels the device was rotated by two men. Once the vase was hollowed out, the surface was polished with a sandstone rubber to give it a fine finish.

From the earliest times, the Egyptians had used paints to outline their eyes. These were probably first introduced to shade the eyes from the glare of the sun, and to give protection against eye diseases. Kohl, used to delineate the eyes, was made from the minerals malachite (green) and galena (grey). These were ground up using a palette and pebble, and the substance was then stored in kohl-jars. Even in the predynastic graves, the deceased was provided with slate palettes and pebbles and little bags of galena or malachite for use in the next life.

Later, tube-shaped kohl-pots were used, which were either single or compound and probably included different colours in the separate sections. The kohl was removed from the jars and applied to the eyes by means of a bulbous-ended kohl-stick. However, in the 12th Dynasty town of Kahun, most kohl containers were dumpy stone vases. Sometimes they had small handles and were always of stone-alabaster, serpentine and diorite being favourite materials. Almost all these vases had broad, flat neck-pieces, which were fixed on separately.

Dried herbs and fruits were also discovered, which were ground down for use in cosmetics and one small wooden box contained juniper berries. The Egyptians also used minerals for cosmetics. These included red and yellow ochres and blue and green copper ores, which were ground to a fine powder with a stone pestle and mortar and then mixed with animal fats to make face colouring and eye-shadow. At Kahun, rectangular trays of syenite, granite and basalt were discovered for grinding paint and ink; there were also rubbers – pebbles flattened at one broad end and stained with red paint – and the colours included haematite (for red colouring), yellow ochre, and blue pigment.

Other toilet articles included bronze mirrors, one of which had a magnificent ivory handle in the form of a lotus flower; another, already mentioned, had a wooden handle which represented the head of the goddess Hathor. There were many ivory hairpins which took a variety of forms; the head of one was shaped in the form of an animal's head, while the head of another took the form of an outstretched hand. Wooden combs were also found; one example was a double comb, with rows of fine and coarse teeth. Pieces of ivory carving in the form of lions came from some toilet boxes, and the bowls of fine wooden toilet spoons (used to scoop the perfumed cream from the jars or to pour scented oils over the body) were carved, in one instance, to represent a duck's head with a red ivory beak, and in another, to resemble a shell. Petrie also found examples of a bronze hair-curler, a rotating razor, and pairs of tweezers.

The evidence suggests that luxury goods were an accepted part of life at Kahun, and it is also interesting that some features of the female residents' beauty equipment reflected the royal fashions of the period.

Jewellery was also widely worn, and it is evident that various industries had developed to supply this need. Ivory and glazed ear studs were found, which were inserted into large holes pierced in the wearer's ear-lobe. The manufacture of beads was also well developed, and Petrie suggested that, because only small numbers of any one kind were found, they may have been made to order rather than mass-produced. With regard to style and design, there was less variation than in later times, but the quality was generally better. The beads were perforated by means of a bow-drill, and sand was probably used as an abrasive. Materials which were distinctively of the Middle Kingdom period included amethyst, garnet, blue glazed quartz and green glazed steatite, and examples of these were common at Kahun. No glass beads were found, since these mostly date to a later period, but other typically Middle Kingdom decorative forms which were found at Kahun included small figurines of birds and animals in blue or green glaze. Generally the jewellery at Kahun was distinguished by the bright colour of the glaze and the fineness of the decorative lines.

Scarabs were a particularly favoured type of amuletic jewellery in ancient Egypt. Modelled to represent the sacred dung beetle, they symbolised the eternal renewal of life and were considered to provide protection in life and in death for the possessor. The flat undersides of scarabs, although sometimes plain, more frequently bore a carved design which often incorporated the names of kings or gods or a motif designed to bring good fortune and health to the wearer. At Kahun, Petrie also discovered much later scarabs of the 18th Dynasty which belonged to the intrusive burials of that period. However, those of the 12th Dynasty were also recovered, often with distinctive patterns on the base, and one was found in the masons' spoil heap of chips near the pyramid of Sesostris II at Lahun. Scarabs are useful in dating sites, because they are frequently inscribed with the names of current rulers. Here, a scarab inscribed with the name of King Neferhotep of the 13th Dynasty, found in a room near the centre of the town together with some papyri, is the latest dated excavated object from the first occupation of the town, and can assist in establishing a chronology of events at Kahun.

Toys and games

Although 'toys' and 'dolls' have been found in Egyptian tombs, the exact nature of their purpose is never entirely clear. Were these objects intended as playthings for the deceased owner in the next world, or, as has sometimes been claimed, did they have magico-religious significance, as models to be 'brought to life' to provide enjoyment for the tomb-owner?

There can be no doubt, however, about the intended use of the toys and games found at Kahun. They were made for and used by the children as they played in the streets of the town; indeed, the children probably modelled some of the toys themselves, for their own amusement.

An abundance of toys has survived. First, there were the clay figurines, assiduously modelled perhaps by the children from the grey Nile mud. They include a small model of a man, a hippopotamus, a pig, a crocodile, an ape in black clay with beads inserted to represent eyes, little vases, and an unidentifiable animal which was perhaps the handiwork of a less artistically able child. There is also a model of a boat with two seats (one of which is pierced with a hole to take a mast) and the remains of a rudder. Limestone toys, carved and often painted, were also popular. The hippopotamus was a favourite form, and also occurs as a unique flint toy chipped in outline from a thin flint flake. One limestone toy is carved to represent two boys wrestling; the arms and figures are in relief, and the detail on the heads is carefully worked. Another shows the figurine of a seated boy nursing a monkey on which traces of red paint remain.

It is also evident that a doll-making industry existed at Kahun. Parts of painted wooden dolls with pegged, movable limbs were found, as well as dolls of blue glazed pottery which were truncated at the knees and held their hands at their sides. These were decorated with tattoo patterns of spots or lines on their thighs and with a girdle line around the waist. In one house – presumably the doll-maker's home – Petrie found a large stock of dolls' hair. This was constructed so that fine threads, all about 6 inches long, were placed together and rolled with mud, and a conical lump of mud was placed at the end of each section of hair. He suggested that this style, with mud pellets at the ends, may have been copied from the hairdressing of the day, which, in his time, could still be seen in parts of modern Sudan. The hair sections would have been inserted into holes in the doll's head and these were obviously treasured and quite sophisticated toys.

Ball games were also played at Kahun. Some balls were roughly shaped in wood, while others were made of leather. One has six gores sewn together and is stuffed with dried grass; one of the gores had obviously cracked and had been carefully re-stitched in antiquity.

The streets of Kahun also reverberated to the noise of whip tops and tip-cats, and a number of wooden whip tops were found, each being a circular piece of wood, flattened at one end and worked to an obtuse point at the other.

Wooden tip-cats were also discovered; these were sticks, ranging in length and diameter from 16 cm and 3 cm to 6.9 cm and 1.5 cm, and pointed at each end. The game, which is known from other parts of the world (and particularly from Lancashire, where it is called 'Peggy'), was played by hitting the tip-cat into the air with a bat or stick; before it landed on the ground, it would be hit again, and the person who could hit the 'cat' farthest would be the winner.

Board games were known at Kahun and two kinds were discovered. The first, well known from other sources, is called *Snt* (Senet). Two senet-boards were found in the town. One is marked out on the inside of a wooden box lid which was once attached to a box of the kind used for the baby burials. The board is marked out in red lines on a white background; there are three horizontal rows, each containing ten squares which average 3.38 cm. In the bottom row, in the seventh square from the left, there is an indistinct trace of Hieratic writing. Counting from the left-hand side along the top ten squares, the second is marked with the hieroglyphic for '2', the third '3', the fourth 'X' and the fifth '*nfr*'. Along the top edge, the second and third squares have a line which brackets them, and another line curves around the fifth square. The gaming pieces which would have accompanied this board were not discovered.

Another, incomplete senet-board was found. This was made of a slab of limestone, on which the lines are lightly incised. When it was complete, this board would have been marked out in three horizontal rows, each containing ten squares. In the top row, the hieroglyph '*nfr*' is marked in black in the square first on the left, and in the middle row, in the square immediately below it, a cross occurs, also painted in black.

Examples of another game, played or marked with pegs inserted in a pottery board, were also discovered by Petrie and, as far as he was aware, no similar game had been found elsewhere in Egypt. Each of the symmetrical sides of the board was marked with thirty holes, and every fifth hole was marked by a cross cut. The 20th hole formed a common pool at the end, in which the lines joined before returning, and each player had both an up and a down track of holes.

In general terms, the toys and games found at Kahun range from comparatively sophisticated pieces which were probably produced commercially on a small scale, to the simple toys which the children and their parents made. They are particularly appealing, and recapture glimpses of life in the town – the men sitting on benches outside the houses, playing an engrossing game of senet, the children noisily spinning their tops and batting their tip-cats in the streets, and small girls proudly clutching the treasured dolls with their movable limbs and elaborate hairstyles.

Craftsmen at Kahun

A most important aspect of the Kahun material is the wide range of craftsmen's tools discovered there, which not only show the

type of crafts which were carried on but are also important in-
dicators of how Egyptian technology was developing in the 12th
Dynasty.

The tools were found in various locations throughout the town
and its vicinity, but those discovered at three specific sites are
particularly interesting.

One group had been left in the corner of a room, close to the
floor, in a house in the workmen's quarter. These tools were
contained within a circular rush basket, formed of small bundles
closely bound together with single rushes. It had a cover and cord
for suspension and is still in a remarkably good state of preservation. Because the basket was buried in the dry dust, and nothing
came into contact with the metal tools inside, the original polish
and hammer marks on the bronzes are also perfectly preserved.
These tools included two copper hatchets and two copper chisels;
traces of hafting could be seen on the backs of both the hatchets
but there was no mark of either hafting or hammering on the
chisels. The larger hatchet was broken across the body – a strange
discovery, since there was no indication that sufficient strain had
been applied to the hatchet.

There was also a hammer-wrought copper bowl inside the
basket, and a copper knife was found lying nearby on the ground.
The whole group obviously comprised a workman's set of tools,
kept in a basket in readiness for use.

Another major discovery was the caster's shop. Here, Petrie
found metal tools and also five moulds for metal casting which
were made from pieces of earthenware. These were trimmed
square, and the mould was cut out on the face of the block. This
was then lined with a coat of fine ash and clay to give the mould a
smooth surface, and these moulds would be used to take the
molten metal. Petrie found moulds in the shop for various tools,
including flat chisels, one with two lugs at the narrow end; a knife,
which subsequent to casting would probably have been hammered out to a larger size; and a small hatchet. This mould may
have been used to produce the object that he found in a house a few
doors away.

Other items discovered in the shop included the socket-head of a
drill or firestick, two pieces of sandstone whetstone, a horn haft,
some pieces of wood of uncertain use, flint flakes, and a spindle
whorl.

The discovery of this shop and its contents enabled Petrie to assess the skills of the Kahun metalworkers and the techniques which they employed.

He also found the masons' tools, near the royal monuments at Lahun, where they had been left by the workmen. These included metal tools and other wooden pieces used in stone-working.

From these and other discoveries, it is possible to consider some of the technologies which were employed at Kahun. Some of the residents were evidently skilled in woodworking and carpentry and produced furniture, tools, funerary goods and coffins. These techniques are often shown in tomb scenes, and this was obviously a major industry in Egypt. However, here at Kahun, not only the products but even some of the actual tools were discovered. Egypt produced relatively little wood and most was provided by date and Dom palms, sycamore, tamarisks and acacias. It was therefore necessary to import wood from abroad to meet certain demands; deal and cedar were brought in from Syria, and ebony and other rare woods were obtained from Asia and Africa.

Specific woods were used for different purposes: sycamore and sometimes imported cedar were employed for objects which required large, thick planks, such as boxes, doors, tables, coffins and large statues. Tamarisk was used for items that required hard wood, and was especially favoured for tools and tool handles. Acacia provided planks and masts for boats, handles of tools and weapons, as well as some furniture. The foreign woods were mainly put to ornamental uses, and some elegant furniture was produced, including boxes, chairs or tables, by inlaying ebony with ivory. So desirable were the goods made from exotic woods that some native woods were sometimes painted to resemble the foreign types, and the paint was applied on a thin coating of stucco. The sections of boxes were glued together, and a box lid was usually fastened to the base by means of two knobs which could be tied together with string and then sealed.

A range of tools was used by the carpenters. These were of the usual type, and the blades, made of copper or bronze, were fastened by means of leather thongs to the hard wooden handles. First, a hand saw (a large knife with a toothed edge) was used to reduce the wood to the required size. Since the double saw was not employed, each piece of wood had to be cut single-handed. To do this, the wooden beam was placed upright in a simple vice, held between two posts which were firmly fixed into the ground, and it was kept in place by cords. Other tools – the axe and the adze – were used for rough shaping. Smaller holes were made with the socket-drill, worked by a bow, but mortices and carving were done with a wooden-handled chisel. This was struck with a wooden mallet; two types of mallet were found at Kahun – the club mallet shown in early tomb scenes, and the later headed mallet. The 12th Dynasty is obviously the period when the form was undergoing change. A final polish was given to the wood with planes of sandstone. Plummets and right-angled pieces were also used by the carpenter, and he stored his bronze nails in a leather bag.

At Kahun, both metal and flint tools continued to be used side by side for woodworking. The axe and chisel, which originated as stone or flint tools, were now produced in copper, but stone was still employed for some purposes. The development of these tools enabled the Egyptians to produce properly jointed furniture, and as most examples of the above tools have been found at Kahun, they provide an invaluable source for our understanding of Middle Kingdom technology.

Since Kahun was the town of the pyramid workmen, the stonemasons were obviously an important sector of the community. The Egyptians' expertise in stoneworking goes back to the Predynastic Period, when magnificent vases and vessels were carved from hard stones. However, by the Old Kingdom, the masons had developed the skills necessary to quarry and dress large blocks of stone for pyramid-building.

At Kahun, various masons' tools were recovered. Wooden wedges were found, and clamps (flat pieces of wood with expanding ends) for holding stones in position. Petrie noted the existence of holes for such clamps in the pyramid pavement at Hawara. Stone and clay plummets were also discovered as well as some very interesting wooden offset pieces which were used by the masons to face their stone blocks. These are three flat-ended wooden sticks of equal length; one is plain but two have a hole pierced at one end, which is worked through to the side, and these holes were originally threaded with string. From the evidence of tomb scenes at Thebes as well as those pieces found amongst the foundation blocks of Sesostris II's temple at Lahun, Petrie was able to deduce how they were used.

Stoneworking was a skilled and important industry, and using simple tools the Egyptian masons were able to cut and work stones which ranged from the fairly soft limestone to the hard granites and basalt. Probably by the judicious addition of certain alloys and by tempering the metals, they were able to produce tools of sufficient strength to cope with these materials.

With its range of stone and metal tools, and the discovery of the caster's shop, Kahun is an important site for consideration of workmen's tools and there is ample evidence that stone and metal tools were used here alongside each other. The Egyptians, with their inherent conservatism, evidently retained stone tools where they admirably suited their function and could hardly be improved. Indeed, the evidence from this town illustrates the transition stage between the old and new technologies as the Egyptians gradually perfected their metalworking techniques. It is apparent that, in some cases, the metal forms were strongly influenced by the older stone tools, but also that some of the new metallic forms were also now influencing the stone forms.

The stone implements from Kahun provide a unique collection, first because they provide the earliest group of artefacts where the style of chipping can be identified as typical of one period, and secondly, because the tools were known to have been used for domestic or trading purposes rather than for ceremonial use.

Flint-working had, of course, been practised in Egypt from earliest times. The methods here, as elsewhere, evolved from the production of simple hand axes, where a series of flakes were detached from a lump of flint by hammering it with a second stone. This produced a tool with a cutting edge down one side, a point, and a rounded, smooth butt. This tool, which could be used for a variety of purposes, such as chopping, cutting, and scraping, continued in widespread use in Africa, Europe and parts of western Asia for a long time. The flakes cut off in the process of producing the hand-axe were at first thrown away, but later they too were used as small tools, and were finally individually trimmed to make knives and scrapers.

Thus, there arose the beginnings of a tool-making industry. Gradually men evolved the highly skilled activity of striking a wide range of specially designed tools from the parent flint. As knives, scrapers, chisels and gravers, these in turn were used to produce a secondary range of tools and implements from other materials, including wood, horn, bone and antler.

A study of the stone implements found at Kahun was undertaken by F.C.J. Spurrell, F.G.S., shortly after their excavation. His examination showed that the tools were mostly made from an opaque flint which was easier to cut than other varieties; also, it was evident that most of the carefully formed flakes had been struck off the core by repeated blows. The implements included axe and adze blades, saw flints and flints inserted into large sickles, as well as knives, scrapers and flakes.

With the axes, there was evidence that they quickly broke up; the bold flaking showed that the craftsmen had great mastery of their skill and they experimented with different methods of fastening these blades to handles. A hornstone axe was found which was probably used for squaring blocks of stone. The blades of adzes, which were fitted to wooden handles, were comparatively rare but on these, the new cutting edge was carefully trimmed and well rounded. No implements were found which could have been used for stone-facing nor as saws, because metal tools were by now being employed for these purposes.

Numbers of knife blades were discovered which were all well chipped in broad flaking. However, when a knife became blunt, it was not re-worked but was used as a disposable item. There was one particularly fine example of a flint knife with the remains of a handle made of fibre and cord bound around the stone, with which two flint flakes were found. Indeed, the evidence throughout the town indicates that flakes were widely used without any preliminary preparation and that probably many of the inhabitants were able to produce the less elaborate flint tools.

Stone also continued to play a part in the production of agricultural tools. It has already been shown how flint 'saws' or teeth were fixed with cement into bone or wooden sickle handles. The sickle resembled an animal's jaw, and painted examples similar to the Kahun sickles occur in tombs of the Old Kingdom at Giza and Saqqara. In use, the sickle would be brought, tilted slightly upwards, towards the reaper as he cut the corn, and the Kahun examples, with their sharp teeth, would have produced excellent results.

Although flint and metal tools continued to be used together at Kahun during the first period of occupation in the 12th Dynasty,

Petrie claimed that by the beginning of the New Kingdom (the 18th Dynasty), flint had almost ceased to be used, and bronze had replaced copper as the most popular metal. An analysis of the metal tools from Kahun was undertaken shortly after excavation by Dr Gladstone. He claimed that the tools of the 12th Dynasty were of copper, whereas those of the New Kingdom were of bronze. He also maintained that the small impurities which existed in the copper of earlier times and hardened the metal were accidental occurrences in particular ores, rather than a deliberate mixture to produce a certain type and strength of metal.

Metalworking posed a number of problems for early peoples. Copper ores were found to occur naturally in certain areas, such as Eastern Turkey, Syria, the Zagros Mountains, Sinai, the Eastern Desert of Egypt and Cyprus. The earliest method of working copper, as well as gold, was to hammer the small pieces of metal using rounded pebbles. However, the metal became brittle and cracked beyond a certain point. Then there came the discovery that the stresses built up within a piece of hammered metal could be relieved by heating the metal to quite a high temperature. The cooled metal could then be hammered to the required shape, until it began to harden, when it could be reheated. The development of this process, which is known today as annealing, marked an important step forward in metalworking techniques because it showed that high temperatures could be used to alter metals.

Another important discovery was that metallic copper, reduced from its ores, would become molten, and could subsequently be poured into moulds. The idea of using moulds had long been established in the production of faience seals and mud-bricks, but gradually special moulds were designed to cast metal objects. The earliest of these were very simple; a negative was cut into a piece of stone, the molten metal was poured into it and then hammering and annealing of the metal object would produce the required shape.

Later developments included the introduction of two-piece moulds, made of fired clay; these were sometimes first moulded around a carved wooden pattern, which was then removed, and the two pieces were fired and joined together, to receive the molten metal in the hollow centre. Later, an additional clay core was included in the mould so that objects such as socketed axes could be cast.

A number of pottery moulds were discovered in the caster's shop at Kahun which would have been used for casting such items as knives, chisels, and hatchets. One double mould was discovered, intended for the production of two knives, one straight-backed and the other curved.

Sometime before 3000 BC, a major discovery was made in metal working that marked a significant advance. It was found that a harder and more easily worked metal could be produced, by adding a small quantity of tin-ore to the copper ores during the smelting process; this produced an alloy-bronze.

Egypt had large quantities of copper but no tinstone, so there was a considerable delay before the working of bronze could be introduced. Thus, whereas elsewhere bronze became a common metal, in Egypt copper continued to be used for a long time for most purposes. However, bronze gradually replaced copper and became widespread for tools. Experiments with methods of alloying and heating the furnace where the metals were smelted produced increasingly sophisticated results.

Bellows (made of skin or skin-covered drums and used in pairs) were introduced to replace those of a reed or pipe attached to a bag. The new type raised the temperature of the furnace even more efficiently to a level not previously reached when the fire was blown by mouth. This innovation resulted in larger-scale production, and greater quantities of items and larger castings became possible.

A new method of alloying tinstone to copper was now developed; tinstone was reduced to metallic tin in the furnace before heating it together with copper to form bronze. This meant that the relative proportions of the two metals could now be closely scrutinised, and the resulting experiments with bronze, adding low or high tin contents, meant that different materials could be produced for specific purposes. For tools and weapons, strength was the quality required above all others, and a proportion of about 8 percent tin was retained in producing these.

Gradually, therefore, bronze came to replace both stone tools and even those made of copper. However, as the examples from Kahun show, copper tools of that period were relatively hard and their strength was considerably increased by continual hammering. Their importance as a group of objects has warranted a modern analysis which is discussed in Chapter 10.

Weights and measures

When Egypt and Mesopotamia became commercial centres of the ancient world, it became necessary for each area to devise its own standardised system of weights and measures for business to be conducted.

At an early date, the Egyptians devised methods of surveying and land measurement following the annual inundation; their knowledge of geometry and mathematics used effectively in the construction of the pyramids was also considerable. Their units of measurement were based on distances between various points on the human body; thus, a cubit was the distance from the point of the elbow to the tip of the middle finger, a span was measured from the tip of the little finger to the tip of the thumb on an outstretched hand, and a palm was usually measured across the knuckle of a hand. There was also a finger-width and a foot, based on the relevant parts of the body. The cubit, the largest unit, was generally subdivided into the other units – the Egyptian royal cubit was made up of seven palms and each palm had four finger-widths.

However, from early times, Egypt and Mesopotamia had followed different courses in this respect as in many others, and although each area used the cubit, they divided it into different sections, to which they gave different names.

Egypt also had a different system of weights from those in use elsewhere in the Near East. The trade in metals, carried on by the great civilisations, had brought into existence the need for a system of weights; these were all based on a theoretical unit – the weight of a grain of wheat. In different countries, multiples of this grain were used to make larger units, and a shekel could vary from 120 grains in one place to over 200 in another. Also, larger units which were multiples of the shekel were introduced; these, the mina and the talent, were in use throughout much of the ancient Near East.

Egypt, however, had a different system and used metric weights. The balances – simple scales with pans – must have been fairly sensitive and the weights were made of hard polished stones, into which the weight mark was cut. Again, Egypt differed from Mesopotamia; the Egyptian weights were geometrically shaped blocks of stone with rounded corners and edges, whereas the Mesopotamian weights were more decorative and were often carved in the form of a duck. Indeed, so varied were the systems in the different countries of the ancient world that visiting merchants carried appropriate sets of weights to meet the requirements of trading in the various countries.

It is important to understand this background in order to appreciate the statement which Petrie made concerning the weights and measures he discovered at Kahun.

Of the measuring sticks which he found, he claimed that none was the usual Egyptian cubit. One was a bar of wood of the customary form for a cubit; it had one bevelled edge, on which the cuts were marked off, dividing it into six palms. So, although its length was in exact agreement to the usual Egyptian standard, it had only six instead of the customary seven palms. Two other measures were found on slips of wood; both were very roughly made, and may have been used as temporary aids. One was divided into seven palms in the Egyptian manner, but the total length was of the same standard as the double foot of Asia Minor. The other scale had seven and a half spaces.

Petrie formed the opinion that these rods combined elements of the systems of measurement in current use in Egypt and elsewhere, and that they were attempts, presumably by foreigners resident at Kahun, to imitate the Egyptian system.

The weights found in the town also added support to his theory, for he maintained that there was a significant number of foreign weights amongst the group and that, of the total, not one sixth were Egyptian; even those, he claimed, were made of soft materials not normally used for Egyptian weights.

It will now be necessary to consider the evidence which supports Petrie's theory of a substantial foreign community at Kahun. However, the general appearance of the town, despite any cosmopolitan occupation, must have conformed fairly closely to other settlements throughout Egypt. From the distribution of the objects within the town and, as far as we can assess, from the incomplete records, it seems that areas of Kahun were probably allocated to specific trades and crafts, rather like the divisions of eastern cities in medieval and later times.

There may have been some permanent shops, like the caster's, but probably many of the commercial transactions would have been carried out at a regular market. In more recent times, Winifred Blackman found that at Lahun the shops stocked a few provisions but that most were bought at the weekly market. During this stay, she was accommodated in a house built of sun-dried mud-brick (fashioned in a mould like those of ancient Kahun) with ceilings made of ribs of palm branches. On the flat roof of the house there were small mud granaries, and bundles of dried stalks, as well as flat cakes of cow dung, used for fuel. Her experiences in the Fayoum during three winters showed her that some techniques had survived from antiquity. The making of bricks, baskets and pottery were still major occupations of the area. At harvest time, the corn was cut with sickles very similar to those discovered at Kahun, before it was taken to the threshing floor, and winnowed in the open air. She also noted another ancient survival – that the wages of the labourers were paid in grain.

PLATES

1 (*Left*) Portrait of Dr Jesse Haworth, patron of Egyptology in Manchester, who supported Petrie's excavations at Illahun, Kahun and Gurob. In recognition of his generosity to the Manchester Museum, and of his position as one of the first patrons of scientific excavation in Egypt, the University of Manchester conferred on him the honorary degree of Doctor of Laws in 1913. In return for his continuing support of Petrie's excavations, the Manchester Museum received artefacts from sites throughout Egypt, which form the nucleus of this important collection.

2 (*Right*) Portrait of Sir William Flinders Petrie, about the time when he became Edwards Professor of Egyptology at University College London. Miss Amelia Edwards, one of the co-founders of the Egypt Exploration Fund (later Society), bequeathed a sum of money in her Will to found the first Chair of Egyptology in Britain, and expressed a wish that Petrie should be appointed to this post, which he subsequently held for forty years. It was through Miss Edwards's intervention that Petrie and Haworth first met and Haworth was persuaded to provide financial support for the excavations.

3 General view of the first Egyptology gallery at the Manchester Museum, University of Manchester in 1913. By 1911, the University considered a scheme to extend the existing Museum to provide suitable accommodation for Jesse Haworth's continuing donations of Egyptian antiquities. The Manchester Egyptian Association opened a fund for subscriptions, but Haworth's generosity enabled the scheme to be realised, and The Jesse Haworth Building was opened in 1912. The artefacts from Kahun and Gurob were displayed to the public for the first time. In 1927 a further extension, incorporating a Second Egyptology gallery, was opened. This too was the result of Haworth's generosity.

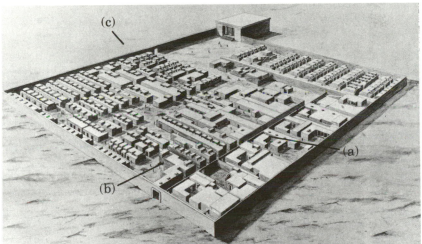

4 (*Above*) Photograph taken at Kahun, showing Flinders Petrie (centre), his wife, Hilda, and C.T. Campion. The photograph (in the Manchester Museum archive) was accompanied by a letter from Campion to Miss W.C. Crompton, Curator of Manchester's Egyptian collection, dated 18 March 1914. Writing from Lahun, Campion says that Petrie had just finished the enclosure immediately around the pyramid, and that seven gangs had started to clear the North Court, where the eight Mastaba tombs were situated. He continues, 'On Monday week, four of us went over to see the place [i.e. Kahun], about a twenty minute walk from here, and I took two photographs . . .'

5 (*Below*) Artist's reconstruction drawing of the town of Kahun. Like the other workmen's towns, Kahun was enclosed by a thick mud-brick wall which kept the inhabitants separate from others living in the area. The town was built to adjoin a temple in which King Sesostris II was worshipped; both the town and the temple were known as 'Hetep-Sesostris'. The town was laid out on a regular plan and arranged in two areas – separated by an internal wall. The western part (a) contained the blocks of workmen's houses, while the Acropolis (b) had a palace. Large villas (c) were situated in the eastern area.

6 Part of a group of objects found in a house in the workmen's western quarter at Kahun. The mirror has a handle of hard brown wood, carved with the head of the goddess Hathor on either side. The torque (bottom) is the only example so far discovered in Egypt which was obviously worn in the owner's lifetime. The few other examples found in Egypt have come from burial sites. However, the torque, although so rare in Egypt, was a distinctive ornament which was worn for over five centuries in areas of Western Asia.

7 A selection of stone and faience jars used to hold perfumed ointments and oils, and kohl. The three alabaster jars at the back were found in the house in the workmen's quarter, together with the mirror and torque described in (6). The small, dumpy stone vases with broad, flat neck-pieces fixed on separately were containers for kohl, the substance used by the Egyptians to outline their eyes. The tube-shaped kohl-pots familiar at other sites were not in fashion at Kahun.

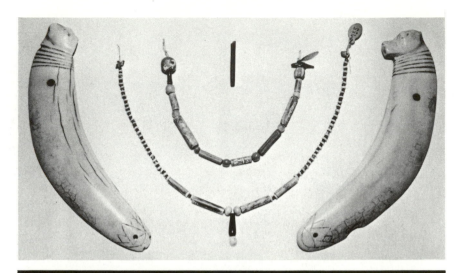

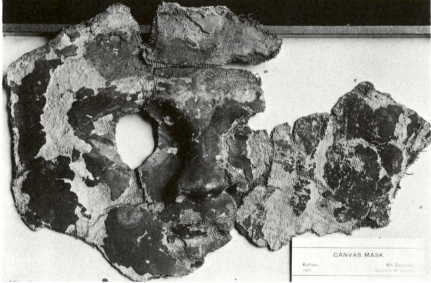

CANVAS MASK

Kahun.
[93]   XII Dynasty.
                                        Dublin, H. M. [...]

8 (*Above*) Jewellery was widely worn at Kahun, and this shows a selection of beads. Here also is a pair of ivory clappers, found with a wooden figurine in the chamber of a house; in the next room was a dancer's mask made of canvas. The wooden figurine was of a dancer in a costume with a head-dress or mask representing the god Bes, and a tail. The clappers and the figurine were discovered buried in a hole in the floor of the chamber.

9 (*Below*) A dancer's mask found in the same house as a pair of ivory clappers and wooden figurine. It is made of three layers of canvas stuck together and moulded to form the face of the household god Bes. Painted black, details such as arches over and under the eyes, spots on the cheeks and red lips are also shown. Some of the surface stucco has been knocked off during use, and the canvas base has been painted black to camouflage the damage. Holes are made at the eyes and nostrils to allow the wearer to see and breathe.

10 (*Left*) One of the curious stone stands used in the houses at Kahun. These were probably used to support dishes holding bread and other food which was offered to the gods in a regular household ritual. This example, carefully cut out in pierced work, shows two primitive figures of men, standing back to back. The strange design of these stands suggests a purely local artistic development which may indicate either that these worshippers at Kahun were foreign with different religious customs, or that native Egyptians here simply introduced a different style.

11 (*Above*) Basket-making and rush-work were important industries at Kahun. An example of a well-made fibre brush, in almost perfect condition, was discovered (*left*). On the right is a plaited rush sandal, an alternative form of foot-wear to the leather shoes and sandals also found at Kahun. The rush basket (centre) was found in the corner of a house chamber, close to the floor. It was obviously used by a workman to transport his tools, for it was found to contain a copper bowl, chisels and hatchets.

12 (*Above*) A great variety of pottery was made at Kahun for domestic purposes. Incised dishes are a representative style for this period and site. They were perhaps used to serve food, since one dish has a raised centre. On the inside of the dishes the incised patterns include designs derived from basketwork, or incorporating animals and, as in this example, fish and lotus flowers. Usually oval in shape, they were of fairly coarse red pottery with a rough surface, which probably indicates that they were not used for cooking, nor for serving wet or juicy food.

13 (*Below*) An oblong wooden stool cut from a single block of wood, and roughly finished. It is possible to imagine the owner sitting outside his house in the evening, the day's work over, in the way people relax today in villages throughout Egypt. Stone seats were also found at Kahun, each cut from one block of stone, with a section cut away underneath to create two legs and the seat slightly hollowed out to provide more comfort. Parts of carved wooden chairs were also discovered, which indicated that some of the inhabitants possessed furniture of a finer quality.

14 (*Above*) Craftsmen's tools discovered at Kahun provide one of the most important aspects of the site. They indicate the type of crafts carried out in such a community and also illustrate the development of technology in Egypt during the Middle Kingdom. Skilled carpenters and woodworkers were obviously well established in the town, and in this modern artist's reconstruction, a carpenter is shown making the wooden stool found at Kahun. Carpenters used a range of tools, many with bronze blades fastened to wooden handles by means of leather thongs. Wooden mallets of the type shown here were found at the site.

15 (*Below*) Small wooden boxes were used at Kahun to contain cosmetics, jewellery and trinkets. One shown here held powdered haematite and juniper berries for colouring the face, and a bulbous-ended kohl-stick. The sections of each box were glued together, and the lid fitted into the box in such a way that the lid could not be raised at one end. At the other end, there was a knob on the lid that could be fastened to a knob on the box; these knobs were tied together with string (still visible) and sealed.

16 Larger wooden boxes, probably used originally to store clothing and other possessions, were discovered underneath the floors of many houses at Kahun. They contained babies, sometimes buried two or three to a box, and aged only a few months at death. Protective beads and amulets adorning some of the babies were inscribed with the names of kings and thus fixed the date of these burials. Interrment of bodies at domestic sites was not an Egyptian custom, although such practices occurred in other areas of the ancient Near East, particularly at Mesopotamian sites.

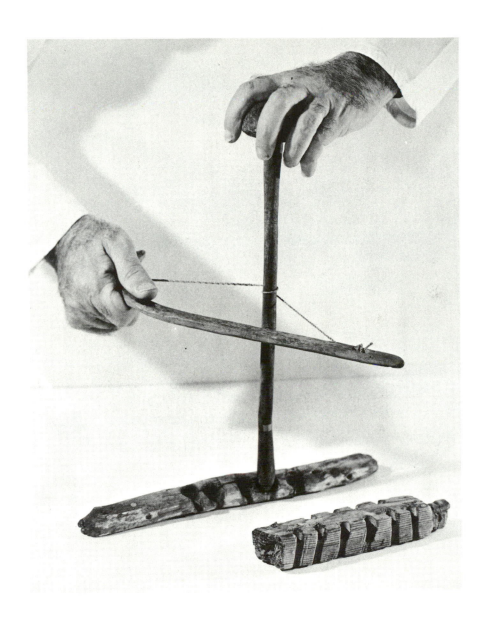

17 Before the discovery of firesticks at Kahun, no fire-making tools from ancient Egypt had ever been found, and the method of fire-production used by the Egyptians was unknown. Essentially a bow-drill, the firestick has four parts. The user would exert heavy pressure on a conical stone drill-cap, which pushed down a wooden firestick. This was thus pressed into the wooden matrix hole underneath. The simultaneous action of pressing down the firestick and pulling the drill-bow caused sparks to ignite at the matrix.

18 (*Above*) Builders' tools were found at Kahun. Petrie discovered a wooden mud-brick mould (*top*), into which alluvial mud mixed with water was packed. Although tomb scenes elsewhere illustrated the method, this was the first tangible evidence of the industry ever found at a site. Once constructed, a building was plastered with a layer of mud. The plasterers' float (*right*) found at Kahun is similar to ones used today; here some plaster still remains where the ancient workman forgot to clean it. On the left are two wooden butterfly cramps which were used for stonework.

19 (*Below*) Metal and stone tools continued to be used side-by-side at Kahun, and illustrate the transitional stage between old and new technologies. Inherently conservative, the Egyptians retained stone tools at Kahun where they particularly suited their function, and the later metal forms were often influenced by the designs of the stone tools. Here, there is a selection of stone, copper and bronze knives from the site. The flint knife, with the handle of fibre and cord, is a good example of Egyptian flint-working which had been practised since earliest times.

20 A major discovery at Kahun was the caster's shop, where Petrie found metal tools and five earthenware moulds for bronze-casting. The mould (*left*) used to take molten metal was for an axe; the mould was lined with a coat of fine ash and clay to produce a fine surface. The metal hatchet (*right*) was found in a workman's basket in his house, ready to be taken to his place of work. The obvious break across the body in antiquity is curious since there is no indication that sufficient strain had been applied.

21 Carpenters and woodworkers at Kahun used a range of tools. A selection of these can be seen here. On the left is a wooden adze handle; this tool was used for rough-shaping the wood. A chisel (*centre*) with a wooden handle and a metal tip was used to produce carving and mortices. A wooden socket drill (*right*) was worked by means of a bow, and used to make small holes. In carpentry, as well as other crafts, metal and flint tools were used alongside each other at Kahun.

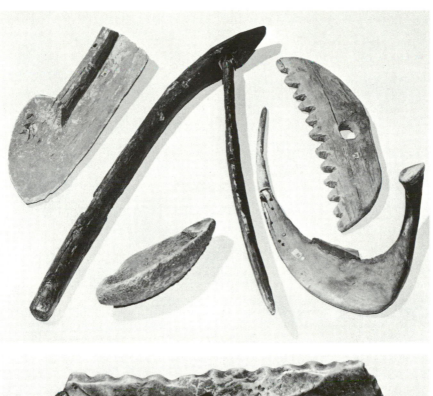

22 (*Above*) Agricultural tools found in the houses at Kahun are similar to those depicted in tomb scenes elsewhere in Egypt. A simple wooden hoe (*centre*) and rake (*top right*) were used to clear the ground before ploughing commenced. The hoes from Kahun had either broad and flat, or thick and narrow wooden blades; the rakes were roughly cut from a single piece of wood and were much worn. Sickles (*bottom right*) were used for reaping; the grain was later winnowed, being tossed with wooden scoops (*top left*), before it was finally collected off the threshing floor using wooden grain scoops (*bottom left*).

23 (*Below*) The sickles used in Egypt to reap the crop were based on the shape of an animal's jawbone. Sometimes an animal jawbone was utilised, but otherwise the body of the sickle was made of wood. Flints were either set into the teeth sockets of the jawbone to form a cutting edge, or in the wooden sickle, a line of short flint blades was set into a groove and held in place with cement made of mud and glue. A detail of a wooden sickle, with the flint saws held in position, is shown here.

24 Ball games were played by children in the streets of Kahun. Wooden balls (*top left*) were
found, as well as a leather ball (*top centre*) with six gores, one of which had obviously been
re-stitched in antiquity. Wooden whip-tops were discovered (*top right*), and also tip-cats
(*bottom row*). These wooden sticks, each pointed at both ends, are known in other parts of
the world. Kahun has provided evidence of a wealth of toys and games which were quite
obviously used and enjoyed by their owners.

25 (*Above*) Clay figurines were modelled perhaps by the children themselves, as toys. This selection, all made from Nile mud, includes an ape with beads inserted to represent eyes (*top left*), a pig (*top right*), an unidentifiable animal (*bottom left*), a crocodile (*centre bottom*), and a model boat with two seats (one of which is pierced with a hole to take a mast) and the remains of a rudder (*bottom right*). In addition to these, there was a minor doll-making industry at Kahun, which produced wooden dolls with pegged, movable limbs, as well as dolls of glazed pottery.

26 (*Below*) Kahun was a centre for fishing, fowling and hunting activities. However, in the gardens and vineyards, it was also necessary to frighten away the birds, a purpose for which this sling was probably used. Beautifully woven, it has long cords, one of which ends in a loop, to retain it on the finger. It was found with the three small sling-stones, which were probably flung from the sling simultaneously, to produce a scatter effect. This may be the earliest example of a sling yet discovered.

27 Although Kahun had its own pottery-making industry, some of the pottery discovered at the site, because of its style, was claimed by Petrie to be of foreign origin. He believed that some of these pieces may have been introduced into the town by an immigrant section of the community. Recent investigations of the Kahun pottery, using advanced scientific methods, have indicated that the visually 'foreign' pots are indeed made from clay which was derived from different sources. Examples of three of these 'foreign styles' are shown here.

28 (*Above*) Scene from the tomb of the Vizier Rekhmire at Thebes (18th Dynasty), showing the process of mud-brick manufacture. Bricks were made from alluvial mud, mixed with water and packed into wooden moulds which could be lifted to allow the moulded brick to fall to the ground. Laid out thus in long rows, the bricks dried in the sun. Kiln-baked bricks were only widely introduced throughout Egypt in the Roman period, for, in the dry climate, sun-dried bricks survive for many years and indeed, are used in buildings in parts of Egypt today.

29 (*Below*) The remains of the village of Deir el-Medina at Thebes, where the community of workmen lived who were engaged in the building and decoration of the royal tombs in the Valley of the Kings. The village was inhabited by these men and their families from the 18th to the 21st Dynasties. Like Kahun, it occupied an isolated position which afforded easy surveillance, and the original town was enclosed inside a thick mud-brick wall. The houses were quite cramped and dark, and followed a basic pattern, although variations in decoration reflected differences in status and wealth.

30 (*Above*) The pyramid of Lahun was built for King Sesostris II and introduced several new features in pyramid design. The architect moved the entrance outside this pyramid, to provide greater security for the burial. However, when it was located by Petrie, he discovered that the burial had been plundered in antiquity. The core of this pyramid was cut from a mass of solid rock, and the framework of retaining walls was built of mud-brick. The original limestone casing of the pyramid has long since been removed, so that today only the brick structure remains.

31 (*Above*) Reproductions of the wig ornaments and crown of Princess Sit-Hathor-Iunut from Lahun. Petrie found four shaft tombs at Lahun, to the south of the pyramid, and the most easterly of these contained the famous royal treasure. This gold crown, with fifteen rosettes, a uraeus, representations of feathers and a pair of streamers seemed to be a ceremonial head-dress, to be worn over a wig. It introduced a new design, and had obviously been worn during the owner's lifetime. It is an outstanding example of the craftsmen's skills in the 12th Dynasty. (Originals in the Cairo Museum and the Metropolitan Museum of Fine Art, N.Y.)

32 Model of a weavers' workshop from the Theban tomb of Mekhet-Re, a Twelfth Dynasty
noble (c.2000 B.C.). The Egyptian Museum, Cairo.

All the workers shown are women. *Top:* two weavers kneel at a horizontal loom, to the
right of which a heddle-jack can be seen; one of them touches a long, curved beater-in.
Centre and *Bottom Right:* seated and standing women pot-spinning; the figures holding
two spindles are demonstrating their great skill in using this difficult method. *Left:* two
workers are preparing warps by winding finished thread round pegs set into the wall.

CHAPTER 7

The Foreign Population at Kahun

From his excavations at Kahun, Petrie formed the opinion that a certain element of the population there had come from outside Egypt. However, before considering the Kahun evidence, it is necessary briefly to outline some facets of Egypt's relationships with her northern neighbours.

The theory has been advanced that Aegean elements evident in some areas of ancient Egyptian civilisation may have come indirectly through Syria, and that the city of Byblos on the Syrian coast probably played an important intermediary role in a trading network. Egypt had long had close connections with Byblos, since this port controlled and exported the 'Cedars of Lebanon' which were in much demand in Egypt. This argument suggests that Byblos acted as a link between Egypt and Crete, for it is known that Byblos and Crete had commercial and technical links, and it is therefore necessary to consider Egypt's early relations with both Asia and the Aegean.

There has been much discussion of how and when the earliest links were established between Egypt and the Aegean. Some scholars have suggested that, from Neolithic times, there was always a close relationship and that this was based not just on trading requirements but that the two peoples had a 'community of blood'. This theory argues that Egyptian and Libyan cultures had strongly influenced Crete since the beginning of Minoan civilisation and this, it claims, could be explained in terms of an emigration of people from North Africa into Crete. The idea remains conjectural, however, and some archaeological elements cannot be explained by this theory.

There are indications of contact between Egypt and Crete in the Early Dynastic and Old Kingdom Periods. Sir Arthur Evans's excavations at Crete showed that the Minoan (prehistoric Cretan) civilisation was nearly, if not quite, as old as that of Egypt. This Cretan or 'Minoan' civilisation, able to develop unaffected by foreign incursions, gradually spread northwards and absorbed the culture of the Aegean islands and possibly that of the Peloponnese, before extending over central mainland Greece. Here, where it becomes the prehistoric culture of the mainland, it is known by the term 'Mycenaean'. Evans divided the 'prehistory' of Crete into three main periods – Early Minoan (EM I, EM II and EM III), Middle Minoan (MM I, MM II and MM III) and Late Minoan (LM I, LM II and LM III). He based the dates of the Cretan chronology on Egyptian synchronisms, but the sequence of the periods was based on the archaeological evidence from the Cretan excavations. The Early Minoan Period synchronised with the Old Kingdom and earlier periods in Egypt. Middle Minoan (when the Minoan culture had not yet reached mainland Greece) correlated with the 11th to 17th Dynasties in Egypt, and this synchronism was confirmed by the discovery of polychrome pottery in a cave at Kamares in Crete which indicated that Crete, or the Aegean Islands, were the sources for similar pottery (known today as 'Kamares Ware') which was discovered in the 12th/13th Dynasty deposits at Kahun and other Egyptian towns. Finally, the Late Minoan Period corresponded to the 18th/19th Dynasties in Egypt, before catastrophe brought Crete and the Minoan/Mycenaean civilisation to an end.

Various elements suggested links between Egypt and Crete in the Old Kingdom period, but the most convincing evidence is provided by the remnants of stone vases of Egyptian style which were found at Knossos. Some, made of liparite from the Lipari Islands, were of the Middle Minoan I period, and thus were of a slightly later date than the Egyptian Old Kingdom. However, their carinated form is typical of the 3rd and 4th Dynasty styles in Egypt, and therefore, they may either have been imported from Egypt earlier on and kept as treasured heirlooms, or they may represent a Cretan imitation of a form which was fashionable in Egypt at an earlier date. Other examples of Egyptian syenite or black porphyry vases appear to have been imported early on and handed down in Cretan families before being buried as treasured possessions. The evidence suggests that some Egyptian vases, carved from hard stone, were introduced into Crete, but also that the Cretans produced their own vessels which, although carved in the Egyptian style, were of soft stone. Therefore, although there was undeniable Egyptian influence, it is difficult to establish when direct contact actually occurred, and one scholar (Vercoutter) has suggested that the presence of Egyptian stone vases in Crete may not be due to trading contacts. He suggests instead that, during the troubled period at the end of the Old Kingdom, foreign vandals pillaged the old Egyptian cemeteries and removed the stone vases, which finally reached Crete, where they then occur, Predynastic and Old Kingdom types together, buried in the same contexts. By the Egyptian First Intermediate Period, Cretan artists, inspired by the plundered vessels, then sought to produce imitations in soft stone.

Other evidence for association includes the button seals which were found contemporaneously in Crete and Egypt, and Early Minoan II/III seals in Crete bear a close resemblance to the Egyptian seals of the 4th to 6th Dynasties. There has also been consideration of the term *H3w-nbwt*, the hieroglyphic name found in Old Kingdom texts. This term, later applied in Egyptian texts to the peoples of the Aegean, may indeed indicate Old Kingdom connections between Egypt and Crete, but it has also been suggested that, since the term may not have had the same exact meaning throughout two and a half thousand years of Egyptian history, it need not necessarily indicate an Old Kingdom connection with the Aegean islands. Alternative theories have identified the *H3w-nbwt* of the Old Kingdom texts either as the non-Egyptian population on the maritime border of the Egyptian Delta, or as a general and vague term for the peoples of the coast of Asia.

However, during the Middle Kingdom (Dynasties 12 and 13) and the Middle Minoan Period, it is evident that connections existed between Egypt and Crete and that there was an interchange of ideas and products between the two peoples. One of the most important discoveries relating to this period is that of Middle Minoan pottery found at various Egyptian sites, and this has posed some major problems for archaeologists, for Egyptologists use the term 'Minoan' pottery in the Middle Kingdom context to refer not only to vessels which appear to be genuine imports, but also to those which, although they resemble the Minoan style, can be seen by visual inspection almost certainly to have been made in

Egypt from local clay. However, only fabric analysis, which is described in Chapter 9, can finally determine the original home of this pottery.

Archaeologists have never found great quantities of Minoan pottery in Egypt; also, apart from pieces from Abydos and Qubbet el-Hawa, the cases and sherds were all discovered within the stretch of the Nile between Lisht and Lahun. However, the apparent distribution of this evidence may be misleading, since relatively few living sites have been excavated in Egypt, where this type of pottery seems mainly to have been found. All the known 'Minoan' vases and sherds are from excavated sites, and apart from the Abydos and Kahun finds, the material is not considerable.

Sherds were found at Kahun, Haraga and Lisht, but so far it has been impossible to determine if these all date to one specific chronological Minoan period or whether they extend over a longer time. The pottery found at Lisht, a site in the Fayoum selected as the burial place of the first king of the 12th Dynasty, Amenemmes I, may have come either from the tombs or the village.

Haraga was an important site which lay about two to three kilometres from Lahun. It included the cemeteries on the edge of the desert, which were perhaps used for the burial of the inhabitants of the important Middle Kingdom town of Rehone (Lahun), and these provide the largest, well-documented cemetery series for the Middle Kingdom. Additionally, it is possible that the site may have incorporated the refuse dumps and perhaps even a settlement of the workers who were involved in the various stages of funeral preparations. The site was excavated by Engelbach in 1913/14, and he reported that he found there 'about twenty pieces of Cretan Kamares ware, similar to those found by Petrie, twenty five years before, at Kahun'. The total collection of Minoan ware from the site emerges as the largest concentration of such pottery yet to have been found in Egypt.

The excavated sites in the vicinity of the Lahun pyramid of Sesostris II probably represent a single major building development which grew up at the place which the king had chosen for his burial. There was a significant Middle Kingdom growth in the area, with the arrival of administrators, court officials, and religious personnel, as well as the workmen, and this increase in size and quality of occupation was reflected in the cemeteries. In Kemp and Merrillees's study, they consider that the Minoan

pottery from Haraga is probably comparable with the Kahun
Minoan ware, in terms of use. Sherds from light buff storage jars
which were found at Haraga were described as 'natron-jars' by
Engelbach, and some examples of these sherds, now in the Manchester Museum collection, bear 'natron' labels. It is argued that
the material evidence from Haraga – large numbers of vessels
used for the transport and storage of natron, as well as refuse
material such as natron, resin, sawdust and cloth – indicates that
this was probably the place where mummification was carried
out, near to the cemeteries. The men engaged in this work and in
associated occupations may have lived at the site, and therefore,
the Minoan sherds found here, as at Kahun, would suggest that
imported wares of this type were used by the members of a
workmen's community.

However, it was the Minoan sherds from Kahun, excavated by
Petrie in the 1880s, which first aroused interest. Petrie included
these amongst a whole group of material which he described as
'foreign', and more specifically as 'Greek'. However, not all these
'Minoan' sherds were true imports, and some have been identified
stylistically as local Egyptian imitations of Minoan vessels. Other
sherds, although they have polychrome decoration, may have
come from vessels which were of purely Egyptian style and
manufacture. However, true Minoan sherds from Kahun can be
identified as Classical Kamares ware, with patterns incorporating swirls and spirals. Petrie presented this collection to the Greek
and Roman Department of the British Museum where they were
subsequently published.

The Kahun sherds were received into the British Museum
collection and accessioned in three groups, in November 1890,
February 1912, and September 1914, and this has enabled Kemp
to assign the pottery to specific seasons of excavation. The material accessioned in the first two groups appears to have been
presented to the Museum by Petrie's sponsor, Jesse Haworth.
Petrie's journals and other sources do not provide complete information on the find-spots of the sherds. However, on additional
evidence, it appears that all except two sherds from the second
season were discovered in a large rubbish dump at the north-west
corner of the site. The archaeological facts indicate that the
Minoan sherds and the imitations at Kahun were not luxury
items which were used exclusively as fine imported ware by the
upper levels of the town's society, for it appears that none of it was

discovered in the vicinity of the north row of mansions. Rather, it seems to have been domestic ware used by some of the ordinary people of the town. However, Kemp cautions that such 'evidence' should be carefully interpreted, since the scanty representation of Minoan pottery in the wealthier areas may simply be due to the fact that their rubbish was more completely and effectively cleared away in antiquity.

Again, caution must be exercised in establishing the exact date of this pottery. Petrie claimed that the Egyptian pottery found with the Minoan sherds was entirely of a 12th Dynasty date, and he thus established a similar date for the foreign ware. However, the stratification in the rooms, filled with loose sandy material, was probably not straightforward, and it is unlikely that correlation between the depth of a find-spot and the age of an object can be accurately established at Kahun.

Petrie's claim that all the Kahun Minoan pottery could be attributed to the time when Sesostris II's pyramid was being built cannot therefore be substantiated. These pieces, as well as other types of object from the site, need not necessarily be attributed to the early years of occupation when the workforce was obviously at full strength, because the total evidence points to a much longer occupation by a community not simply composed of pyramid workmen. The Minoan material at Kahun can therefore only be attributed to the general history of occupation. Nevertheless, if we consider the evidence of Aegean archaeology, the Minoan material at Kahun could have belonged only to the Middle Kingdom Period and not to the 18th Dynasty occupation.

Another archaeologist, Von Bissing, claimed that only a brief connection had existed between Egypt and the Aegean and that it was during the 18th Dynasty, and not the 12th Dynasty, that the Minoan pottery had come to Kahun. He also tried to show that the occupation of the site had been continuous, and that a group of Egyptian pottery from there – wavy-necked jars – was of the 18th Dynasty.

However, Garstang's discovery of Tomb 416 at Abydos and of a fine 'Kamares' pot in a 12th Dynasty tomb provided substantial evidence against Von Bissing's theory that the Kahun Minoan pottery was later than the 12th Dynasty. His discoveries at Beni Hasan also showed that the Egyptian wavy-necked jars were to be identified with the 12th Dynasty.

The Abydos tomb, from its other artefacts, could be clearly

identified as Middle Kingdom, dating either to the 12th or 13th Dynasties. It provided a dated, funerary setting for the Minoan pottery which could then also be applied to the Minoan ware found in less well-defined contexts in the domestic rubbish heaps at Kahun and Haraga. At Qubbet el-Hawa – another tomb context – another vase was found which may be an imitation of a Minoan one. However, here, re-use of the tombs meant that this find could not be closely dated.

In general terms, therefore, Middle Minoan pottery was found at a few sites in Egypt during the Middle Kingdom. These were mainly situated in the Fayoum area, and the advent of this pottery there probably dates to a time between the reign of King Sesostris II and the end of the 13th Dynasty. However, at this stage, although we can say that the pottery entered Egypt and was imitated there between c. 1890 and 1670/1650 BC, it is not possible yet to assign it to specific historical divisions of Minoan chronology.

Kamares ware would appear to have two major sources in Crete – the palaces at Knossos and Phaistos. However, the route and method of entry for this pottery into Egypt has given occasion for much discussion, and several possible routes have been suggested. These include the journey from Crete to a Delta port and then on to Memphis or another centre by an inland river route; from Crete to Cyrene and thence along the North African coast to the Nile Delta; or from Crete to the Syrian coast, sometimes passing via Cyprus, and following the coasts of Anatolia and Palestine to the Nile Delta. This latter route has a certain amount of archaeological support, including the fact that some Syrian coastal sites, such as Byblos, showed evidence of cross-cultural influences. Evidence for a direct Egyptian-Crete trade is lacking at present; although it would appear that at certain periods their royal courts exchanged presents, there has as yet been no major discovery of groups of imported material in either Crete or Egypt which are not also found in Syria. The Syrian ports appear to have played an important role receiving imports and then exporting them, and no convincing alternative to the Syrian role as trade intermediary can yet be proved.

Apart from the pottery, the only other evidently Minoan import at Kahun was a stone pyxis lid. However, throughout this period, there was a general awareness of each other's artistic styles, which found some degree of expression in shapes and patterns, but, despite this interchange, the influence was rather one-sided and there is less evidence of Egyptian material found in Crete during the Middle Kingdom and Second Intermediate Period. This includes a small statue of an Egyptian, Abnub, son of Seker-user, and some twenty scarabs as well as an alabaster lid bearing the name of a Hyksos king of Egypt, named Khyan, discovered by Evans at Knossos. The Egyptians may also have introduced the Cretans to the idea of writing with pen and ink on papyrus, instead of their usual custom of inscribing on clay with a stylus for two clay cups, inscribed in ink in the Egyptian manner, were found in Crete. Possibly incision on clay was used for everyday purposes, and papyrus was kept for important documents, but most of these texts, if they existed, would in any case have perished.

In architectural and artistic terms, the Middle Minoan and Middle Kingdom Periods possibly saw a constant exchange of ideas and techniques. It has been suggested that some architectural connections existed during this period, and that these were perhaps evidenced in buildings such as the Labyrinth built by Amenemmes III at Hawara, which later visitors compared to the Labyrinth of Minos at Knossos. However, in other instances, such as the columns used in buildings in Egypt and Crete, there were few similarities. Also, the resemblances between the wall-paintings seen in the two countries are superficial, for the materials at hand were very different. The Cretans never carved their walls before painting; poor stone supplies forced them to invent other decorative forms, and they sometimes substituted modelling the plaster ground in relief for the wall-carvings executed by the Egyptians. The Cretans also painted straight on to the plaster while it was still wet, unlike the Egyptian artists. Again, because of the scarcity of suitable stone, they never embarked on large stone statuary, but perfected the skill of carving small objects such as seals. Their metalworking techniques showed an independent style, and although the forms of some Egyptian pottery were copied, the Minoans introduced their own lively and increasingly extravagant and naturalistic decorative designs.

By the New Kingdom, which corresponded to the Late Minoan Period, the cross-fertilisation of ideas was perhaps less marked, although there has been much discussion of the possible 'Minoan' influence on Egyptian tomb-art of the period. Again, scholars have discussed the possible effect of the naturalism of

Cretan art on the artistic representations which occurred in Egypt during the period of King Akhenaten's reign, towards the end of the 18th Dynasty. Alabaster vases continued to be exported to Greece, and Minoan and Mycenaean pottery was imported to Egypt until the twelfth century, when the links with the Aegean ceased.

However, not only do we have the material evidence of this continuing connection, but in some New Kingdom tombs it is probable that the Aegean islanders themselves are depicted on the walls. A fresco from the Tomb of Senmut shows Minoans bringing tribute to Egypt and similar events occur in the scenes in the tomb of the Vizier Rekhmire. These tribute-bearers, described as the men of Keftiu and of the 'Islands in the Midst of the Sea', carry gold and silver objects for the Egyptian Treasury.

There has been much discussion regarding the true origin of Keftiu and the Keftians. Were they from Crete or were they from other parts of Asia? Many people accept that they were in fact representatives sent to Egypt from Minoan Crete, and that the people of the 'Islands in the Midst of the Sea' were envoys sent by the other islands under Crete's control. They were probably not just tribute-bearers, but ambassadors sent with gifts to the Egyptian court, and the Egyptians would have reciprocated with other gifts. The envoys and retainers probably remained as a small group at the Egyptian court for some months. Kemp has posed the question whether, although these people first appear in Egyptian scenes and inscriptions in the New Kingdom, they first came to Egypt during the Middle Kingdom. This would coincide with the period when most Minoan pottery imports are found in Egypt. However, Kemp cautions that the presence of quantities of this pottery in Egypt is not sufficient evidence to indicate that the Keftians were in Egypt at the same date, for the pottery may have been imported through quite a different route and via a middleman, whereas Egyptian and Cretan envoys would have made a direct exchange. Nevertheless, it is strange that the New Kingdom, the period when the Cretan visits are best documented in Egypt, was the time when the quantity of Minoan vases found in Egypt falls below that of imported Mycenaean, Cypriot and Syrian wares. Another major difference is that, whereas the Middle Minoan pottery mainly occurs in domestic sites, in the New Kingdom the foreign wares occur as treasured possessions in the tombs.

The Minoans disappear from the scene some time towards the end of the fifteenth century BC, overwhelmed by a major catastrophe, which would have coincided with the later years of Egypt's 18th Dynasty. Relations between Egypt and the Greek mainland and Aegean islands then reopened and continued until the late New Kingdom. The subsequent upheavals of Egypt's Third Intermediate Period and the generally unstable political conditions in the Mediterranean and Near East finally brought relations between the two peoples to a close, until a new phase re-opened between Egypt and Classical Greece.

It is already clear that connections between Egypt and Crete involved other areas of the ancient world. The towns of Syria were particularly important and major discoveries underline contacts between these areas of the ancient world. In 1921–2, the archaeologist Montet, in his first excavation campaign at Byblos in Syria, discovered a spread of broken offerings above the ruins of a building dedicated to the goddess known as the Lady of Byblos, which was in use during the third millennium BC. Amongst these were fragments of stone vases with the names, written in hieroglyphs, of most of the Old Kingdom kings, culminating with that of Pepy I. In his second campaign, Montet discovered a magnificent jar which originally contained nearly a thousand objects. This, known today as the 'Montet Jar', was a closed deposit and formed the basis of a detailed study.

The jar, coil-built and of red ware, was locally produced, and could be dated by its stylistic features to the time between the Early Bronze and Middle Bronze periods. One opinion held that it was contemporary with the Middle Kingdom in Egypt. None of the objects inside the jar was inscribed with a royal name, but the seals and scarabs could be classified, compared with Egyptian parallels, and dated accordingly. The seals – there was no other closed deposit from Egypt or elsewhere – could only be judged on style and Egyptian examples. They were mostly made of steatite, and included scarabs, seals and cylinder seals.

The rings were all of a type that was known from the Egyptian sites of Dahshur and Lahun. Pendants and figurines included baboons that were similar to examples of the First Intermediate Period found in Egypt. Figures resembling the Egyptian god, Harpocrates, were also discovered and these probably dated to the time between the end of the Old Kingdom and the First Intermediate Period.

Carnelian was used for most of the collection of beads, and the forms followed the four traditional shapes of Egypt – cylinders, barrels, rings and spheroids. An Old Kingdom bead collar was one of the best dated examples found in the jar, and generally, the beads dated from c. 2130–2040 BC.

There were also over forty torques and pins which were made locally at Byblos. These torques, perhaps introduced into Syria by an intrusive ethnic element, have already been discussed in connection with the rare example found in a workman's house at Kahun. Metal torques or representations of them on statuettes have been found at many sites from Ras Shamra to Tell el 'Ajjul, as well as the few isolated examples which have come to light in Middle Kingdom contexts in Egypt.

Some jewellery, especially the metalwork, shows evidence of a possible Mesopotamian origin, and the Montet Jar contains a miscellaneous collection of objects – both ornaments and utensils. Some Mesopotamian elements were present but essentially the contents were acquired mainly from Egypt. They probably arrived in Byblos c. 2130–2040 BC, either through trade, barter, booty or as personal souvenirs. These dates would correspond to the First Intermediate Period in Egypt, and the discovery is yet another indication that relations existed between Egypt and Syria, as well as Syria and Mesopotamia, in this period.

Another important find which illustrates a strong association between Egypt, Asia and the Aegean is the El-Tod treasure. This was discovered in 1936, buried in the stone foundations of a temple at El-Tod in Egypt which, the archaeologists believed, was built by King Sesostris I of the Middle Kingdom.

The treasure was contained within four copper chests, two of which were inscribed with the name of a later 12th Dynasty king, Amenemmes II. The contents of the chests were all of foreign origin, but they reflected a wide diversity of traditions also seen in objects known to come from Crete, Syria and Mesopotamia. There has been some difference of opinion expressed regarding the date of the items which show Minoan influence and some scholars attribute them to Middle Minoan II, while others place them in Middle Minoan IB. Although it is generally accepted that the caskets were deposited in Egypt some time during the Middle Kingdom, even this has been challenged and a later date suggested. It would seem that the treasure was not originally packed inside the Egyptian caskets, because ink inscriptions in Hieratic have been added to some items. However, even if the imported treasure was packed into the caskets in Egypt, it can be argued that the treasure and the chests need not necessarily be of the same date, since chests from a previous era could have been used. Therefore, although the treasure may have been packed and buried during the Middle Kingdom (thus indicating an association between the sources from which the various contents were derived), no firm conclusion can be drawn regarding either the date of the treasure or of its burial.

However, generally, there is sufficient evidence of contact between Egypt, Asia and the Aegean during the Middle Kingdom to set the background for the situation at Kahun.

The theory has been suggested, and received support from a number of scholars, that foreigners, either from Syria or Crete or elsewhere, were resident workers at the Egyptian sites where the Minoan pottery was found. Petrie was the first to advance this theory and his reasons for doing so should now be considered.

Petrie's excavations at Kahun revealed a diversity of objects which persuaded him that foreign workers were resident there during the Middle Kingdom occupation. First, there was the evidence of a number of types of pottery which he classified as 'foreign' and of the pot marks which he believed were a link in the chain of the development of the alphabet; secondly, the weights and measures which he found at the site included a high proportion of non-Egyptian pieces which he believed had been introduced by the foreigners; and there were also isolated instances of 'foreign' items such as the torque found in one of the houses. Additionally, there were some religious practices which did not seem to be entirely Egyptian in origin.

Considering the pottery first, Petrie classified one group as 'Aegean' but intended this term to cover not only the Greek islands but also the coast of the Peloponnese and Asia Minor. He described three major groups as distinctively 'foreign', including the black ware with bright yellow, red and white patterns which was quite different from any known Egyptian pottery, and the distinctive wave pattern of Aegean ware, also unknown on Egyptian examples. These pieces were apparently found in rubbish heaps which Petrie maintained were entirely of the 12th Dynasty. He argued that, from their position, the heaps would not have been accumulated by later residents; he claimed also that the Middle Kingdom residents, once the pyramid had been completed

and the houses of the workmen deserted, heaped up their rubbish
in the houses. The people who had lived at Kahun when the town
was fully occupied (during the building of the pyramid) would
have used the extra-mural rubbish heaps and the 'foreign' pottery, found in and under these heaps, must therefore, Petrie
argued, belong to the time of Sesostris II.

Petrie also discovered other foreign ware. One group of black
pottery was found, the pieces being uncovered in various places in
the town. Most of the fragments of these vases were decorated
with a chevron pattern, with alternate spaces filled with rows of
dots, or a double chevron blank, with dots on each side of it. Petrie
identified this with pottery found by Naville in deep, undisturbed
burials of the 12th and 13th Dynasties at Khatanah near Fakus.
These were found with other objects of the Middle Kingdom,
including 12th Dynasty scarabs, and Petrie argued that the black
pottery found at Kahun, which he indicated had a marked similarity to Italian black ware, should also probably be dated to the
12th and 13th Dynasties. He believed that the Kahun black
pottery shared a common origin with the Italian black ware,
although the latter continued in use until later times. Finally, he
classified some other pottery, which was decorated with non-
Egyptian styles, as 'foreign'. He claimed, as negative evidence to
prove the Middle Kingdom date for the Kahun 'foreign' wares,
that none of these types had ever been found in sites of later
periods and that no pottery of the later periods had ever been
uncovered in the Kahun rubbish heaps which he claimed were
12th Dynasty.

At the time of his discoveries, Greek archaeologists objected to
such an early date for this pottery. However, he maintained that
the Kahun 'Aegean' pottery could not follow the Mycenaean
pottery styles and that they did not fall into place in the historical
development of pottery from the Mycenaean downwards. Yet
they were certainly from Greece or Italy, and Petrie suggested
that the pottery was the product of the earliest Libyo-Greek
civilisation of the Aegean and Italy, c. 2500 BC.

This last statement was made in the light of insufficient evidence, since in Petrie's day, the state of early Aegean civilisation
was unknown. However, his claim that this pottery had nothing
to do with the historic civilisation of Greece was correct, and some
of it has subsequently been identified either as Minoan, or as
Egyptian imitations of that type. It has also been shown that

other types of foreign pottery were present at Kahun, including Syro-Palestinian pottery and El-Lisht juglets of the late Middle Kingdom. El-Lisht ware juglets have a highly burnished black or brown slipped surface and, although many were produced locally in Egypt, and were therefore an imitation, the original examples were Syro-Palestinian. These juglets occur in Western Asia mainly in areas (such as the Syrian coast) where other evidence also indicates links with Egypt. At least nineteen pieces of El-Lisht ware juglets were found at various sites throughout the town, and these probably entered Kahun in the 13th Dynasty. Kahun also produced a number of other vessels and sherds which, in recent times, have been identified as foreign.

Therefore, although Petrie's assessment of 'foreign' wares is not entirely accurate, since he included not only examples that were made abroad and imported into Egypt but also Egyptian imitations and even locally made wares that merely had unconventional features, it is undeniable that the inhabitants used foreign wares which were derived from the Aegean islands or from Syria-Palestine. Whether these wares entered Egypt through trade or were brought in by the foreign immigrants at Kahun is still uncertain. It is also unclear whether the Minoan wares came directly to Egypt, or via the Syrian trading ports. The answer to this question would help to clarify whether Kahun's foreign residents came both from Syria and from the Aegean, or only from Syria.

Other material finds Petrie made at Kahun which he considered to be imports included small vessels of bluish marble, which he claimed originated in the Mediterranean or Aegean areas. He also stated that the weights and measures used at Kahun included a high proportion of non-Egyptian examples. Not only were many of the standards foreign, but the materials of which the weights were made were not the customary ones used by Egyptians.

However, it was the pot marks – signs scratched on the pottery, in some cases by the potter before baking and in others by the owners – that Petrie regarded as the most important evidence of foreign influence at Kahun. One mark was found on a large jar sunk in the floor of a chamber and used to store corn or water. Above this, tools and a papyrus of the Middle Kingdom were uncovered. Therefore, Petrie claimed that the pot and its mark dated to the period when the house was in use – that is, the 12th

Dynasty. Other evidence – potter's marks on jars in the temple foundation of Sesostris II and the style and manufacturing methods of this pottery – strongly suggested a 12th Dynasty or possibly early 13th Dynasty date for the pot marks.

Petrie considered that these marks presented evidence of a time of trial and error at Kahun, when various alphabets were used concurrently, before the clear evolution of the final alphabet emerged. He argued that the Phoenician and Cypriot alphabets (the forerunners of the Greek and Western alphabets), which, according to one theory, were derived from Egyptian Hieratic of the 12th Dynasty, were in a state of evolution and development before 2000 BC, and that, at Kahun, with its other evidence of a cosmopolitan population, there was ample scope for experimentation with written forms.

What, then, was Petrie's hypothesis? He suggested that during the troubled times of the 11th Dynasty, the Egyptians had fought with the Aegean peoples and become acquainted with Mediterranean races. The 'foreigners' may first have been brought to Egypt as captives to work on public projects, but the discovery of weights at Kahun indicate that a commercial association also existed with their homeland. Uneducated to the Egyptian system of writing, the foreigners learnt the use of the Egyptian masons' marks, with whom they lived. The masons' marks had been derived from hieroglyphs and many of the pot marks resembled them. The marks were then used for the sounds attached to them, and eventually, words were written down in new signs. Commercial concerns then carried these signs from Egypt into the Mediterranean areas. Thus, the system, founded on the workmen's signs, developed into a simple mode of writing which became the starting point for the true alphabetic system.

We must now consider other evidence which, during the years since Petrie first excavated at Kahun, has further revealed some idea of the extent of relations between Egypt and Asia during the Middle Kingdom.

A famous papyrus (the Brooklyn Papyrus) was left to the Brooklyn Museum in New York in the Will of the Egyptologist, Charles E. Wilbour. The legal and administrative contents of this document enhance our knowledge of the period between the end of the 12th Dynasty and the Hyksos period (c. 1786–1670 BC).

On the *verso* of this papyrus, a woman named Senebtisi attempts to establish her legal rights to the possession of ninety-five servants. A list of them is included which states their titles, names and surnames, and their occupations. Of the seventy-seven entries which are presented well enough to enable the individual's nationality to be read, twenty-nine appear to be Egyptian while forty-eight are 'Asiatics'. Of the Asiatics, seven were men, employed as domestics and cooks, thirty were women who were shopkeepers or involved in weaving and making clothes, and nine were infants.

It is evident that the foreigners were associated with the Egyptians in work, and that a further attempt at integration was made, by giving the foreign children and some of the adults Egyptian names. Although the foreign names were not precise enough to enable the exact homeland of these Asiatics to be identified, it can be said that they were from a 'Semitic group of the north west'. It is possible that they changed their names because the Egyptians found them difficult to pronounce, although it may have been part of an Egyptian integration policy.

The Brooklyn Papyrus is important here because it shows that one household employed a large proportion of Asiatics and this household was situated in Upper Egypt and not in the Delta; therefore, it is apparent that Asiatic servants were by now dis-seminated throughout the community.

There is also other evidence of Asiatics working in households at this time, although in smaller numbers. Mention of them is made throughout many texts. On stelae, they appear in domestic service, usually listed after the members of the family; sometimes, only one Asiatic occurs, but in other instances they are present in groups of two, three, four or six. They have Egyptian names, clothing and hairstyles, but are usually distinguished as Asiatics by the title ^c3m (feminine: ^c3mt). Some came to hold important and trusted positions in Egyptian households, and, since they were sometimes engaged in the funerary cult on these stelae, it is probable that they followed Egyptian religious practices.

At Kahun, there is significant literary evidence of the presence of Asiatics. In one of the legal documents mention is made of Asiatic household servants. Others are listed as dancers in the festival celebrations in the temple of Sesostris II, and in another document we learn of two Asiatics employed as porters in the same temple. It is also evident that there were Asiatics in some of the military or police units, since there was mention of an officer in charge of Asiatic troops. Kahun also had a 'Scribe of the

Asiatics'. It is apparent that the Asiatics were present in the town
in some numbers, and this may have reflected the situation
elsewhere in Egypt. It can be stated that these people were loosely
classed by Egyptians as 'Asiatics', although their exact homeland
in Syria or Palestine cannot be determined, and that they held a
variety of posts in public institutions and private houses, and were
apparently given some fairly responsible positions.

However, the reason for their presence in Egypt remains unclear, but various suggestions have been made. There is historical
evidence to indicate that Egypt had troubled relations with her
northern neighbours in the First Intermediate Period and possibly at the beginning of the 12th Dynasty. Although there are no
inscriptions from the Middle Kingdom (as there are from the New
Kingdom) relating that prisoners-of-war were brought from Syria
and Palestine to Egypt, it is possible that Egypt pursued similar
policies in the earlier period.

During the First Intermediate Period, Egypt was plagued with
incursions of Beduin, who infiltrated the Delta. It is probable that
such conflicts did not cease at the beginning of the 12th Dynasty,
and indeed, the first king, Amenemmes I, is reputed to have built
a line of fortresses – the 'Wall of the Ruler' – to keep the Asiatics
out of the Delta. This is known from allusions in the two Egyptian
texts, the 'Prophecy of Neferty' and the 'Story of Sinuhe'. A stela
in the Louvre, belonging to a General Nesoumontou, also states
that in Year 24 of the king's reign, he made war on the Asiatics
and destroyed fortresses, although the site of this is not stated.

Classical sources (Herodotus, *The Histories*, Bk II, 102–3, 106,
107–8) mention that King 'Sesostris' was victorious against the
Orient and that he captured many prisoners who were brought to
Egypt to work on building projects.

The Asiatics, or a proportion of them, may indeed have entered
Egypt at this period as prisoners-of-war. However, some probably
arrived in various other ways, for it is obvious from the literary
and material evidence that there were also peaceful contacts
between Egypt and her northern neighbours. In the Story of
Sinuhe, during the early 12th Dynasty, Sinuhe found other
Egyptian residents in Palestine when he went there; he met men
who travelled between Egypt and Syria, and generally, the impression is of cordial relations between the two areas. The imported objects of Egyptian or Syro-Palestinian manufacture in
both areas also suggests friendly association, and in Sinai, there

was collaboration on mining projects between Egyptian and local workmen. The general trends in Egypt from the beginning of the 12th Dynasty suggests that some of the Asiatics came as traders, and that these or other travellers introduced some new styles and techniques to the Egyptians.

Apart from military or commercial reasons, some of the immigrants may have come, as they did later, to seek work in Egypt. To do so, they would have sacrificed their nomadic freedom, in exchange for regular employment and food.

Animals, as well as humans, entered Egypt in the 12th Dynasty. A tomb scene at Meir shows cattle entering Egypt from Asia and a similar scene occurs in a tomb at Bersheh, belonging to a commander who lived under Sesostris III. He had lived at Megiddo in Palestine, where his statue was found, and the Egyptians probably controlled this area and exploited its resources subsequent to Sesostris III's campaign to Sichem in Palestine. The cattle in the scene may represent booty brought back as plunder from this campaign.

Thus, the scattered documentation gives no clear answer as to how or why the Asiatics came to Egypt in the Middle Kingdom. By the New Kingdom, the sources are more specific, and at Gurob, the Fayoum town which replaced Kahun in the New Kingdom as the centre of the area, Petrie again claimed that there was a substantial foreign population. He based this on the evidence of some of the pottery and the pot marks, on the weights, and on the discovery of bodies with light hair, as well as on his belief that some burial customs there were non-Egyptian. Although some of his arguments have since been refuted – for example, the foreign pottery may be attributed to trade rather than to the immigrants – there is nevertheless firm literary evidence that Asiatic slaves, women and children were at Gurob and that some received instruction in the workshops. However, the foreigners here may well have been in the minority, and seem to have merged successfully with the Egyptian residents.

No firm conclusions can therefore be drawn about the Middle Kingdom foreign population at Kahun – why they came, who they were, and how they were employed. It is not clear whether the pottery of Syro-Palestinian and Aegean origin arrived at Kahun through trade or was brought in by the foreigners. It can only be stated that the population at Kahun provided a ready market for exotic pottery which was met either by imported goods or local imitations, and that the Minoan wares do not appear to be luxury items, reserved for the tombs or the houses of the wealthy, but were apparently purely domestic wares for which the humbler inhabitants had a preference. Similar pottery from Haraga (if it was thrown out from the embalmers' workshops) and at Lisht (where it may have come from a living rather than cemetery location) would suggest that the Minoan ware was particularly associated with the poorer social elements. The question must therefore be asked, although no accurate reply can be given: did these foreign workmen bring the pottery with them, use it at Kahun and elsewhere, and then imitate it in their new homeland?

Again, it is unclear whether the Minoan and Syro-Palestinian pottery came from two direct provenances – perhaps Byblos and Crete – to Egypt, or whether the Minoan ware was brought into Egypt indirectly via Syria. Again, we can ask whether the immigrants themselves came from one or more homelands? The other evidence – literary and material – indicates an 'Asiatic' presence, but there may have been Minoans at Kahun as well.

We can further question the occupations which the foreign residents held at Kahun. Literary evidence indicates that their range of employment was fairly wide – in temple service, in private households, and in the army or police. Although there is no direct evidence, some of the artisans and craftsmen may also have been brought from elsewhere. The wife of one workman possessed a torque – rarely found in Egypt – and there is subtle evidence in the royal jewellery of the Middle Kingdom that the artisans were influenced directly or indirectly by Asiatic styles. It would be reasonable to assume that there were a significant number of foreign workers in the town, who required administrative supervision by a 'special scribe' allocated to them, although it is impossible to determine their numbers in relation to their Egyptian neighbours.

It is also difficult to assess how completely they assimilated Egyptian ways. Such evidence as we have regarding the religious customs of the town indicate that there may be some differences at Kahun, although the Asiatics were employed in the temple cult. The scanty evidence excavated from the surrounding cemeteries provides insufficient skeletal and other material to allow a complete study to be made either of the inhabitants' burial customs, or their ethnic origins and physical illnesses.

A further question remains to be answered – why did the inhabitants of this first occupation at Kahun leave their homes? Before looking at possible answers to this, it is necessary first to consider the evidence for the date of the conclusion of that period of occupation.

CHAPTER 8

Last Years at Kahun

We know that Kahun was built to house the pyramid workmen, artisans and officials connected with the construction of Sesostris II's pyramid complex at Lahun. It is also clear that although it may have been during the early years that the greatest activity occurred, when the population of the town was at its height, nevertheless the community did not fade away once the pyramid was finished. Indeed, there is every indication that Kahun continued to flourish throughout the 12th Dynasty and into the 13th Dynasty, and was a place of much greater significance than that afforded to a mere pyramid workmen's residence town. The cult of the founder, Sesostris II, was still observed in his funerary temple at Kahun long after his death, and the various trades and industries which had grown up at Kahun in its heyday were still pursued. It is evident that the completion of the king's pyramid was not the reason why Kahun's inhabitants eventually deserted the town, abandoning their tools and other possessions in the shops and houses.

However, it is difficult to assess the extent to which the life of this community continued to flourish during the later years of the 12th Dynasty and the 13th Dynasty. Evidence which includes written material, pottery, scarabs and seal impressions indicates that it remained a centre of some importance throughout this period. In the papyri, the kings of the 12th Dynasty are well attested, but there is also reference to early kings of the 13th Dynasty – Sekhemre Khutawy and his successor, Sekhemkare.

The historical evidence of the papyri is also generally supported by the information derived from detailed studies of the important group of clay seal impressions, cylinder seals and scarabs which were found at Kahun. Together, they assist in establishing the length of occupation of the site.

The clay sealings were used to mark ownership of boxes, vases and bags, and on the underside of some of these Petrie found the impressions of the vessel and cord bound around it, to which the seal had been attached. Grains of resin were found with others, indicating that a number of these packages contained resin. The sealings were picked up by small boys from the modern village of Lahun whom Petrie employed to hunt over the dust and the earth after the workmen had cleared a room. Sometimes, these children discovered small objects which had been overlooked in the preliminary excavation.

Nearly all of the sealings were found in two or three rooms of a house which was situated on the road leading up to the Acropolis. Such was their concentration in this one area that Petrie suggested that the house where they were found may have been occupied by the staff of the Governor's house and possibly acted as an office for parcels and provisions sent for the governor. The sealings not only have a useful role in determining the town's chronology, but also provide names and titles of some of the officials; we find 'The citizen, Sebek-user . . .' on one, and 'Inspector of the Prince's geese' on another, while a third refers to the 'Keeper of the Office of Agriculture, Iyab'.

As well as the clay seal impressions, cylinder seals and scarabs were also discovered at Kahun. The royal names of the 12th Dynasty rulers which occur on the sealings and cylinder seals include those of Sesostris I, II, III and Amenemmes III. The name of King Amenemmes II, however, is missing. There appear to be no scarabs which can be attributed to Amenemmes I, and only one surviving impression bears the name of the town's founder, Sesostris II. However, cylinder seals bear the name of Sesostris III, although he is not mentioned in the papyri. A scarab was also found, inscribed with the name of a 13th Dynasty king, Khasekhemre Neferhotep I.

There is a notable absence of scarabs and sealings attributable to the Hyksos kings. These were the rulers whose infiltration into Egypt finally swept away the native kings of the 13th Dynasty. The design elements which distinguish scarabs of the Hyksos period are missing from the Kahun examples. A wooden stamp bearing the name of Apepi (Apophis) was found at the site but, although this was the name of a Hyksos ruler, this example may refer not to the king, but to a private individual who lived during the 12th or 13th Dynasties when the name was already in use. After the hiatus of the Hyksos period, the royal names at Kahun then resume with the New Kingdom rulers – Amenophis I, Tuthmosis I, II and III, and Amenophis II, III, IV. This provides support for Petrie's theory that the town of Kahun was partially re-occupied in the 18th Dynasty.

In general, it is difficult to determine whether most of the artefacts discovered at Kahun date to the earlier years of the 12th Dynasty, or to the 13th Dynasty. However, it seems that the town continued to prosper without interruption throughout the whole of this period, and the local situation would have reflected the general conditions throughout Egypt at this time.

The writings of the ancient historian, Manetho, described the 13th Dynasty as a time when 'Sixty kings of Diospolis . . . reigned for 453 years', and, at one time, some scholars accepted that these brief and numerous reigns indicated a period of chaos at the end of the 12th Dynasty, with a time of difficult transition between the 12th and 13th Dynasties.

However, the currently held view is that the change-over of dynasties was in fact peaceful, and that the first king of the 13th Dynasty may have been related by ties of blood or marriage to the previous rulers. The brief reigns of the 13th Dynasty may be explained in terms of a series of 'puppet' kings, perhaps dominated by a powerful line of viziers, who were possibly selected by election to rule for a limited period.

There was obviously no marked political upheaval in Egypt, and for more than a hundred years, the central government continued to wield power. Egypt's prestige abroad remained high, the royal building programmes flourished at home, and the kings still ruled the land from Memphis and used the Fayoum town of It-towy as a royal residence.

However, eventually the weakness of the king's position, and the rapid succession of rulers undoubtedly lessened Egypt's power and prosperity at home and abroad, and the lack of a strong ruler, as always in Egypt's history, brought the country to a state where outside intervention became possible.

Their exact place of origin and the extent of their overlordship of Egypt is still uncertain, but during the 15th and 16th Dynasties a group of foreign rulers whom we know as the 'Hyksos' took over control in Egypt. This 'invasion', now believed to have been a gradual and progressive infiltration rather than a rapid military conquest, probably represented a change of rulers rather than a massive influx of a new ethnic group. However, it has been suggested that the earlier introduction of perhaps substantial Asiatic elements into Egyptian households and other occupations throughout the Middle Kingdom may have facilitated this development. The gradual awareness of Asiatic cultures and the intermarriages which took place between some native-born Egyptians and the Asiatic immigrants would have created a climate, it is argued, in which the indigenous population were less resistant to the Hyksos conquest.

Whatever the background to the conquest, by c. 1674 BC the Hyksos king, Salitis, who founded the 15th Dynasty, had occupied Memphis and It-towy. The Middle Kingdom fell and the last rulers of the 13th Dynasty were probably reduced to the status of local rulers, as vassals of the Hyksos kings.

Our knowledge of the Hyksos kings and their rule rests largely on historical sources which are based on the propaganda of the period which immediately followed. A new line of native rulers emerged at Thebes and founded the 17th Dynasty, c. 1650 BC. These warrior princes drove the Hyksos from the land, and their descendants, the triumphant pharaohs of the 18th Dynasty, established Egypt as the major power of the ancient Near East. These kings justified and advanced their claims to rule Egypt using a variety of methods, including an effective propaganda which emphasised the miseries which the Egyptians had previously suffered under the Hyksos. It is difficult to establish the truth in this matter, although other evidence indicates that the population may not have suffered under severe Hyksos domination and in some areas at least, their arrival in Egypt may not have been too unwelcome.

Nevertheless, towards the end of the 13th Dynasty, the country would certainly have passed through troubled times, and this is reflected in the Fayoum area. The royal support which the area had enjoyed from the reign of Sesostris II onwards now seemed to fade away and from the start of Hyksos rule, there is a noticeable decline in the prosperity of the whole region around Lahun. Indeed, there is a suggestion, albeit based on a single piece of evidence, that there may have been a limited immigration of desert peoples into the area.

A single sherd of so-called 'pan-grave' pottery was discovered at Kahun by Petrie. This fragment from a hand-made bowl formed part of a series assembled by Petrie, which bore the potmarks that he believed belonged to an early form of the alphabetic script. The sherd was presented to the Department of Greek and Roman Antiquities at the British Museum by Jesse Haworth in 1890, and was later transferred to the Department of Egyptian Antiquities. Subsequent research has indicated that it may have come from one of the smaller houses in the western sector at Kahun.

The sherd belongs to the culture for which Petrie created the term 'pan-grave'. The evidence for this 'culture' included certain distinctive features, such as the shape of the graves, and some elements of the grave goods, particularly the pottery with its incised decoration. The 'pan-grave' burials, discovered by Petrie at a number of cemeteries, led him to theorise that the culture had been introduced to Egypt between the 12th and 18th Dynasties, by immigrants from a desert region.

The 'pan-grave' pottery was discovered not only in graves, but also in some towns and Egyptian military fortresses in Nubia. In his study of the Kahun sherd, B.J. Kemp reaches the conclusion that it is not possible to state that there was a pan-grave phase at Kahun on a single piece of evidence and that, although desert immigrants may have been present in the area, the sherd may simply represent an isolated example of a trade in these goods which was carried on in the town.

Nevertheless, it is obvious that, whatever the local conditions may have been, there was a marked decline in royal support and patronage for the Fayoum towns during the Hyksos period. The archaeological evidence – the absence of scarabs and seal impressions bearing the characteristic Hyksos designs – indicates that Kahun had now ceased to be a major centre of activity.

There are different opinions of how this first period of occupation at Kahun drew to a close. It can be argued that declining local economic conditions, and perhaps even foreign infiltration and harassment, finally drove the residents of Kahun from their homes. The quantity, range and type of articles of everyday use which were left behind in the houses may indeed suggest that the departure was sudden and unpremeditated.

Another interpretation of the evidence is that there was no total evacuation of the town, but that the population declined and dwindled until, by the New Kingdom, only a token occupation of some of the houses remained.

Petrie advanced the theory that, following the abandonment of the Middle Kingdom town, a second phase of occupation occurred during the 18th Dynasty, probably mainly in the reign of Amenophis III. This occupation, he argued, was sparse, with only some of the rooms in the western section (the workmen's quarter) now being occupied. Here, in a house at the east end of the fourth street, he discovered a remarkable set of bronze tools which were dated by the discovery of an associated papyrus to the reign of Amenophis III. Other items found in the area included pottery, other tools, and scarabs dating to the reign of the same king. Apart from the discoveries in the western sector, he claimed that only one other object of the 18th Dynasty was found elsewhere, apart from a few burials in the eastern part of the town.

One of the major discoveries of this New Kingdom occupation, however, was that of the tomb of Maket. This 'tomb', situated in one of the rock-cut cellars under the old houses in Kahun, had obviously been cleared to take the burials of one family. It held twelve coffins and two boxes for baby burials and each coffin contained as many as five or six bodies. Petrie described how the bodies and their wrappings had all been reduced to a black powder, but he carefully recorded the position of all the coffins and the minor objects. He believed that the tomb had been used from the mid-18th Dynasty to the 20th Dynasty. The seventh coffin contained the body of 'Maket', the 'Lady of the House', and her jewellery; this find, providing the name of the owner, was particularly important and, therefore, the group is usually referred to as the 'Tomb of Maket'. The artefacts from this group were presented to the Ashmolean Museum, Oxford.

The extent of the New Kingdom phase of occupation at Kahun remains uncertain. Despite Petrie's theory of limited residence there, other scholars have maintained that, because of the large number of 18th Dynasty funerary deposits uncovered in the town and the quantity of New Kingdom pottery which turned up in the houses, the occupation at this period may have been more significant.

Although, by the 18th Dynasty, the position which Kahun held as the pre-eminent town of the Fayoum dyke had passed to Gurob, it has been suggested that in the New Kingdom, Kahun may once again have housed workmen who, this time, were engaged in dismantling the Temple of Sesostris II at Kahun, and using the temple as a quarry for other royal building projects in the area.

A small community may even have continued to live at Kahun into the 19th Dynasty, although, by this period, both Kahun and Gurob had entered a state of final disintegration and a new town was soon to take their place as the main centre of the Fayoum.

This new town was probably situated in the vicinity of the modern village of Lahun and may have been founded so that the residents could attend to the regulation of water-works which were established in the area by King Osorkon I. The town was occupied at some period between the 20th and 26th Dynasties, although Petrie was unable to determine the exact dates for this. The inhabitants of the town cleared out the old rock-cut tomb shafts which lay at the base of the Lahun pyramid, and re-used them for burials. Petrie's excavations here showed that the tombs were probably continuously used between the 22nd and 25th Dynasties.

The final chapter in Kahun's history occurred during the Roman period, when the long-deserted town was dug for limestone. The discovery of pottery and coins attest to this last phase, before the site, which had once bustled with all the noise and activity of an important religious and commercial centre, was finally left to the sand and the jackals. It was to remain deserted and hidden, until some two thousand years later, when William Flinders Petrie once again revealed the streets and houses of Kahun, and gave the modern world a glimpse of how this ancient community had lived.

PART III

THE INVESTIGATION

In order to examine the material from Kahun which is now housed in the Manchester Museum, a programme of investigation was set up which has so far involved the use of a number of multidisciplinary techniques. One aim of this project was to develop the concept, initially employed on the Manchester Egyptian Mummy Research Project, of subjecting certain museum collections to modern analytical techniques so that new information could be gained. More specifically, it is hoped that the Kahun Project will provide new insight into the development of various technologies at a particular period of history, and will also supply answers to questions relating to the provenance of pottery and metals found at Kahun.

The present account of this work includes the first descriptions of these studies. It is planned both to extend the scope of the current investigations and also to widen the range of techniques so that important studies such as the analysis and identification of the wood used in the artefacts at Kahun may eventually be incorporated in the project.

CHAPTER 9

Analysis of Egyptian Pottery

By Dr G.W.A. Newton

Pottery has been produced in Egypt for more than 7,000 years and the raw materials and techniques have hardly changed. This reflects the outlook of ancient Egyptians who showed a strict adherence to religious traditions. There have been many studies of the fabrics and designs of the pottery, both archaeological and scientific. A former Disney Professor of Archaeology at Cambridge defined archaeology thus: 'It is, I conceive, the science of teaching history by its monuments of whatever character those monuments may be.'

In Egypt monuments, such as temples and pyramids, dominate the scene. However, the beauty of a Badarian pot, made between 5000 and 4500 BC, cannot fail to impress. These pots are delicate, reducing to about 1 mm thick at the rim in some cases, and burnished in red and black. It is clear that the technology was well developed early on, and there is evidence that it deteriorated at later periods.

The development of some technological aspects of pottery-making is reflected in tomb-paintings. The series of pictures shows the development of the potter's wheel. In (a) the pot is hand turned on a block but it is unlikely that sufficient rotational energy could be generated to 'throw' the pot as in (b). This second picture is from the region of Niuserre, 2416–2392 BC (5th Dynasty), and probably marks the origin of the potter's wheel in Egypt. An 18th Dynasty (1575–1308 BC) painting (c) shows a further development where two people are involved, one to rotate the wheel leaving the potter's two hands free to work the clay. The technological development of the kick wheel (d) (taken from a temple relief dating from the reign of Darius, 518–485 BC) allowed one person to rotate the wheel and also have two hands free to work the clay.

For any civilisation changes in style, technique, shape and patterns reflect changes and developments in that society. In this respect pottery is very important. In our own society we are aware of changes in types and patterns of tableware and ovenware: for example the introduction of pyrex or the changes in shape of a ketchup bottle. This type of change was as true in ancient societies as it is today. In ancient Egypt the most abundant pottery was undecorated and used for cooking, storage, eating and drinking. Painted pottery, very important in some societies (e.g. Hellenistic Greece), was in Egypt rather restricted to a few periods and localities.

Petrie was one of the first to realise the importance of shape and style and used this to establish a sequence dating technique of pottery in Predynastic Egypt which is still valid to the present with only minor modifications.

At Naqada and a site known to the Greeks as Diospolis Parva, Petrie discovered thousands of pots. Every grave contained some pottery. From this he built up a corpus of 700 kinds of pot in nine principal groups. One group from Naqada, a wavy-handled type, was particularly distinctive and was influenced by jars imported from southern Palestine. Petrie placed the shapes in a sequence which corresponded with a line of development from a broad-shouldered jar with functional handles like the imports, to cylindrical jars with just a wavy line. Pots of other kinds found in association with those with wavy handles could be tied into that sequence. Gradually all Predynastic pottery was organised in this way establishing a great series. This involved considerable trial and error and the study of other material such as stone vessels and slate palettes.

TABLE Sequence dates of Predynastic Egyptian pottery

PERIOD	SEQUENCE DATE	BC (PETRIE)	BC (MODIFIED)
Tasian	20		
Badarian	21–29	7400	5000–4500
Amratian	30–37		
Gerzean	38–60	5500	4500–3200
Semainean	61–78		
First Dynasty	78–82	4000	3200

Eventually 62 sequence dates (SD) from 20 to 82 were established as shown in the Table.

This sequence has been modified slightly: the Tasian would not be separated from Badarian, post-Badarian would be grouped into Naqada I and II, and the dates are later. Otherwise the essentials of the sequence are those derived by Petrie. The similarity between imported wavy-handled jars from southern Palestine and the local product was so strong that they could not be distinguished by traditional methods. The introduction of scientific measurements of the fabric (in the past decade or so) has revealed that clays of different origin had been used. This emphasises one important factor in scientific measurements on pottery which will be discussed later.

In the Old Kingdom and the First Intermediate Period there is an absence of imported pottery and a sharp change in shape. The variety of shapes disappears and during the First Intermediate period there seems to be a deterioration in the quality of the pottery produced.

The Middle Kingdom and Second Intermediate Period are interesting because the pottery has a wide range of shapes and styles and is marked by the introduction of a two-man pottery wheel. This seems to be a period of well-organised professional potters who were developing new techniques and who were probably influenced by pottery from the Levant and Cyprus.

The New Kingdom is also an interesting period: the blue-painted vases appeared and trade with the Eastern Mediterranean was booming, with the import of such commodities as perfumed oil, cosmetics and perfume from Mycenae and opium from Cyprus. This trade was not just a rich person's prerogative, for Mycenaean sherds have been found in dwellings of the rich and poor. This trade seemed to take place on a large scale: in some minor official's graves one-third of the burials contained imported pottery from the Levant.

Pottery is a very important factor in unravelling the trading habits of ancient man, and this is equally true in Egypt. Archaeologists have developed techniques, based on shapes and styles together with a visual study of clay fabric (colour and texture), for discriminating local production from imported material. Further, they are able to distinguish several types of local ware. This exercise of distinguishing local wares from each other and from imported material is extremely important. As a general rule pottery produced hundreds of kilometres apart is very different and can usually be distinguished visually. However, there are problems as mentioned earlier: for example copies of Palestinian wavy-handled jars were so good that visual techniques were inadequate and more objective methods are required. When sites are close, ten kilometres or so, visual distinction can be hampered by the fact that potters were using similar techniques and raw materials. Colour can be very misleading, because the firing process can change the colour of a pot even when the potter and starting materials are identical.

Over the last century various scientific methods have been developed to offset these difficulties:

(a) classical analysis;
(b) thin section;
(c) atomic absorption;
(d) neutron activation analysis.

These methods are listed in order of development and sophistication, and this is the order they should be applied to a problem. Ceramics produced large distances apart, probably on different continents, can usually be distinguished by methods (a) or (b). As the problem gets more difficult method (c) could help, and method (d) should only be used for the more intractable problems such as distinguishing pottery produced at kiln sites operating within 10 km of each other.

(a) Classical analysis

This technique has been applied to archaeological problems since the middle of the nineteenth century. In the case of pottery the problem is to distinguish one potter's products from another. This is done by identifying differences in the clay used and/or in technique. Classical analysis can be used to measure the major elements present in clay: aluminium, silicon, magnesium, sodium, potassium, calcium and iron. The ratio of these seven elements to each other may distinguish one clay source from another: possibly a Nile silt from a marl clay, but more readily an Egyptian clay from a Greek clay.

In addition, major element analysis can help in identifying the pigments used to colour pottery. The blue-painted pottery of the New Kingdom was thought to be coloured by the blue pigment calcium copper silicate (Egyptian Blue), but analysis has shown that this is more probably a cobalt aluminate. It is possible to indicate that this cobalt aluminate first arose as a by-product of the silver smelting process. An interesting fact, evolving from chemical analysis, is that the cobalt containing silver ore that led to the discovery of this blue pigment most probably came from Bohemia and was introduced to Egypt by the Mycenaeans; there is certainly none in Egypt. It is interesting also that Egyptian Blue is somewhat of a misnomer because large quantities are found in Mycenae and the Levant and little in Egypt.

(b) Thin section

This is the traditional method of the geologist for studying rocks. It involves taking a thin section of the material to be investigated, a few millionths of a metre thick, and examining it under a microscope. The minerals present are identified by their appearance. A semi-quantitative estimate of the concentration of each mineral present can be obtained. This will identify the major minerals and the presence of inclusions like quartz and limestone. In addition, the method gives an indication whether the potter deliberately added limestone or sand as a temper to change the texture of his product.

This is a tedious but relatively cheap method of distinguishing different pottery types and is a useful precursor to more complex methods like neutron activation analysis.

(c) Atomic absorption

With this method, as in (a), the ceramic has to be dissolved, a procedure not without problems. The solution is then sprayed into a flame where the atoms are excited; a light, specific for one element, is shone through the excited atoms and the amount of light absorbed is a measure of the concentration of that element in the ceramic. A different light source (lamp) is required for each element to be determined. For this reason it is unusual to measure more than about ten elements for each sample. This is adequate if the samples to be distinguished are very different, but is unlikely to be successful if the production centres were within a few kilometres.

(d) Neutron activation analysis

The advantages of this method are:
(i)   small samples required;
(ii)   it is very specific, that is, identification of a trace element, say gallium, is unambiguous;
(iii)   element concentrations can be obtained precisely;
(iv)   more importantly, large numbers of elements (about 35) can be determined on one sample.

The disadvantages are:
(i)   a nuclear reactor is required;
(ii)   additional expensive equipment is essential; and
(iii)   the technique is rather slow.

Given that the reactor and expensive equipment are available, this is the only technique to distinguish samples of similar origin.

In essence, the method involves placing the small sample from each pot or sherd in a nuclear reactor where it is made radioactive. This radioactivity is measured carefully to give the concentration of a large number of elements. If 50 samples have been measured, each for 35 elements, then this is a large amount of data which requires a considerable amount of work to unravel. This detailed information, with careful manipulation, is capable of making fine distinctions between samples. For example it is possible to distinguish different silts by their trace element concentrations.

Applications of neutron activation analysis

There have been several applications of neutron activation analysis to Egyptian pottery. A detailed study has been made of Tell el Yahudiyeh ware which was distributed throughout the Levant and Egypt as far south as Nubia in the Middle Bronze Age. The chemical analyses indicate that the most common source of clay is Nile alluvium; interestingly there is also a widely used material defined by the author (Maureen Kaplan) as 'Nile mixture', that is a mixture of alluvium and Pleistocene clay. Since the Pleistocene clay lies below the alluvium, the 'mixture' can be adventitious or deliberate. The latter is more likely because the 'mixture' always contains 20–30 per cent Pleistocene clay. The chemical analyses showed that there were two major production sites of Tell el Yahudiyeh ware using Nile alluvium; these were on the island of

Elephantine at Aswan and the other group consisted of vessels from Faras and Verma.

Kahun is an interesting site, being the home of labourers who built the Sesostris II pyramid. In addition to local pottery made in Egypt there is considerable evidence for imported pottery being found at this site. There have been two separate analyses by neutron activation of pottery from Kahun. It would seem that Egyptian ware is made from Nile alluvium, and the imported pottery (on stylistic grounds) is very different chemically from Egyptian ware. More detailed analyses are in progress to see if differences can be established for Nile alluvium. Professor Noll has pointed out that Nile alluvium is a material low in lime content and there are calcareous clays, high in lime, for example marl clays. Indeed, Professor Noll has indicated that lime content is a useful criterion for the classification of ancient Egyptian pottery. It is interesting to note that lime has a physical effect on pottery production: it makes the clay easier to sinter and hence more waterproof. It would reduce the porosity of the final pot, which is an unsatisfactory result for water containers which need to lose water by evaporation through the pores to keep the water cool. The Kahun pottery is non-calcareous, typical of a pot made from Nile alluvium. There are several analyses of Nile alluvium which indicate that it is a fairly uniform material in that the concentrations of many elements are very similar. Neutron activation analysis is the ideal technique to use in such a situation and this will probably reveal, as some already suggest, slight differences in Nile alluvium at different periods and in different places.

The Manchester Kahun project team has analysed, using neutron activation analysis, some of the pottery excavated by Petrie from rubbish dumps and workers' homes in Kahun. There is no doubt that some of the pottery is imported, the concentration of trace elements being very different to the locally made ware. This confirms previous findings and the archaeological visual inspection of the samples. The local material is very similar to that expected for Nile mud, but interestingly there appears to be more than one type of Nile mud. Further analysis of the data may enable the team to identify the source of the imports, and also, if there is more than one type of import. In the future the project team intend to study the problem of Nile mud in more detail, particularly with respect to variations with time and location.

Related problems could be concerned with Predynastic pottery which is also made from Nile mud.

Problems arise in the study of Egyptian pottery because a large amount of it is made from Nile mud which tends to have a uniform composition. Differences can arise because of different proportions of sand, clay and mud present in the pot. These could be present in the raw material (different flood conditions) or added deliberately by the potter. The Manchester project team will contribute to the study of Egyptian pottery by looking for these additions and measuring a large number of elements (about 30) by neutron activation analysis. This is the only approach for this complex problem and so far is untried.

CHAPTER 10

The Chemical Analysis of the Kahun Metals

Dr G. Gilmore, Universities Research Reactor, Risley

The metal objects found at Kahun were everyday items such as knives, chisels and needles together with mirrors, bowls and, most unexpectedly for an Egyptian site at this time, a neck ornament called a torque. In later times many of these items, particularly the tools, would have been made of iron, but at the time of Kahun iron was unknown and the objects are made of copper alloys. Although Kahun is classed an Early Bronze Age town, not all of the metallic objects were actually made of bronze. This period was one of transition from the copper age, which originated in Pre-dynastic times when naturally occurring 'native' copper was found to be a satisfactory alternative to flint for making tools, to the Bronze Age proper when the superiority of copper alloyed with tin was recognised.

Kahun presents us with an opportunity to examine everyday life in the Middle Kingdom of Egypt in some depth and many interesting questions spring to mind when we consider where the ordinary day-to-day objects, the pottery, the tools and fabrics, might have come from. Were they made in the town itself or were they brought in by way of trade? If they were indeed imported – was this from near or afar? For example, much of the pottery was clearly Aegean in style and the weights and measures were identifiable as Middle Eastern, suggesting these items had been imported in some way. When we look for the source of the copper tools we can not be so sure. There are three possibilities we can consider: that the tools were made in Kahun itself; that they were imported from metal-producing centres in Egypt; or that, in common with some other items, they were imported from distant parts.

At most sites known to have carried out smelting, evidence is available in the form of furnace sites, slags, metal globules and such like. At Kahun, Petrie excavated a caster's shop, complete with moulds for manufacturing knives and hatchets, but this operation would only involve the remelting of copper and there is no direct evidence that smelting was carried on in the town itself.

Some 2000 years later than the lifetime of Kahun, Pliny the Elder, in his *Natural History*, described the qualities of copper from different sources with sufficient confidence to list them in order of excellence. To understand why one copper should be different from another we should look at how the primitive smelters produced their metals.

Metals such as copper are manufactured by smelting. Chemically the process is one of reduction of an oxide to the metal and in antiquity would have been brought about by heating a suitable ore with charcoal – the latter being both fuel for the heating and the agent bringing about the reduction. Copper containing minerals which were not oxides or carbonates (which easily form oxides on heating) could also be used, but these needed pretreatment such as roasting to convert them to a form suitable for smelting.

In ancient times the quality of a metal would depend on the skill of the smelter and on the composition of the ores available to him. Apart from the ores themselves, various other materials are needed in order to free the metal from its chemical combination in the ore.

The metal is associated in the ore with unwanted components collectively referred to as 'gangue' which is separated from the metal by slagging. Extra materials are added to the smelt to produce a silicate – the slag – which is liquid at the temperature of the furnace. In a well-regulated, efficient furnace, the more dense metal will then fall to the bottom of the furnace to form a pool. The lighter slag remains at the top of the furnace and is removed mechanically after the furnace cools or, in a more advanced type of furnace, by tapping off the liquid slag while hot.

We must bear in mind that the primitive smelter lacked the means to analyse his materials chemically and he would have been dependent upon his ability to recognise satisfactory ores and fluxes by their colour or hardness – indeed by any visual or tactile information he could get, perhaps aided by folklore. It is therefore not surprising that a metal could be identified as a product of a particular place by virtue of its quality.

Excavations in the Negev desert at Wadi Timna since 1964 have unearthed several primitive smelting sites. This large area, not too far distant from Kahun, was largely undisturbed and the Israeli archaeologists discovered smelting hearths, some of which predate Kahun and others which were active long afterwards. We can suppose that the site would have been active during the occupation of Kahun and, although there is no evidence to suggest this, we might suppose that copper from Timna could have found its way to Kahun. Whether or not this is true, Timna provides an example of how copper would have been produced at the time of Kahun whether in the town itself or elsewhere.

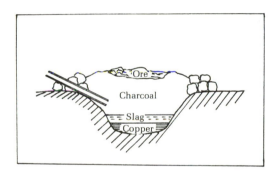

FIGURE 6   An impression of the type of smelting hearth which might have been in use in Egypt at the time of Kahun. The inclined pipe is a tuyère for supplying a forced draught using bellows.

The type of furnace used would probably have been a bowl furnace, little more than a shallow hole in the ground perhaps 20 to 30 cm in diameter. There may have been some sort of arrangement for producing a forced draught possibly blown by bellows. The bowl would have been charged with a mixture of copper ore, charcoal and flux. The copper ores which would have been used then, and are still present now at Timna, were of the oxide type and, since such ores are generally associated with excess silica, we can deduce that an iron-containing flux such as haematite must have been used.

Both the ore and the flux contain impurities and, just as the copper oxide is reduced in the furnace to metallic copper, so some of these impurities would be reduced as well. They would then be incorporated into the copper to an extent depending upon the solubility of the impurity in the copper and the conditions within the furnace. For example, if the temperature of the furnace were high enough the copper would, quite readily, absorb iron from the slag. The resulting iron would be brittle and most unsuitable for tools liable to encounter shock, such as chisels. On the other hand impurities such as arsenic harden copper and are beneficial. Indeed, in some cases arsenic-containing mineral was probably added to achieve just this effect. The smelter himself may not have known what he was adding – just that a little bit of 'this and that' made his copper more desirable.

At first sight, it would be expected that arsenic, a very volatile metal, would be vaporised in the furnace and lost. However, experiments with models of these early furnaces have shown that most of the arsenic is retained in the copper. More knowledgeable smelters might remelt their copper to remove the excess iron and this would further alter the impurity concentrations of the copper. We know that such a process would cause heavy losses of the volatile elements.

The addition of tin to copper, to make a bronze, was almost certainly intentional and represents an advance in technology. Mixed copper/tin ores are rare and the accidental incorporation of tin is much less likely. The tin would probably have been added as the tin oxide, cassiterite, mixed with the copper ore before smelting.

It would seem, then, that the elemental composition of a metal may tell us something of the technological capabilities of the smelters. A high iron concentration, for example, might indicate that the makers of a particular item were not aware that remelting would produce a better copper. Over and above these technological aspects, themselves of considerable interest, we expect that the copper produced would bear, to some extent, the signature of the raw materials used. If each ore has an individual impurity 'pattern' then the copper produced from the ore may retain some of this individuality and, in principle at least, allow the ore to be identified from the composition of any object made from it. We cannot rely upon elements such as arsenic and iron, which might have been deliberately modified, and we must look instead at the trace elements. The hope is that if copper is found with an uncharacteristically high, or low, concentration of a particular element this would reveal a particular source of copper ore. This principle has been of great value in other contexts in identifying the source of silver ores by reference to the concentration of their gold impurity.

In his publication of the Kahun finds Petrie stressed the presence of weights, measures and pottery not native to Egypt, which suggested that immigrant workers were employed in Kahun. If these workers imported their pottery perhaps they also imported their tools. By analysing these tools and comparing them with material from other areas we might find some aspect of their composition, perhaps only in the trace element composition, which would label them as 'foreign'. A decision was therefore made to analyse as many as possible of the Kahun copper objects in the Manchester Museum. There was one factor in our favour, for there were in the Manchester Museum just two samples of copper ore found at Kahun, and an analysis of these might provide an indication of the composition of a locally smelted copper.

The analysis

Several methods of analysis would have been suitable for this study but that chosen was Neutron Activation Analysis (NAA). The technique is exceedingly sensitive and can measure several elements at one time. The major disadvantage of the method, the need for a nuclear reactor, was already solved by the availability of the Universities Research Reactor, owned jointly by Manchester and Liverpool Universities, a short distance away. NAA involves irradiation of the samples within the reactor which, as one might expect, makes them radioactive. It so happens that each of the components of the metal produce a different radioactive isotope which, using suitable equipment, can be separately measured to allow calculation of the concentration of each constituent of the sample.

Although most of the radioactivity is of short half-life and would decay away fairly rapidly, it is not desirable to have museum specimens radioactive to any degree, and instead, small samples were taken from each of the tools. Of course, taking samples from museum exhibits can be a contentious matter but the sensitivity of NAA is such that samples of as little as ten milligrams of copper are sufficient without compromising the ability to determine a range of elements including some trace elements. Moreover the samples need not be destroyed but can be retained for re-analysis in the future should there be a need, avoiding further sampling of the objects. The samples were taken by either drilling or filing tools using a hand-held model-maker's drill and a range of rotary tools including dental burrs. For some samples drills as small as 0.5 millimetres in diameter were used – a test of nerves for the sampler and no room for shaking hands. The drillings, or filings, were carefully collected and eventually weighed into polyethylene irradiation containers.

FIGURE 7   A drill, 0.5 mm in diameter, points to the hole drilled in one of the Kahun axes. The inset shows, at the same scale, the hole drilled in 1898 when the axe was first sampled for analysis.

Different radio-isotopes have different rates of growth and decay. For example, one of the isotopes of copper has a half-life as short as 5 minutes while iron produces an isotope of 45 days half-life. The general procedure in NAA is to use short irradiations, with short decay periods, to measure the short-lived isotopes and long irradiations, followed by long periods of decay, to measure the long-lived isotopes.

Accordingly the samples were irradiated twice – a short irradiation of 3 minutes, to selectively activate copper, tin and indium, and then a much longer irradiation of 7 hours to allow the longer-lived arsenic, antimony, gold, silver, iron, zinc, chromium, cobalt and selenium activities to 'grow'. After each irradiation the samples were measured using a gamma spectrometer. This instrument sorts out the many different gamma rays emitted by the sample by energy and presents them as an understandable spectrum. The position of each peak in the gamma ray spectrum allows each element to be identified and the size of the peak represents the concentration of the element in the sample. Twelve elements in all were measured in each sample. The Achilles Heel of neutron activation analysis, with respect to metals, is lead. This element, although becoming radioactive, does not give an isotope suitable for gamma ray spectrometry. Fortunately, lead is not usually found in substantial amounts in copper or bronze until much later in the Bronze Age and we assumed that the lead concentrations would not be significant. In fact, this assumption does appear to be reasonable since, in most cases, the analysis does account for the whole of the sample.

The reckoning

Kahun stands at a technological cross-roads. In the early history of metalworking use was made of native copper, that is copper occurring naturally as the metal. This was easily recognisable and needed no smelting. Later in his development, man learned how to smelt the simple oxide ores and such pure, or at least unmodified. coppers were in use in the Egyptian Archaic Period of the First and Second Dynasties. Somewhat later, in the Old Kingdom, arsenical coppers made their appearance. Perhaps, in the first place, certain ores which contained high levels of arsenic were found to produce more useful copper. Later it may have been realised that this 'high-tech' copper could be produced from other ores by adding arsenic-containing materials during the smelting.

This technological progression is common to all metal-producing societies and eventually leads to a Bronze Age proper. Egypt is no exception. By the time the New Kingdom arrived almost all copper-based metal which was made was bronze, produced by adding substantial amounts of tin to the copper. Kahun flourished during the period of transition between the arsenical copper age and the bronze age and this is reflected in the analysis of the metals.

All of the Kahun coppers analysed contain arsenic. With one exception the concentrations are such as could have arisen, by chance, from impurities in the copper ore. However, the ore fragments found in the foundation deposits contain less than one

FIGURE 8   The Universities Research Reactor at Risley – a surprising ally for
the Egyptologist.

hundredth of the arsenic found in the samples. If these particular
ore samples are indeed representative of the local copper ores we
would have to conclude either that the metals were not made from
local ores or that arsenic was deliberately added in some way.
Most of the samples also contain tin although in many cases it
would be misleading to call the alloy a bronze. For example, a
particular needle contains 0.55% of tin and 0.46% of arsenic. A
typical bronze would contain, say, 5 to 10% of tin as do some of the
Kahun samples which we can clearly designate as bronze – among
them the torque.

   While a tin concentration of, say, 5% is readily explained away
as deliberate addition, a 0.5% tin is more difficult. This is much
more than would be expected from impurity in the ore and rather
less than we might expect from deliberate addition. Does such a
concentration represent a 'bad lot' of tin ore or was such a low
concentration intended?

   The iron concentration in the tools, averaging 0.6%, is consistent with that expected from copper produced by the smelting of
oxide ores and the refining by remelting. Some of the samples
contained over 1% of iron and it may be that these coppers were
not purified. The highest concentration of iron measured was

3.4% in a *broken* chisel – perhaps no accident bearing in mind that iron renders copper brittle.

Other minor and trace element concentrations present a confusing picture. Certain items contain strangely high levels of particular elements – a needle with almost 1% of silver, for example, whereas all other samples contain less than one tenth of this amount. It would be satisfying to be able to assign significance to the fact that the torque and the bowl contain considerably more gold than all the other samples. It is tempting to suggest that the atypical composition of the torque indicates a foreign origin, a conclusion supported to some extent by the rarity of the torque in Egypt at this time. Such a temptation must be resisted when we consider that the differences in composition are so marginal.

One possible way of looking for order in such a large body of analytical data would be to group together items related in some way and to search for statistical differences between the mean compositions of these groups. For example, we might expect the items designated as 'Group 9' by Petrie, which were all found together, to be more alike in composition than the whole mass of objects. Alternatively, we might suppose that all the knives, or chisels, taken together might show a more consistent composition than the whole. However, this is not the case. It seems that whichever 'meaningful' group of objects are taken it will contain just one or two rogues which destroy the cohesion of the group.

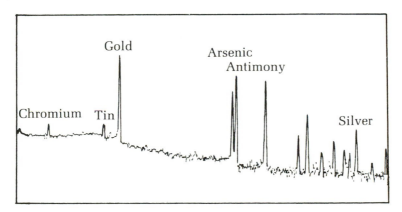

FIGURE 9   A small portion of the gamma spectrum of an irradiated sample taken from a Kahun knife. The position of each peak identifies an element, the area of the peak is related to the concentration of the element.

Comparing the Kahun coppers with those from other areas gives little help either. Copper alloys of the same period from Greece, for example, exhibit the same general patterns – a mixture of copper, arsenical copper and bronze with no obvious distinguishing features.

The model tools, together with one of the copper ore samples, were found in the temple foundation deposits. Most of the Kahun metals were in an excellent state of preservation, but unfortunately the models were found on examination to be completely corroded, without even a metallic core remaining. It would appear that they were immersed in water during their burial. In spite of the obvious possibility that corrosion would itself modify the relative concentrations of copper and the other elements it was decided to analyse the models as far as possible.

In fact, the group of models does turn out to be the most homogeneous group of items. All are arsenical coppers with less than 0.5% of tin and reasonably low iron. But even here we have an 'odd-man-out'. One sample unexpectedly contains 0.3% of silver and a relatively high gold concentration. Again we note the high purity of the copper ore found with the models compared to the composition of the models themselves.

The simplest hypothesis to account for the presence of metal objects at Kahun is that copper was mined, smelted and formed locally. Although there is no direct evidence for this, let us examine the indirect evidence which would suggest that smelting could have been carried out at Kahun. Petrie described in his account of the excavation of Kahun 'fragments of peculiar materials may be noticed, black fibrous haematite; obsidian; large pieces of red oxide of iron, for paint; green carbonate of copper ore; . . .' Now here we have, albeit only in token amounts, two of the materials needed for copper smelting – copper ore and an iron flux. Apart from charcoal, which we may assume to be available, the only other essential ingredient is expertise, for which we need look no further than the immigrant workforce. On several occasions Petrie suggests their origin as Cyprus – an island renowned throughout history for its production of copper. Maybe we see at Kahun not the import of objects, but the import of technology.

At Gurob only 15 miles or so from Kahun, Petrie discovered direct evidence for smelting in the area – but 400 years later in time. In this 18th Dynasty town were found copper ore, copper slag in a crucible, haematite (of several grades), pure tin and orpiment. Orpiment, a mineral used as a dye and pigment, is a significant find, for it consists of arsenic trisulphide – one of the few materials which could have been added to a copper ore to produce an arsenical copper.

Most tantalising of all is a fragment of a papyrus rescued from the cartonnage case of a mummy which refers to 'the copper mines'. Great would have been the rejoicing had sufficient been recovered to tell us where these mines were! Now, of course, none of this proves that extensive metalworking was carried on at Kahun. What it does tell us is that the necessary raw materials were available.

Is the analytical information consistent with the hypothesis? The Kahun coppers are just what we would expect from the smelting of a carbonate ore using an iron flux with the probable addition of an arsenical mineral, such as orpiment, using a simple type of forced draught furnace. We must assume that a tin ore was available for bronze making. It is interesting that copper ore was placed in the foundation deposits along with tools. Would the ore have been placed there at all if the village were not familiar with smelting as an everyday occupation? It has been suggested that the foundation deposits laid beneath the temple were intended for the 'kas' (spirits) of the builders of the temple to enable them to keep it in good repair. Surely there would have been little point in depositing copper ore unless those 'kas' were able, as in real life, to use the ore to make and repair their tools.

It is more than likely that if, as we now suppose, smelting were carried out at Kahun, the actual site would be outside the township itself – near the mine source of the copper perhaps. Then, as now, the smelting industry would not make a pleasant neighbour. We should not, perhaps, be surprised that in an excavation limited to the town itself no direct evidence was found of metal production. We can but hope that any future expedition to Kahun will give some attention to the outlying parts of the town and its surroundings to search for more tangible evidence.

CHAPTER 11

Kahun: The Textile Evidence

by Joan Allgrove McDowell

'Who could have ventured a hope for a complete, untouched and unencumbered town of the 12th Dynasty? It is a prize beyond all probability.'

So W.M. Flinders Petrie wrote in his *Journal*, which survives in manuscript at the Petrie Museum, London. It is typical of the man that he was so excited by a mere workmen's village – an emotion not shared by many archaeologists of his day. As busy as ever he was, he supervised during two seasons, 1889–90 and 1890–91, the four sites of Illahun, Kahun, Gurob and Hawara. His careful recording, aided by his impressive knowledge of tools, techniques and terminology, has given us a unique insight into the textile crafts carried out in the houses of the Kahun workforce, where previously there was only pictorial evidence of 12th Dynasty workshop production.

The collections of tools, now in Manchester Museum and the Petrie Museum, London, cover flax preparation (with a rare flax-stripper), spinning, weaving and finishing of linen cloth, cording and netting with linen, palm and rush fibre, as well as basketry, matting and sandal-making of rush and palm. Every-where there are signs of the careful use of materials and of the recycling which is still part of Egyptian life – nothing was wasted, it seems – and since handles were made of textile fibre, where today they are of plastic, tools and containers used by Kahun's inhabitants can be reconstructed. The fragments of dyed wool are perhaps the single most important find, but quite extraordinary is the almost total absence of woven cloth or garments, a problem we shall return to later.

FIGURE 10   a) and b) Weaving sequence. Tomb of Khnumhotep, Beni Hasan. (Newberry, op. cit.) and H. Hodges, *Ancient Technology*, p. 98).

Egypt's linen cloth was famous in the ancient world for, as well as making prodigious amounts for mummification, it was one of her chief exports. Despite the millions of metres of bandaging now in the world's museums, however, no systematic study has been made of this superficially unexciting material and the opportunity of recording an important collection from a Middle Kingdom dwelling site like Kahun is indeed welcome.

Some of Egypt's earliest textiles are also the finest, and cloth of the Predynastic period shows fully developed techniques. This disconcerting phenomenon, familiar to Egyptologists, has presented modern scholars with evidence of the taming of the Nile, a sophisticated, centralised government, and the mastery of crafts like hard stone-cutting at the beginning of the Dynastic period, all arguing a long history as yet unknown to us. In the case of textiles, their making is such an early and fundamental activity that in many cultures, including nomadic ones, weaving goes back to their early history but, even so, is preceded by plaiting, cording, basketry and mat-making. But, whereas rushes, skins and wool can be utilised by hunting and herding societies, linen can be produced on any scale only by a sedentary population.

The Egyptian language included hieroglyphs for *linen*, and for *fine linen*, and all showing a weaver's comb or beater: indicating an organised industry and quality control when the written language was in its infancy.

The 12th Dynasty, towards the end of the Middle Kingdom, is an important watershed in Egyptian textile history, when old techniques were about to meet competition from new tools and methods which are thought to have been introduced by the Hyksos, and which include a different form of spindle-whorl and the vertical loom.

Of the four major natural textile fibres: linen, cotton, wool and silk, linen and wool were known in Egypt from earliest times. And, whereas the wool of prehistoric Europe has disappeared, leaving only a partial picture of textile activity, Egypt's dry and sterile soil has preserved both animal and vegetable material, giving evidence of wool and of vegetable fibres like linen, rush, papyrus and palm-fibre, dating from about 5500 BC.

A number of Predynastic sites have provided indications of cloth production. In 1913 Peet discovered, in the dwellings of a small farming village at Abydos of about 5500 BC, spindle-whorls of groundstone and bone, loom-weights and needles, pointing to domestic activity. The Predynastic settlements of Omari, south-east of Cairo, and investigated between 1944 and 1952 by Debono but not yet published, yielded skins, flax seeds (*L. usitatissi-mum*), mats, spindle-whorls, bone needles and cloth. Even earlier is the Neolithic site of Kom W. in the northern Fayoum, dating from 6000 BC and excavated by G. Caton-Thompson in 1924–6. Whorls and signs of flax-growing were found on this site, dating from the long transitional phase of climate changes between c.7000 and 6000 BC, when hunter-gatherers were altering their lifestyle, first to seasonal settlements, then to village and mixed-farming communities. In this respect, and in trade links and communications with desert peoples, the Fayoum was a crucial area in Egypt's development, but its independent culture was to be submerged by that of Upper Egypt after unification.

The recent reassessment and fresh investigation of old sites by a new generation of archaeologists and prehistorians like M. Hoffman puts the pioneering work of Petrie and those like him in their proper perspective, and the picture which is emerging is an exciting one. A continuous history – with gaps caused by lack of evidence – of life along the Nile and in the adjoining regions goes back to the Palaeolithic Age, and the independent growth in North and South does not necessarily require the incursion of a

FIGURE 11   Weaving sequence. Tomb of Khnumhotep, Beni Hasan. (Newberry).

'dynastic race' to explain the high level of culture in the land after unification.

The flax plant, which is believed to have originated in the Near East, does not seem to have grown in its wild form (*L. angustifolium*) in ancient Egypt, for seeds of only the two main domesticated varieties, *L. humile* and *L. usitatissimum*, which superseded it, have been found. At first possibly only the seeds were gathered for their oil, which would augment other food oils like sesame and castor oil, and other plant-fibres such as grasses, reeds and papyrus were used for the plaiting and making of non-woven cloth, mats and rope. Even after the properties of its fibres were known, the plant may have been gathered in its wild state, before it was grown as a crop. It requires a settled agricultural community to grow and tend the crop, a rich soil and a good water supply – which would pre-suppose taming the waters of the

FIGURE 12   Horizontal loom. Tomb of Khnumhotep, Beni Hasan. (Ling Roth, *Ancient Egyptians & Greek Loom*).

Nile – and the skill to carry out the quite complex processes of preparing the fibres for spinning.

The growing, harvesting and preparation of flax was hard manual work, and was done by men. It grows to a height of about one metre in a short time, and favours a sandy soil. The earliest evidence of its growth is in the Fayoum and Delta regions, as we have seen. In the Dynastic Period, as today, it was a winter crop, sown in mid-November and harvested toward the end of March of our calendar, the harvesting dictated to some extent by the use to which the crop was to be put. The stem has a thick, woody core and a hard outer covering, with the bast fibres between. Half-ripe yellow stems were soft enough to produce good quality thread, but if the plant was harvested too early the fibres would be weak, and if left until the plant was completely ripe the fibres would be fit only for mats and rope. It was pulled out of the ground, not cut, an activity often shown in tomb-paintings, and sorted into evenly-sized bundles. After drying in the sun for a short time, the rippling process was carried out with a coarse comb-like wooden tool known as a flax-stripper, of which one from Kahun is in the Manchester Museum. This would break up the hard outer fibres of the flax stalks and separate the seed capsules, from which oil was made. Rippling facilitates the next operation of retting, or soaking the stems in water. This could last for up to fourteen days, allowing fermentation which helped to soften and separate the bast fibres from the woody parts. Retting is often shown in Middle Kingdom tomb-paintings, taking place in a square tank, though sometimes the fibres are seen boiling in a pot. After retting, it was possible to separate the bast fibres from the rest. This was done by hand before the New Kingdom. Then they were beaten to soften them further, scraped (scutching), and combed or hackled with a heavy saw-toothed beater. It is said of flax that the rougher it is treated the better, although a skilled operator knows how far he can go without damaging the bast fibres. There is no doubt that the time and effort put into fibre preparation by the ancient Egyptians contributed in no small way to the excellence of the finished cloth. The combination of drying, soaking and beating resulted in smooth, silky grey fibres ready to be combed and rolled into bundles of parallel fibres known as rovings, for spinning.

At some stage scouring and bleaching must take place; if textiles are to be dyed, before dyeing. Linen fibres could be put through this process either before or after weaving, or both, and it will be described later, as part of cloth finishing.

The object of spinning is to make a long, continuous thread from fibres too short to weave in their natural state, and spinning and twisting cause individual scaly projections of the fibres to adhere to each other along their irregular surfaces. The resulting thread should have strength and elasticity. Hand-spinning is simple to do but nevertheless requires skill, which has always been abundant in Egypt. Tomb-paintings and models, which generally depict workshops, show women spinners, though from the time of Herodotus to today men have spun as well. It has been traditionally a domestic activity, taken up when there is leisure for it and easily put down again, whether in the home or at today's tourist sites, where one encounters an occasional male guard spinning between parties of visitors. 'In the production of clothing and thread these people were not at all behindhand', wrote Petrie, and at Kahun spindles and whorls were found in the workmen's houses, to be taken up and put down at will, as women and children still do all over the Near and Middle East while minding the sheep, cattle or goats or gossiping with their neighbours. As well as providing thread for the family's use, it could earn the maker a little extra income.

The most primitive form of spinning was done with the finger and palm of the hand, or by rolling the fibres between hand and thigh (seen at Beni Hasan), but the spindle was a very early invention, as we have seen.

There are two important and near-contemporary sources of evidence for the use of the textile tools from Kahun. The first is at Beni Hasan, about 150 kilometres south of Kahun, on the Nile's east bank and in the old Oryx nome of Upper Egypt. The provinces had enjoyed comparative independence since the First Intermediate Period, and the rulers and high officials lived much like the feudal princes of medieval Europe and were buried in their own lands. The end of the 12th Dynasty saw the end of decentralisation, however, and direct power invested again in the Pharaoh's person. At Beni Hasan the last of the great figures of the period built themselves rock-cut tombs in the limestone cliffs, with painted scenes. Many of these belonged to nomarchs of the 12th Dynasty (c. 1991–1786 BC), and their families, and can be dated by inscriptions; four were painted with scenes showing textile production.

Tomb 2 of the North Group was built for Amenemhet, Governor

of the Oryx nome, who died in the 43rd year of the Pharaoh Usertsen I (Sesostris I, 1971–1928 BC). He calls himself 'Sem-Master of all the tunics' and 'Superintendent of Weaving' and on his tomb walls, among other industries for which he was responsible, are scenes of flax cultivation, steeping flax in water (retting), in what looks like a small enclosure, beating flax, rovings being placed in a box, rope-making and the folding of cloth. All the operators are men. In the tomb of Khnumhotep II (Tomb 3, North Group), who bore the same titles as Amenemhet and who was buried in the sixth year of Usertsen II (Sesostris II), the Pharaoh who built the pyramid at Illahun and Kahun, are the same scenes of flax-beating as well as rope-making, women weavers and a woman holding a spindle, watched by a male overseer. Tomb 17 of the South Group was occupied by Khety, among whose titles were 'Master of linen and linen manufacturers', 'Superintendent of weavers' and 'Superintendent of washing of linen'. The north wall of this tomb was painted with rows of women spinning, netting and weaving while opposite, on the south wall, is a colossal painted figure of Khety himself, holding his staff and baton of office while an attendant holds a parasol over his head and another carries his sandals. Baqt III (Tomb 15) goes one better as 'Superintendent of linens and linen-makers, spinners and twine-makers', and his tomb shows similar scenes.

Many of the paintings, until recently in parlous condition, were copied during the nineteenth century, at different dates and each differing slightly in detail. They undoubtedly record one of the important industries of the region during the Middle Kingdom, cloth production, the organisation of which was apparently in the hands of the Governor. Although they display workshop conditions, the various tasks carried out by individuals would not be beyond a worker at home. Although restored in the 1980s, the Beni Hasan paintings still present problems. Flax preparation, spinning and rope-making are repeated often enough for comparison, and are identical. It is the looms which have caused difficulties of interpretation, as they appear to be vertical in the tomb scenes, which has caused some scholars to assert that Egyptians of the Middle Kingdom knew the vertical loom. We shall return to this matter later, when discussing the loom. Suffice it to say that the other source of evidence for textile production of the Middle Kingdom, tomb models, which were the predecessors of servant statuettes or *shabtis* and which were placed in tombs from the 5th Dynasty onward, to ensure that the deceased owner had squads of labourers and craftsmen to hand in the afterlife, agreed with the Beni Hasan scenes where flax-preparation, spinning and rope-making are concerned.

To return to spinning, the spindle and whorl shown at Beni Hasan and found in numbers at Kahun was in common use at least from Predynastic times (and whorls are found much earlier) up to the end of the Middle Kingdom, when alternative forms were introduced, although it was never entirely abandoned. The spindle is a slender, shaped wooden stick, at Kahun varying from 7 to 15 cm long, pointed at one end for insertion into the whorl and rounded at the other, with a spiral groove into which the thread was attached. The whorl has a central hole to take the spindle end, and can be made of bone, pottery or wood. The Kahun whorls are of wood and are of the early type, namely a flat, round disc. Spindles and whorls are smoothed and polished, to avoid catching the thread, and several whorls in this collection have traces of mud or stucco, which might have supported paint on their surfaces.

Before beginning, the spinner must place the roving comfortably, leaving both hands free. The distaff is a much later invention, introduced into Egypt in the Roman period, and at this time the bundle of fibres was held under the arm or rolled into a ball and placed in a pot. Beni Hasan shows the pot method and in one painting the spinner is standing, scantily clad to avoid tangling the thread with her clothing.

The three types of hand-spinning with this spindle and whorl were used in ancient Egypt – all appear in the tombs of Baqt and Khety at Beni Hasan. They are the grasped spindle method, when spindle and thread are held in the hands, the supported spindle, when the spindle is rolled against the thigh, and the suspended spindle method, which is probably the most common since it produces stronger thread. To start spinning with the dropped spindle method, a length of prepared fibres is fastened in the groove at the spindle end, below the whorl, then the spindle is rotated and more fibres are paid out through the spinner's finger and thumb. The spindle's weight causes it to fall slowly, pulling the rotating thread with it, and when it has reached the ground, the spinner will pick it up, wind the spun thread into a ball and start again.

The fibres are wetted before spinning, often between the lips, and linen has a predisposition to twist naturally to the right (known as S-twist) when wet. Although the spinner can choose the spin direction, she is unlikely to slow down the work by going against the natural inclination of the fibre, so the vast majority of ancient Egyptian thread is S-twist, a useful criterion when the origin of a specimen is unknown.

Thread is spun with its ultimate purpose in mind, and a skilled spinner knows which type of spin to choose: tightly-spun or 'high-twist' thread for warps, which must be strong, coarse fibres for heavy cloth, and finer fibres and looser twist for wefts when a smooth surface for the cloth is required. Middle Kingdom tomb scenes and models show women spinners seated or standing to spin, and also depict spinning with two spindles at once, a method needing very great skill which does not seem to have survived.

Spun yarn could be made thicker and stronger by plying or twisting several threads together, generally in the opposite direction to that in which it was spun, so that ancient Egyptian plied thread is most commonly S-spun and Z-plied. However, a considerable number of S-plied threads were found among the Kahun examples. What Petrie called 'string' is 3 to 6-plied coarse linen thread, tightly plied for strength.

The comparatively small amount of spun thread from Kahun is S-spun, and most of it is medium fine, with some coarse. There is also some very fine and tightly spun linen among the weaver's waste, arguing that high-quality cloth was woven, and a fragment of netting made with very fine yarn. There is 2-, 3-, and 4-plied thread but some of it is unusual in being S rather than Z-plied. Sewing thread is consistently S-spun, Z 2-plied linen.

The wool is all S-spun and Z 2-plied, loose and medium tight. The weaving tools from Kahun may be few in number but, with the spindles and spun thread, they tell us a good deal about the weaving practice of the town. There is no trace in Egypt of very primitive weaving apparatus like the back-strap loom; the earliest and only loom until the Second Intermediate Period, the horizontal or ground loom, is simple but by no means primitive. It is still used by village and tribal weavers in the Near and Middle East because it is versatile and can be easily packed up and transported on migration. It first appears in Egypt painted on a pottery dish from a Badarian woman's tomb, and is the loom used by weavers of Kahun, who left a loom beam and heddle-jacks behind them. The vertical or upright loom is thought to have been introduced into Egypt from Western Asia by the Hyksos in about 1600 BC. This loom has a row of weights attached to the bottom end of the warps instead of a cloth beam, can produce wider cloth and the weavers shown using it are generally men. However, the horizontal loom, in true Egyptian fashion, remained in use.

It consists of two strong wood beams, the warp and the cloth beam, each of which is supported by pegs driven into the ground. The warps are stretched over the beams and the weaver weaves from the cloth-beam end. It is more difficult to roll up finished cloth, so very long lengths are easier to weave on the vertical loom, but one advantage of the ground loom is that it allows the insertion of a number of heddle-rods. Despite theories that loom-weights on a site indicate the vertical loom, they can also be used to hang from the four corners of the ground loom, to keep the warps evenly spaced.

To manufacture plainweave two heddle-rods are inserted across the warps, each carrying an alternate set of warps wrapped round it and fastened by string loops. By raising one rod a complete set of alternate warps is lifted higher than the others, making a space or shed through which the weft shuttle is passed from one side of the loom to the other. Then this rod is lowered and the other is raised to make the counter-shed which allows the weft to return. The heddle-rods are supported by pairs of stones or heddle-jacks. No fewer than seven of the latter were found in Kahun, all of them of wood, roughly shaped to fit the heddle-rod, four of light weight and the other three of heavy, hard wood. One has also been used as a mallet. In addition, three small model heddle-jacks of painted wood survive, possibly made to amuse children and awaken their interest in weaving.

As previously mentioned, some scholars have interpreted the type of loom in the Beni Hasan tomb paintings as the vertical loom, for instance, where it appears upright in the tomb of Khnumhotep, with a woman squatting at either side of it. But clear indication of heddle-rods and jacks points to the fact that we are looking at a horizontal loom which is conforming to the same rules of perspective as painted tables or ponds. The most accurate picture of this loom is given by the tomb-models of weavers' workshops, where it is on the floor, has heddle-rods and jacks and may vary in width from a narrow one with one operator to a wider version with two weavers who pass a thread-loaded shuttle to either side of the loom, lifting alternate heddle-rods. The tomb-model from the Theban tomb of Mekhet-Re of the 12th Dynasty (about 1991 BC), now in the Cairo Museum, shows two seated female spinners and three standing, the latter drawing unspun thread from pots on the ground. Other women are warping and, at the back right, is a ground loom with heddle-rods, jacks and two women weavers squatting at the cloth beam. This loom has woven cloth on it while at another loom a man is adjusting the warp.

This equipment, virtually unchanged, wove all the known types of cloth down to the end of the Middle Kingdom, from very fine, almost transparent fabric to medium-fine for clothing, household purposes and for mummy wrappings, and coarse sackcloth often found re-cycled as packing for mummies.

Before weaving can begin, the warp threads must be arranged on the loom. As tomb-models show us, warping for the ground loom was done by winding spun threads round three or four stakes driven into the ground, or into a wall, in a figure-of-eight, as many times as warps were required. They were transferred direct to the loom and stretched taut between the two beams, with two thin cross-pieces or lease-rods inserted across weftways, to help hold them in place. During warping the warps were separated into two sets on the heddle-rods, as already described.

The loom was now ready for the making of plainweave, for which it was well suited, which is one reason for its success for so long. The Egyptians seem not to have favoured fancy weaves or dyed patterned textiles, possibly because by far the greatest demand was for cloth for ritual purposes, and because of their obsessional attitude to personal hygiene and linen of the purest white. There are, however, some examples of self-patterning, that is, variations in texture given by using warp or weft of looser spin or different thickness, which appears as stripes or bands in the cloth. Pleating has survived from the 11th Dynasty, from Deir-el-Bahri, and a Middle Kingdom example of the weft-loop technique, which gives a looped pile once thought to be no earlier than the Roman period, was found at Qerna.

Simple plainweave, or plainweave tabby, is ideal for linen and is sometimes called 'linen weave'. It is an over-1, under-1 weave and doubtless in very early times weft thread was passed over and under alternate warps with the fingers, or with a needle or peg, before the introduction of the shuttle. And the other innovation which made weaving quicker and gave a more regular surface was the heddle-rod, described on page 236. When several rows of weaving were completed, the wefts were packed closely together with a wood beater or 'weaver's sword'.

Weaving is by no means the end of cloth manufacture, however, for after the cloth is cut off the loom it may still be greyish-brown in colour and the Egyptians preferred better-quality cloth to be almost white. So it would be beaten to improve its surface, washed and bleached in the sun, during which time it was regularly sprinkled with water. The tomb-paintings already mentioned show washing and bleaching being carried out by men wearing aprons and working on the bank of a river or canal. They wet the cloth, rub it with a detergent like natron or potash, pound it on a stone with wooden clubs, rinse it in running water, then lay it out to dry and bleach in the hot sun. This was professional work, 'Chief Royal Bleacher' being an early title. Papyrus Sallier (II.8,2) pities the laundryman and the bleacher:

> The laundryman launders on the banks of the river, a
> neighbour of the crocodile . . . When he puts on the apron of a
> woman, then he is in woe . . . I weep for him spending the day
> under the rod.

Finally, the cloth surface would be polished with a smooth flat stone or something similar of a size and shape to be held comfortably in the hand. Petrie describes four 'curious balls of leather' and states that they were for 'fulling cloth', but fulling is a finishing process for woollen cloth, which mats it and then raises the surface, and the four oval leather balls, filled with leather cuttings, are more likely to have been polishers for linen. Dressing agents, of some kind of sizing or other gelatinous substance, may have been added during the finishing, though none is documented.

Evenly-spun and woven linen cloth has been excavated in Badarian burials of about 5000 BC, with a thread count of 8 to 10 warps and 10 to 16 wefts per square centimetre (expressed as $8{-}10 \times 10{-}16 = 1$ sq. cm), and in Predynastic times finer and closer fabric, $18 \times 10 = 1$ sq. cm, was woven. Among the finest is cloth from the tomb of the 1st Dynasty king Djer at Abydos, with a thread count of 64 × 48 = 1 sq. cm, the equivalent of fine cambric. Compared to these counts, even the few remaining samples of spun linen and cloth from Kahun tell us that its weavers made cloth of as good quality, fine to medium-fine, as some of their ancestors.

According to Petrie, Kahun cloth, almost all of which is now missing, varied from 'the finest', with a count of '94 × 54 = 1 sq. inch' (36–38 × 20–22 = 1 sq. cm), and 'the coarsest about half that number'. This cannot be wholly verified, unfortunately, the surviving scraps being medium-fine, 12–20 × 15–20 = 1 sq. cm. A single exception is a fragment of open-weave linen with a corded, loop-fringe selvedge, which has a count of 30 × 15 = 1 sq. cm.

The pictorial evidence at Beni Hasan, and the titles of several of the nomarchs, argues a considerable linen industry in that region during the 11th and 12th Dynasties. Whether this industry supplied the Royal capital at Lisht we do not know, but it seems likely.

We also know that the labour-force for national building projects was paid in kind with housing, food and oil, sandals and linen. The weaving at Kahun, its quantity, purpose and the manner in which it was produced can only be topics for speculation, based on knowledge of weaving in other, similar communities. A good deal of spinning was done and, although this requires skill, it is not a specialist activity. It would take perhaps three spinners to keep two weavers and one loom supplied with thread. Weaving is more specialised, and even a small loom would take up a room in an average Kahun house, so space must have been set aside for it. We have seven heddle-jacks, and used in pairs they are evidence for four looms, whereas there are scores of spindles and whorls.

Studies of village communities today – and of Britain before the Industrial Revolution – suggest that cloth is often woven by specialists in their own homes but on a professional basis, known as 'cottage industry'. Their cloth may be sold by them, or through middle-men, who buy the cloth or provide thread and pay the weavers for their work. One of the oldest Egyptian words for *weaver* is '*b.t*, and a similar word for maidservant is *b3k.t*, implying that women habitually wove in the home and, where it was a wealthy one, that women servants wove. So we are left with three possibilities: that the Kahun workmen were paid in the form of linen made in a large, state-owned workshop, like those recorded at Beni Hasan, that the Kahun weavers wove the cloth which paid the workforce, or that they wove only for their own requirements.

The latter is unlikely, and the evidence of fine and medium fine cloth suggests that they wove cloth to sell, as well as keeping their families supplied. It is also possible that the preparation of linen fibres for spinning, a lengthy and skilled process and a male activity, was not carried out by the male inhabitants of the town but done by other specialists and the rovings supplied to the spinners.

The other craft requiring linen thread, of which Kahun has provided examples, is netting, which reached a high standard. It is a looping or knotting technique, worked with a continuous thread to make an even, open-work fabric which is ideal in coarser form for fishing-nets and for carrying home the catch, for hunting wild animals by driving them into nets – activities often carved or painted on tomb walls – and in the home, where the Kahun pieces come from, as bags and containers to make the carrying of large jars easier. Netting is another ancient technique, and the earliest specimens are finely and intricately made.

All the surviving netting reels from Kahun are of wood, carefully cut and grooved – one has a short length of thread still in the groove. Only one of them is roughly made. A smooth surface is important for all textile tools, so that the thread does not catch. Netting needles, also known as bobbins or shuttles, were also found. These are flat pieces of wood, some of them curved, and varying in length from 14 to 28 cm, and tapering to a point at one end where there is an eye, Y-shaped, triangular or round. A flat wood gauge is necessary, to make sure that the squares or mesh will be even, but none of these appear to be in the collections and, in any case, a small, flat piece of wood with no distinctive markings would be virtually impossible to identify unless excavated with other netting tools.

Having anchored the thread by tying it in a loop to a stationary object (fishermen traditionally use a toe for this) a series of either knots or loops, depending on the kind of netting under construction, is made round the gauge. At the end of a row the gauge is removed, and subsequent rows are made through the loops of the previous rows, still looping or knotting round the gauge. Netting is illustrated in the tomb of Khety at Beni Hasan.

The netting from Kahun is knotted and made of linen thread,

tightly twisted. There are three fragmentary bags, two of them made with one strand of thread and of 9 cm and 1 cm mesh respectively, and one has the top border and a string tie remaining. The third bag has a ring at the base, and is strongly made of coarse thread doubled, with a close 2 cm mesh.

What little sewing was found is of high quality, and needles, of copper and bronze, are well made. The finest is 1 mm thick, and all of them are long by today's standards, from 10 to 15 cm in length. A bone needle-case containing a threaded copper needle and wood pin or bodkin emphasises the care with which these tools were kept by their owners. In addition, there are thirteen balls of fine S-spun linen thread, some of it pale brown and blue, and each wound on a core of textile waste, ready for sewing.

Perhaps the strangest find at Kahun is what Petrie describes as 'a set of tent-pegs' (*Illahun, Kahun and Gurob, 1889–90*, p.11), with ends of rush-fibre rope still knotted round one of them. Made of wood and measuring about 12.5 cm, each one is cut with a large, round head and a deep groove for rope. They are not loom-pegs, nor are they ordinary, all-purpose pegs, of which several were also found in the dwellings of the town. There are five of them, hardly a 'set' large enough for pitching a tent, although Petrie does imply that they were together when discovered. We cannot know on such slender evidence whether the Kahun townsfolk had any dealings with tented people, but it remains an intriguing possibility.

A number of other fibres are preserved from Kahun. They are all commonly found in Egypt, and all represent techniques which must have predated loom-weaving. Since spindle-whorls have been found on sites as early as the Palaeolithic in Egypt, the Near East and Europe, the use of non-spun fibres must go back to the dawn of mankind's history, when primitive societies were experimenting with plants which were to hand. Their observation of Nature may have prompted them to plait and interlace grasses and reeds to provide shelter, containers and clothing. These techniques, evolved so far back in the past, can still be seen in Egyptian villages today.

P.E. Newberry published the plant material from Kahun, among which was the Nile acacia, common now in villages, where its pods are still used for tanning, and the fruits of two palms, the date and the Dom, the latter a tall palm valued for its fruit and fibre, found on Predynastic sites and the commonest basket fibre in the Dynastic Period. One of the most interesting finds is a body-sling, now in Manchester Museum, made of fourteen fibre cords interwoven with narrow linen strips with a thick loop at either end, through which rope was attached. This kind of sling is still used all over the world for cropping the fruits of tall palm trees by small, lithe men or boys who appear to run up the palm trunk at great speed.

Young, green palm branches, being pliable, were the best material for interlacing and fibres were obtained by shredding, splitting and drying the stems. Five head rings, now in the Manchester Museum, and similar to those worn by village women nowadays to support the heavy water jars they carry on their heads, are made of a palm-fibre core round which is wound tightly Z-twisted fibres, one of three cords and the other of two cords, the ends skilfully knotted together. At the Petrie Museum there is a similar ring made of rush fibre.

The fibres of wild grasses, rushes, reeds and papyrus, which grew in the marshes of the open country beyond the limit of cultivation, were put to innumerable uses and have survived in numbers at Kahun. These fibres require far less preparation than flax. The plant stems were cut with a sickle and reeds and rushes were dried and carefully split, while papyrus fibres were a by-product of coarse rinds left after the inner pith of the plant had been removed to make writing material, and were made into thick rope for heavy use, like hauling stones.

All these fibres were used to make rope, handles, baskets and other containers, as well as sandals, boats and sailcloth. Ropemaking is shown at Beni Hasan, in the tombs of Amenemhet and Khnumhotep, where men stand twisting together by hand two cords which are fastened to a post in the ground, to give greater leverage. The rope was then beaten with a wood mallet and soaked in a vat to increase its strength.

Rope was also made of flax and palm fibre. Petrie comments (*Kahun, Gurob and Hawara*, p.28): 'It was usually of two strands, but sometimes it was thrice doubled, giving eight strands.' Most of this rope is in the Petrie Museum, while plaited linen cords are in the Manchester Museum, and both museums have twisted rope handles for jars and baskets. Cord or rope also made handles for tools, and Petrie describes his first-aid on one specimen, a flint knife with binding on the handle:

made of fibre lashed round with a cord. When found this
was tender, but by wrapping it in paper I took it home*
safely, and then toasting it over a stove I dropped melted
wax on it until it was saturated, thus the binding is now
unalterable. This suggested that other flint knives may
have been similarly handled when in use. Such a handle
would leave no traces on flint after it had dropped away.
(*Illahun, Kahun and Gurob*, p.12)

In addition, there are unused rush fibres, finely split and
twisted into hanks or wound into balls on potsherd cores.

In a home with very little furniture, containers are indispens-
able for storing anything from clothes and grain to chickens.
They are also needed for carrying agricultural and building
materials and even act as coffins for the poor. In ancient Egypt
the most common container for these purposes was the basket.
Petrie found a rush basket with tools in it in a corner of a
Kahun house.

The materials, date-palm (the most common), rush and
papyrus, were all to hand and baskets were doubtless made by
most of the population. Both coiling and twining were practised,
using the fingers. Coiling, which was also used in sandal-
making, is one of the oldest fibre crafts, preceding weaving and
having little affinity with it. Beginning with a base made of a
bunch of fibres wound into a flat coil, the basket is built up by
wrapping the fibres spirally and fastening each row to the previous one with firmly-sewn stitches of the same material, to
achieve the shape required, which is commonly round with a
flat or pointed lid. Twining, where single fibres or bunches of
them are interlaced with the fingers on a square base, does
resemble primitive forms of weaving. Wrapping, although
another form of twining, requires stitching, for a wrapping
thread passes round the fibre or bundle, over two, under one,
etc.

The ancient Egyptians did not decorate these mundane articles with dyed fibres, but relied on the natural texture and
colour of the fibres and the method of manufacture to give
patterning, while the baskets are usually of pleasing shape.
Petrie commends a flat, square type, 'most thoughtfully

* He was living in a tent at the time.

designed, with a wooden bottom bar, rope corners, six fine ropes up the sides to distribute the pressure, retained in place by a cross rope, and ending in a twisted rope handle, the top edge having a fine rope binding' (*Kahun, Gurob and Hawara*, p.28).

Allied to basketry is matting, which can also be made by twining, but another technique evolved using a mat-loom, which is close to weaving proper and is transitional from non-woven fabrics, i.e. made with the fingers, to the weaver's loom. It may have been discovered during interlacing that the flexible foundation fibres, which were probably placed side-by-side on the ground, were easier to handle and gave a better tension if they could be kept taut, and for this purpose the mat-frame evolved. The form of mat-frame used by some Beduin today to make papyrus mats is similar to the one shown in the tomb of Khety at Beni Hasan, with the warps stretched over the frame and the wefts being threaded by hand over and under the warps. No heddle or shed is used. The Beduin mat-frame is semi-vertical, while the one at Beni Hasan appears to be horizontal and a male weaver is putting in the wefts by hand. A wood beam from Kahun, now in the Manchester Museum, may be part of a mat-loom. Measuring 97.5 cm long, 8 cm wide and 3 cm deep, it has 28 holes along its length, 4 cm apart. Petrie remarks on the similarity between the matting of Kahun and the modern *hasira*, but he confuses the mat-loom and the true loom by referring to shuttle and beater. Pieces of this serviceable matting in the Petrie Museum are made with tufts about 1 cm apart, and bound together with thick rope edges. In two examples this is double. Patterning is made by the direction of the fibres.

Matting was used extensively by rich and poor alike, for walls, floors and roofing of their houses. Architecture imitated matting – the false door inside Royal tombs of the Old Kingdom was carved to look like rolled-up matting, a reminder of the palace, where it could be let down as a door or a blind to keep out the sun's heat, while coloured mat-patterns are found on ceilings and walls of the nobles' tombs at Beni Hasan. Matting also made beds, seats and bags and, like baskets, the poor man's shroud or coffin from prehistoric times.

Although not a textile material, leather involves sewing techniques and may be discussed here. Since cattle were reared on a large scale there was no shortage of leather in ancient Egypt,

although Petrie found hippopotamus hide at Kahun as well.
Leather had many uses: for the army it was made into shields,
quivers and even body armour until the New Kingdom. A little-
known use was for loin-cloths for labourers, and a finer type for
religious ritual, of hide skilfully slit at regular intervals to
produce a kind of mesh when worn. Leather strips were also
interlaced across beds and made seats for chairs and stools, as
an alternative to rush. Kahun provides examples of rawhide
thongs, wound or plaited round the handles of tools. But by far
the most common leather artefact must have been footwear,
for the army, the national workforce and for the general
populace.

Sandal-making can be seen in tomb-paintings and, once
again, Beni Hasan gives nearly contemporary evidence of a
sandal-maker's workshop, in the tomb of Amenemhet, Governor
of the Oryx nome. He also bore the title 'Overseer of horns,
hooves, feathers and minerals', and was probably responsible
for collecting the government tax on leather. Part of the tanning
process is seen in the famous 18th Dynasty tomb of Rekhmire
at Thebes. A hide is being taken from a pot containing perhaps
acacia pods or urine, the chief tanning agents, and hides are
being cut to sandal-shapes. One man is using a piercer to make
a hole which will take a thong. The sandal-maker's tools are
clearly shown, and similar tools survive from Kahun – a bone
awl, copper piercers, both round and square, one of them having
a wood handle.

The leather-workers in the tomb-paintings are professionals.
It is a skilled process, but it would be impossible to tell whether
the sandals found at Kahun were made in a government workshop and imported into the town as payment in kind for labour
on the pyramid, or made in the town itself, although no cobbler's
shop came to light.

There is, however, an interesting variety of footwear: a heel
with straps and part of a sole, made up of thick leather layers
compressed together and fastened with metal tacks, and a wide
sandal with a well-preserved thong, made for the broad foot and
splayed toes of the ordinary Egyptian. In contrast, there is a
more slender and elegant woman's sandal, about 22 cm long,
the equivalent of an English size 5. And there are sandals of
rush, made on the same principle as coiled basketry, by stitching
bundles of rush neatly to each other in rows to build the shape,

and finishing the soles and heels by attaching leather strips to them.

More unusual are the sole and part of the upper of a slip-on shoe, stained red. It has a leather toe-piece, with the hair turned inside, stitched to the sole with a leather thong, and part of a corded thong is still attached at the ankle. According to Petrie,

> shoes seem to have been just originating at that period, two or three examples are known but all of them have the leather sandal strap between the toes and joining to the sides of the heel, to retain the sole on the foot, the upper leather being stitched on merely as a cover without its being intended to hold the shoe on the foot. (*Kahun, Gurob and Hawara*, p.28)

In the houses Petrie found doors which had worn down the sockets in which they pivoted at the threshold and, in true Egyptian fashion, the surface had been raised 'by laying pieces of leather, generally old sandals, in the socket'.

Household cloth and articles of dress have a short life, but are often recycled and the absence of woven textiles surviving from Kahun is curious.

The manner in which the 'new town' was abandoned has not been explained. Petrie thought it was inhabited for about a century, but it seems to have been deserted by its inhabitants in such a hurry that some kind of disaster may have occurred, though this could hardly be plague, which has been suggested, since no bodies except the baby-burials were found. Whatever happened, the paucity of cloth is unusual – if sandals and precious needles were left behind, why not unwanted clothes?

There were textiles, however, according to Petrie's account. In his *Journal* (XXV, 14–20 April 1889) he describes 'bits of boxes, string, thread, sandals and even such unconsidered trifles* as linen, of course, come in daily'. And in *Kahun, Gurob and Hawara*, p.12, he mentions 'Miss Bradbury has again taken in hand the textiles and, for the larger and more important pieces, has obtained the careful help of Mr. Wardle and of Messrs. Pullar.'† The string, thread and sandals survive, but of the linen

---

* A Shakespearean quotation. Autolycus, in *A Winter's Tale*, describes himself as 'a snatcher-up of unconsidered trifles'.
† Pullars of Perth, a renowned dry-cleaning company.

cloth there is no trace. However, thanks to Petrie's records and his vivid account, a clear picture of textile activity at Kahun remains.

The professional weaver's status in ancient Egypt was not high, and his lot was an unenviable one, according to the New Kingdom writer of the *Satire on Trades* (Papyrus Sallier, II, 7, 2–4).

> The weaver in the workshop he is worse than a woman.
> His knees are drawn up to his belly, he cannot breathe
> the open air. If he cuts short the day's weaving he is
> beaten with fifty thongs. He must give food to the door-
> keeper that he lets him see the light of day.

Middle Kingdom workshop weavers were women, but their working conditions may have been much the same, and weaving at home must have been preferable. Petrie wrote of the Kahun townsfolk. 'The tomb-paintings of Beni Hasan show us the people themselves as they lived....' (*Kahun, Gurob and Hawara*, p.21), and the picture he has left us is of the wives and children, and perhaps the elderly, spinning, weaving, making nets, baskets and other necessities at home, while the menfolk were working on the pyramid, producing yarn and cloth for the family and possibly enough to earn the 12th Dynasty equivalent of pin-money as well.

Conclusion

It has been shown that the site of Kahun and its related arte-facts are of considerable significance to our understanding both of the way in which a town of the Middle Kingdom functioned in ancient Egypt and also, of the technologies of the period which were developed to meet the needs of the society. Also, the wealth of articles of everyday use found at this one excavated site themselves ensure that Kahun is regarded as a town of outstanding interest to archaeologists and historians.

The place had an additional importance, as a residence for the workmen engaged on the construction of a royal tomb. As such, it can be compared with the other, rare examples of royal necropolis towns, and can illustrate something of the organis-ation, skills and life patterns of these important ancient craftsmen.

However, perhaps some of the most fascinating questions that can be asked about the site and its inhabitants centre around the assumption that there was a presence – perhaps of a signifi-cant size – of foreign residents in the town.

Even if the foreign pottery products are regarded simply as trade imports to the area, there is substantial additional evi-dence to indicate that foreigners lived at Kahun. The legal papyri, the temple lists and other inscriptions confirm the presence of 'Asiatics' in the town, and the occurrence of non-Egyptian weights and measures, as well as individual finds such as the torque, serve to support this theory, which was originally advanced by Petrie. Even in the royal jewellery of the Middle Kingdom, there are indications of foreign influence, but it is uncertain whether these pieces were actually produced by foreign craftsmen resident in Egypt, or by Egyptian jewellers who gained their inspiration from styles and forms which were then fashionable in other areas of the ancient world.

The original homeland, or indeed countries, from which Kahun's foreign population came are also the subject of debate. The Aegean goods found here may simply have entered Egypt through trade, or they may have been brought to the area by immigrants from the Levant. However, the possibility cannot be ruled out that Aegean workers themselves came to Kahun and brought these goods directly with them. When Petrie excavated Kahun, the major excavations on Crete had not then been started, but later, the archaeologist Sir Arthur Evans (*Knossos*, I (London, 1921), p.266) was able to include, in his report on the excavation of King Minos' Palace at Knossos on Crete, that he was of the opinion that a group of Minoan workmen may indeed have been employed on the construction of Sesostris II's pyramid at Lahun. The excavations showed that, at this time, Crete was experiencing a period of stability and prosperity, and quantities of Minoan pottery began to be exported to Cyprus, Syria and Egypt. Although the direct evidence for Cretans residing in Egypt during the Middle Kingdom is at present lacking, it cannot be ruled out that some Aegean traders and craftsmen had already found their way to some Egyptian towns, where they took up temporary or permanent residence.

The existence at Kahun of immigrants from the regions of Syria and Palestine is more demonstrable, for the term 'Asiatic' used in the Kahun papyri probably refers to people from these areas. They may have come from the immediate vicinity of the coastal towns, such as Byblos or from further afield, but at least some of them were probably directly involved in the construction of the Lahun pyramid and were perhaps also engaged in specialised crafts associated with funerary goods. It has also been suggested that Cyprus was one of the homelands from which a group of immigrants may have come to Kahun; these people were perhaps partly responsible for the developments in metalworking in the area.

The workforce at the town may therefore have included various elements from a number of countries, as well as native-born Egyptians. The products found at Kahun certainly indicate a variety of sources, although it must never be forgotten that at least some of these items may have entered the area through trade. Others were produced locally, although they imitated foreign styles, and whether these were made by the immigrant residents of the town, or by Egyptian craftsmen who were copying the imported traded goods, it is impossible to determine.

The reasons which brought the foreigners to Kahun may have been as various as their possible places of origin. Some, especially the Aegean islanders, may have come as traders who then settled at Kahun, or they may have been itinerant artisans who brought their specialised skills. The same may be true of the other groups, although some, especially those referred to as 'Asiatics', may have been brought into Egypt as prisoners-of-war during the troubled years of the First Intermediate Period and even the early part of the 12th Dynasty.

Acceptance of the 'foreigners' in the town seems to have been well established. They may have preserved some of their own religious and other customs, but they were sufficiently well integrated to be included, albeit in specialised roles, in the rituals of the Egyptian temple at Kahun. Even the evidence of the intra-mural burial customs, when baby burials were interred within the town, cannot be clearly explained. Such burials were also found at Deir el-Medina many years later, and may indeed indicate the presence of a foreign custom, although insufficient evidence exists from other Egyptian settlement sites to clarify this. Again, at Lahun, Petrie discovered a baby burial at the pyramid site, which he believed to have been part of the foundation ceremony. This again seems to indicate a non-Egyptian religious practice, and may have been introduced here by some of the immigrant workers.

Nevertheless, in general, Kahun seems to have accommodated its different elements with no great difficulty, and the excavated material presents a picture of a society which, while perhaps combining native and immigrant features, nevertheless inhabited an essentially Egyptian town.

Future work will reveal further details of this unique place and its inhabitants, and it is appropriate that the artefacts from this site, where Petrie was able to develop and perfect some of his earliest archaeological and scientific techniques, should themselves become the subject of an intensive and multi-disciplinary study.

Bibliography

Abbreviations

ASAE   – *Annales du Service des Antiquités de l'Égypte.*

BIFAO – *Bulletin de l'Institut français d'Archéologie orientale.*

CAH   – *Cambridge Ancient History.*

JARCE – *Journal of the American Research Center in Egypt.*

JEA   – *Journal of Egyptian Archaeology.*

JNES   – *Journal of Near Eastern Studies.*

General

Petrie, W.M.F., *Kahun, Gurob and Hawara* (London, 1890).

Petrie, W.M.F., *Illahun, Kahun and Gurob* (London, 1891).

Petrie, W.M.F., *Ten Years' Digging in Egypt, 1881–91* (London, 1892).

Petrie, W.M.F., *Journals*, October 1888–January 1890 (at University College London).

Petrie, W.M.F., *Methods and Aims* (London, 1917).

Petrie, W.M.F., *Seventy Years in Archaeology* (London, 1931).

Chapter 1: The Geography and Historical Background

Aldred, C., *Middle Kingdom Art in Ancient Egypt, 2300–1590 B.C.* (London, 1950).

Gardiner, A.H., *Egypt of the Pharaohs* (Oxford, 1974).

Hayes, W.C., 'The Middle Kingdom in Egypt', in *CAH* (rev. ed.), vol.I, chap. xx (Cambridge, 1964).

Chapter 2: The Lahun Pyramid

Aldred, C., *Jewels of the Pharaohs* (London, 1971).

Andrews, C.A., *Ancient Egyptian Jewellery* (London, 1990).

Brunton, G., *Lahun I: The Treasure* (London, 1920).

Edwards, I.E.S., *The Pyramids of Egypt* (Harmondsworth, 1993).

Gardiner, A.H., 'The Name of Lake Moeris', in *JEA*, 29 (1943), pp. 37–46.

Gardiner, A.H., 'The Harem at Miwer', in *JNES*, 12 (1953), pp. 145–9.

Gunn, B., 'The Name of the Pyramid-Town of Sesostris II', in *JEA*, 31 (1945), pp. 106–7.

Herodotus, *The Histories*, Book II (translated by A. de Sélincourt, *The Penguin Classics*) (Harmondsworth, 1961).

Petrie, W.M.F., G. Brunton, and M.A. Murray, *Lahun II* (London, 1923).

Simpson, W.K., 'The Residence of Ittowy', in *JARCE*, 2 (1963), pp. 53–64.

Winlock, H.E., *The Treasure of El-Lahun* (New York, 1934).

Chapter 3: The Towns of the Royal Workmen

Bierbrier, M., *The Tomb-Builders of the Pharaohs* (London, 1982).

Brunner-Traut, E., *Egyptian Artists' Sketches. Figured Ostraka from the Gayer-Anderson Collection in the Fitzwilliam Museum, Cambridge* (Nederlands Historisch-Archaeologisch Institut Te Istanbul, 1979).

Brunton, G. and Engelbach, R., *Gurob* (London, 1927).

Bruyère, B., *Rapport sur les fouilles de Deir el Medineh (1934–5): Troisième Partie: Le village, les décharges publiques, la station de repos du col de la Vallée des Rois* (Cairo, 1939).

Cerný, J., 'Le culte d'Amenophis Ier chez les ouvriers de la nécropole thébaine', in *BIFAO*, XXVII (1927), pp. 159–203.

Cerný, J., *A Community of Workmen at Thebes in the Ramesside Period* (Cairo, 1973).

Fairman, H.W., 'Town Planning in Pharaonic Egypt', in *Town Planning Review*, 20 (Liverpool, April 1949), pp. 33–51.

Gardiner, A.H., *Ramesside Administrative Documents* (Oxford, 1948).

Gunn, B., 'Religion of the Poor in Ancient Egypt', in *JEA*, 3 (1916), pp. 81–94.

Kemp, B.J., 'The early development of town in Egypt', in *Antiquity*, 51 (1977), pp. 185–200.

Kemp, B.J., 'Preliminary Report on the El-Amarna Survey, 1977', in *JEA*, 64 (1978), pp. 22–34.

Kemp, B.J., 'Preliminary Report on the El-Amarna Expedition, 1979', in *JEA*, 66 (1980), pp. 5–16.

Peet, T.E., *The Great Tomb Robberies of the 20th Egyptian Dynasty*, Vol.I: Text; Vol.II: Plates (Oxford, 1930).

Sauneron, S., *Catalogue des Ostraca Hieratiques de Deir el-Medineh* (Cairo, 1959).

Thomas, A.P., *Gurob: A New Kingdom Town. Introduction and Catalogue of Objects in the Petrie Collection* (*Egyptology Today*, no. 5, vol.I) (Warminster, 1981).

Chapter 4: The Site and its Excavation

Petrie, W.M.F., *Kahun, Gurob and Hawara* (London, 1890).

Petrie, W.M.F., *Illahun, Kahun and Gurob* (London, 1891).

Chapter 5: Legal and Medical Practices, Education and Religion

Abdel-Ahad, G. Wadie, Unpublished Dissertation: 'Concepts of Obstetrics and Gynaecology in Ancient Egypt. The fundamental basis, facts, methods, their survival and relation to modern practice' (presented towards the

DHMSA Examination, London, November, 1983).

Adams, F., *The Genuine Works of Hippocrates* (Baltimore, 1939).

Breasted, J.H., *The Edwin Smith Surgical Papyrus* (Chicago, 1930).

Ghalioungui, P., *Magic and Medical Science in Ancient Egypt* (London, 1963).

Griffith, F.Ll., *Hieratic Papyri from Kahun and Gurob*, vol.I: *Literary, Medical and Mathematical Papyri from Kahun* (London, 1897); vol.II: *Legal Documents, Account Papyri etc. and Letters from Kahun, Gurob Papyri (New Kingdom)* (London, 1898); vol.III: *Additional Notes, Corrections, Indices* (London, 1898).

Griffith, F.Ll., 'The Hieratic Papyri', in W.M.F. Petrie, *Illahun, Kahun and Gurob* (London, 1891), pp. 47–9.

Schaeffer, C.F.A., 'Analyses Metallurgiques', in *Ugaritica*, II, chap. 2 (Paris, 1949), pp. 64ff.

Stevens, J.M., 'Gynaecology from Ancient Egypt: the Papyrus Kahun. A translation of the oldest treatise on gynaecology, that has survived from the ancient world', in *Medical Journal of Australia*, 2 (1975), pp. 949–52.

Stevenson Smith, W., *Interconnections in the Ancient Near East; a Study of the Relationships between the Arts of Egypt, the Aegean and West Asia* (New Haven, 1965).

Chapter 6: Everyday Life at Kahun

Blackman, W.S., 'An Englishwoman in Upper Egypt', in *The Wide World*, vol.I, January, 1924.

Erman, A., *Life in Ancient Egypt* (trans. by H.M. Tirard) (London, 1894).

Forbes, R.J., *Studies in Ancient Technology*, vols I–VI (Leiden, 1956–66).

Griffiths, A.S., *Catalogue of Egyptian Antiquities of the XII and XVIII Dynasties from Kahun, Illahun and Gurob* (Manchester Museum Handbooks, publication 70) (Manchester, 1910).

Hodges, H., *Technology in the Ancient World* (Harmondsworth, 1970).

Lucas, A., *Ancient Egyptian Materials and Industries* (4th ed. revised and enlarged by J.R. Harris) (London, 1962).

Newberry, P., 'The Ancient Botany', in W.M.F. Petrie, *Kahun, Gurob and Hawara* (London, 1890), pp. 49–50.

Petrie, W.M.F., *Tools and Weapons* (London, 1917).

Petrie, W.M.F., *Ancient Weights and Measures* (London, 1926).

Petrie, W.M.F., *Objects of Daily Use* (London, 1927).

Spurrell, F.C.J., 'The Stone Implements of Kahun', in W.M.F. Petrie, *Illahun, Kahun and Gurob* (London, 1891), pp. 51–5.

Ucko, P.J., and Dimbleby, G.W. (eds), *The Domestication and Exploitation of Plants and Animals*: Proceedings of a meeting of the Research Seminar in Archaeology and Related Subjects held at the Institute of Archaeology, London University (London, 1969).

Wilkinson, Sir Gardner, *The Manners and Customs of the Ancient Egyptians*, vol.II (London, 1847).

Winlock, H.E., *Models of Daily Life in Ancient Egypt from the Tomb of Meket-Re at Thebes* (Cambridge, Mass., 1955).

Chapter 7: The Foreign Population at Kahun

Bakir, A.M., 'Slavery in Pharaonic Egypt', in *ASAE*, 45 (1947), pp. 135–44.

Evans, A., *The Palace of Minos at Knossos*, 4 vols in 7 parts (London, 1921–36).

Evans, A., *The Early Nilotic, Libyan and Egyptian Relations with Minoan Crete* (The Huxley Memorial Lecture for 1925) (London, 1925).

Hall, H.R., 'The Relations of Aegean with Egyptian Art', in *JEA*, 1 (1914), pp. 110–18.

Hall, H.R., 'Egypt and the External World in the time of Akhenaten', in *JEA*, 7 (1921), pp. 39–53.

Hayes, W.C., *A Papyrus of the Late Middle Kingdom in the Brooklyn Museum* (Pap. Brooklyn, 35, 1446) (New York, 1955).

Kantor, H.J., *The Aegean and the Orient in the Second Millennium B.C.* (Bloomington, 1947).

Kemp, B.J., and R.S. Merrillees, *Minoan Pottery in Second Millenium Egypt* (Verlag Philip von Zabern, Mainz am Rheim, 1980).

Merrillees, R.S., *The Cypriote Bronze Age Pottery found in Egypt* (Studies in Mediterranean Archaeology, 18) (Lund, 1968).

Merrillees, R.S., 'Palestinian Bichrome Ware in Egypt', in *Australian Journal of Biblical Archaeology*, I (1970), pp. 3–27.

Peet, T.E., *The Stela of Sebek-khu, the earliest record of an Egyptian campaign in Asia* (Manchester Museum Handbook, Publication no. 75) (Manchester, 1914).

Pendlebury, J.D.S., *Aegyptiaca. A Catalogue of Egyptian Objects in the Aegean Area* (Cambridge, 1930).

Pendlebury, J.D.S., 'Egypt and the Aegean in the Late Bronze Age', in *JEA*, 16 (1930), pp. 75–92.

Pendlebury, J.D.S., *The Archaeology of Crete: An Introduction* (London, 1939).

Posener, G., 'Les Asiatiques en Égypte sous les XIIᵉ et XIIIᵉ dynasties', in *Syria*, 34 (1957), pp. 145–63.

Schaeffer, C.F.A., *Ugaritica I* (Mission de Ras Shamra, 3) (Paris, 1939); *Ugaritica II* (Mission de Ras Shamra, 5) (Paris, 1949).

Tufnell, O., and Ward, W.A., 'Relations between Byblos, Egypt and Mesopotamia at the end of the Third Millennium B.C. A Study of the Montet Jar', in *Syria*, 43 (1966), pp. 165–228.

Vercoutter, J., *Essai sur les relations entre Égyptiens et Préhellènes* (Paris, 1954).

Vercoutter, J., *L'Égypte et la Monde Egéen Préhellènique* (Cairo, 1956).

Vermeule, E., *Greece in the Bronze Age* (Chicago, 1964).

Walberg, G., *Kamares: A Study of the Character of Palatial Middle Minoan Pottery* (Acta Universitatis Upsaliensis, Boreas, 8) (Uppsala, 1976).

Ward, W.A., 'Egypt and the East Mediterranean in the Early Second Millennium B.C.', in *Orientalia*, 30 (1961), pp. 22–45, 129–55.

Warren, P., *The Aegean Civilisations (The Making of the Past* series) (Oxford, 1975).

Chapter 8: Last Years at Kahun

Hayes, W.C., 'Egypt: From the Death of Amenemmes III to Seqenenre II', in *CAH* (rev. ed.), vol.II, chap.II (Cambridge, 1965).

Kemp, B.J., 'An Incised Sherd from Kahun, Egypt', in *JNES*, 36 (1977), pp. 289–92.

Tufnell, O., 'Seal Impressions from Kahun Town and Uronarti Fort. A Comparison', in *JEA*, 61 (1975), pp. 61–101.

Van Seters, J., *The Hyksos: A New Investigation* (New Haven, 1966).

Chapter 11: Kahun: The Textile Evidence

Crowfoot, G.M., *Methods of Handspinning in Egypt and the Sudan* (Halifax, Bankfield Museum Notes 2nd series, 12, 1931).

Forbes, R.J., *Studies in Ancient Technology*, vol.IV, *Textiles* (Leiden, 1964).

Hoffman, M., *Egypt Before the Pharaohs, The Prehistoric Foundations of Egyptian Civilisation* (London, 1980).

Kees, H., *Ancient Egypt: a Cultural Topography* (London, 1977).

Lucas, A., *Ancient Egyptian Materials and Industries* (London, 1962).

Newberry, P.E., *Beni Hasan*, 2 vols (London, 1893–4).

Petrie, W.M.F., Relevant Excavation Reports.

Roth, H. Ling, *Ancient Egyptian and Greek Looms* (Halifax, Bankfield Museum Notes, 1951).

Index